# SHAKSPEREAN

# FLY-LEAVES AND JOTTINGS,

## BY H. T. HALL.

# SHAKSPEREAN

# FLY-LEAVES AND JOTTINGS,

A new and enlarged Edition,

BY H. T. HALL,

"To instruct by delighting is a power seldom enjoyed by man, and still seldomer exercised. It is in this respect that Homer may be called the second of men, and Shakspere the first."—LONDON MAGAZINE, OCTOBER 1, 1824.

**AMS PRESS**
NEW YORK

Reprinted from the edition of 1871, London
First **AMS EDITION** published 1970
Manufactured in the United States of America
International Standard Book Number: 0–404–03043–2

Library of Congress Number: 70–135727

**AMS PRESS INC.**
NEW YORK, N.Y. 10003

## PREFACE TO THE SECOND EDITION.

THE first edition of this little work having been out of print for some time, I have ventured to publish a second, considerably enlarged, and as I hope, improved. Much new matter has been added, and the whole work has undergone a thorough revision. Its production has been to me a labour of love and delight, and I now consign it to the care and consideration of the lovers of the great dramatist, whose works are characterised by so strong a love and knowledge of humanity, that they have completely outshone the works of all others in "this narrow world of ours."

THE AUTHOR.

CAMBRIDGE, *November,* 1871.

# CONTENTS.

|  | PAGE |
|---|---|
| On the Genius of Shakspere | 1 |
| Hamlet | 35 |
| The Merchant of Venice | 79 |
| Timon of Athens | 107 |
| As you Like It | 117 |
| Macbeth | 139 |
| King John | 175 |
| King Richard II. | 184 |
| King Richard III. | 220 |
| King Henry VIII. | 233 |
| Shaksperean Jottings: |  |
| Cymbeline | 241 |
| The Winter's Tale | 244 |
| King Lear | 245 |
| Twelfth Night | 248 |
| A Midsummer Nights' Dream | 249 |
| Much Ado about Nothing | 250 |
| The Taming of the Shrew | 251 |
| Antony and Cleopatra | 252 |
| The Tempest | 253 |
| Hamlet, &c. | 254 |
| Shakspere's Morality | 259 |
| Shakspere's Religion | 260 |
| Shakspere's Contemporaries | 262 |
| Shakspere as an Actor | 263 |
| Shakspere's Birthday | 264 |
| Shakspere's Non-observance of the Unities | 266 |
| The Period of Shakspere | 268 |

# THE GENIUS OF SHAKSPERE.

In seeking to consider the genius of Shakspere, the subject should be approached with that reverent admiration which its importance demands. No one man ever fully understood, or can ever fully understand the works of Shakspere in their entirety, nor is Unity of thought and opinion to be expected of one who is so diffuse, so general and so human.* The works of Shakspere are all things to all men, and in this universality is found the power and greatness of his genius. The spirit of criticism, developed by the school of critics, who flourished in the latter part of the seventeenth and the beginning of the eighteenth centuries, of whom, Rymer may be selected as the representative, has happily passed away. The classic school, who believed in the "chorus" as "the root and original," and "as certainly almost the most necessary part of tragedy," no longer exist. Those great admirers of the cuckoo

---

* "Æschylus and Shakspere seem made to prove that contraries may be admirable. The point of departure for the one is absolutely opposite to the point of departure of the other. Æschylus is concentration, Shakspere is diffusion. One must be much applauded because he is condensed, and the other because he is diffuse; to Æschylus unity, to Shakspere ubiquity. Between them they divide God. And, as such intellects are always complete, one feels, in the drama unit of Æschylus, the free agitation of passion, and in the diffuse drama of Shakspere the convergence of all the rays of life. The one starts from unity and reaches a multiple, the other starts from the multiple and arrives at unity."—*Victor Hugo on Shakspere*, p. 246.

school of "rules of art," Dennis and Gildon, were succeeded by Rowe, Pope, Hanmer, Theobald and Johnson, whose preface to an edition of the bard's works in 1765, was looked upon as a remarkable effort of Shaksperean criticism. The influence of Johnson's preface, has been for evil, for he evidently misunderstands our poet, nor has he completely shaken off the trammels of an earlier school, and it so abounds with ponderous and long-sounding words of Latin origin, that there is not much to compensate the reader for his trouble. To Johnson, succeeded Stevens, Capell, and Malone, and their efforts have been highly serviceable to the world of Shakspere literature. The labours of Malone, as displayed in his edition of Shakspere, the best at the time of its publication, (1790), have been adopted by most modern commentators, as the basis for a true chronological arrangement of Shakspere's works.

A more genial school of critics has arisen since Johnson's time, for not fettered by any observance of unities and other such like classic inanities, they have developed the truthfulness and greatness of Shakspere above all other dramatic poets. The works of Lessing, Wieland, Schlegel, Horn, Goethe, Ulrici, Lencke, Bodenstedt, and Gervinius among the Germans, and the works of Hazlitt, Coleridge, Lamb, Jameson, Knight, Collier, Halliwell, Walker, White and Dyce, among the English, have added largely to our means of comprehending Shakspere, and the love of his works which they have generated, hath become so strong, that time will not eradicate the feeling, nor man destroy it.

Shakspere is truly the world's poet, to him all things owe allegiance. He is the genius of humanity, using all things at pleasure, and changing and playing with our purposes as with his own. None other hath so fully developed nor shown such a love of humanity. Our globe and all thereon and all therein he hath turned and played with for his amusement, surveying generations of men, and observing individuals as they passed, with all their acts of folly and wisdom, their vices and their virtues. The simplicity and innocence of childhood, the out-pourings of despair, the ravings of disordered fancy, have been by him most truthfully shown. Like his own Glendower, the "spirits" of the "vasty deep" he has evoked; the demonaic, the wondrous and the terrible, and by his "ways of art" hath made them subservient to his purpose. His "deep experiments," "full of fiery shapes," and deeper knowledge made him familiar with all within the womb of nature. The gentle fays dancing their "ringlets to the whistling wind," paid him respect, so did the "black and midnight hags" who render darkness still darker. The out-pourings of his fancy are wonderful, his creations still more so. He had but to think and all was resolved; all passed before him, as the kings passed before Macbeth. His descriptions are so terse; he condenses into a line, what others take pages to express. "He lays open to us in a single word, a whole series of preceding conditions." With him an epithet carries back the mind for years, the brain reverts to the past, as when Prospero in relating the tale to his daughter of the causes which produced his present sorrow, applies to her, "Me, and thy crying self." The imagination is here thrown back, and we pass from the grown woman to the helplessness of infancy, and immediately is placed before us the first and most trying scene of his misfortunes, and all that he must have suffered in the interval. Again, in *Richard III.* he displays the same power, though the example is of an opposite nature, looking forward instead of reverting back,

"Up with my tent there! here will I lie to-night:
But where *to-morrow?*"

The imagination is again on wing, *to-morrow* awakens thoughts of the coming strife, of death and futurity, with all its calamities or pleasures.

In his high impassioned speeches no word can be substituted for those which he uses; they must be rendered correct, or else the sound is not euphonious, it grates upon the ear, and the beauty of the sentence is marred. Take his description of the approach of night in *Macbeth,* and try to alter one word, and see if the beauty be not destroyed:

"Light thickens,
And the crow makes wing to the rooky wood,
Good things of day begin to droop and drowse,
Whiles night's black agents to their preys do rouse."

Where can a word be substituted? can one be altered without marring the beautiful expression of feeling? Shakspere must have been thoroughly observant of external nature, and have faithfully stored within the chambers of his wondrous brain the results of his observations, to have been so truthful in his descriptions. The account of Ophelia's death displays his closeness of observation, for no other author has marked the difference of the sides of the willow leaf, the upper being green, the underneath being white:

"There is a willow grows aslant a brook,
That shows his *hoar* leaves in the glassy stream."
*Hamlet, A.* iv. s. 7.

In the *Winter's Tale*, how accurately he discriminates between the bandied terms of art and nature, when he observes,

"Nature is made better by no mean,
But Nature makes that mean: so, over that art
Which you say adds to Nature, is an art
That Nature makes. You see, sweet maid, we marry
A gentle scion to the wildest stock,
And make conceive a bark of baser kind
By bud of nobler race: this is an art
Which does mend Nature, change it rather, but
The art itself is Nature.—*A.* iv. s. 4.

How thoroughly he displays his knowledge of humanity, the result of great observation, in *Henry IV.*, when depicting the fickleness of the popular will, he says,

"An habitation giddy and unsure
Hath he that buildeth on the vulgar heart.
O thou fond many, with what loud applause
Didst thou beat heaven with blessing Bolingbroke,
Before he was what thou wouldst have him be.
*Part II. A.* ii. s. 3.

In describing the power of imagination after the brain has resolved upon action, how wonderful is the knowledge he evinces, and how accurately he analyses the courses of human thought. In *Julius Cæsar*, he observes,

"Between the acting of a dreadful thing,
And the first motion, all the interim is
Like a phantasma, or a hideous dream.
The genius and the mortal instruments
Are then in council; and the state of man,
Like to a little kingdom, suffers then
The nature of an insurrection."—*A.* ii. s. 1.

In the Tragedy of *Othello*, one of the grandest of all tragedies, how beautiful is his power of discrimination displayed, how excellently through the character of Iago is effected the jealousy of Othello; how gradually, yet certain, is the coil wound round the unsuspecting Moor; how every circumstance tends to work upon the impassioned black; and when Othello asks Iago, "If he dost not think Cassio honest," how the echo of Iago, "Honest my lord," serves still further to arouse the Moor, causing him to repeat the question, "Honest? ay honest," and when Iago again echoes the words of Othello, the chords are struck, the poison beginneth its work; for Othello immediately exclaims to himself,

"Think, my lord, by heaven, he echoes me,
As if there were some monster in his thought
Too hideous to be shown."—*A.* III. s. 3.

Throughout the whole of this scene the inuendoes of Iago have their weight and succeed in arousing the jealousy of Othello; and when Desdemona importunes the Moor for Cassio, how that passion becomes strengthened, and waxes still stronger through the loss of the handkerchief, so cleverly contrived by Iago, until Othello is completely carried away by his imaginary wrongs and slays his innocent wife. How wonderfully is the remorse of the Moor pourtrayed, when he discovers the treachery of Iago, and what a splendid conclusion the poet puts into the mouth of the Moor, fit compeer for the splendid opening, when addressing Ludovico, he says,

"Soft you; a word or two, before you go.
I have done the state some service, and they know't.
No more of that. I pray you, in your letters,

When you shall these unlucky deeds relate,
Speak of me as I am; nothing extenuate,
Nor aught set down in malice: then must you speak
Of one that lov'd not wisely, but too well;
Of one, not easily jealous, but, being wrought,
Perplex'd in the extreme; of one, whose hand,
Like the base Indian, threw a pearl away,
Richer than all his tribe; of one, whose unsubdued eyes,
Albeit unused to the melting mood,
Dropt tears as fast as the Arabian trees
Their medicinal gum. Set you down this;
And say besides,—that in Aleppo once,
Where a malignant and turban'd Turk
Beat a Venetian and traduc'd the state,
I took him by the throat the uncircumcised dog,
And smote him,—thus

*Lud.* O bloody period!
*Gra.* All that is spoke is marr'd.
*Oth.* I kiss'd thee, ere I kill'd thee:—no way but this,
Killing myself, to die upon a kiss."—*A.* v. s. 2.

In reviewing Shakspere and his works, innumerable are the forms, phases, and guises under which he appeareth. We behold in him the man of learning, the poet, the statesman, the philosopher, and the man of the multitude. If we wish to learn a code of morals, we have only to cull his works, and Minerva like they spring up complete in every page. Do we wish to learn his politics, we shall find his works abound in political truisms, with a knowledge of peoples and governments that seem truly miraculous. Do we wish to view life and know its character, read his pages, and you cannot fail to discover and be bettered by your discovery.

"To-morrow, and to-morrow, and to-morrow,
Creeps in this pretty pace from day to day,
To the last syllable of recorded time;
And all our yesterdays have lighted fools
The way to dusty death. Out, out, brief candle!

> Life's but a walking shadow; a poor player,
> That struts and frets his hour upon the stage,
> And then is heard no more: it is a tale
> Told by an idiot, full of sound and fury,
> Signifying nothing."—*Macbeth, A.* v. s. 5.

This may seem materialistic, but is it not true? Doth not life partake of "a walking shadow," which for a few brief moments is seen, "and then is heard no more." How peculiarly happy is the expression of life being "a tale," one "told by an idiot," and how expressively it falls upon our senses, and stamps the correctness of the opinion upon the brain, when the sentence is concluded, of its being "full of sound and fury signifying nothing."

In *Measure for Measure,* Shakspere again dwells upon the subject of life; and he here delineates with unerring power, the hopes, desires and dreads which all mankind have of death, that insatiate fisherman into whose nets all classes of society must come. He says, and mark the correctness of the saying,

> "Reason thus with life:
> If I do lose thee, I do lose a thing
> That none but fools would keep: a breath thou art,
> Servile to all the skyey influences,
> That dost this habitation, where thou keep'st,
> Hourly afflict: merely, thou art death's fool;
> For him thou labour'st by thy flight to shun,
> And yet runn'st toward him still. Thou art not noble;
> For all the accommodations that thou bear'st
> Are nursed by baseness. Thou'rt by no means valiant;
> For thou dost fear the soft and tender fork
> Of a poor worm. Thy best of rest is sleep,
> And that thou oft provokest; yet grossly fear'st
> Thy death, which is no more. Thou art not thyself;
> For thou exist'st on many a thousand grains
> That issue out of dust. Happy thou art not;
> For what thou hast not, still thou strivest to get,

And what thou hast, forget'st. Thou art not certain;
For thy complexion shifts to strange effects,
After the moon. If thou art rich, thou'rt poor;
For, like an ass whose back with ingots bows,
Thou bear'st thy heavy riches but a journey,
And death unloads thee. Friend hast thou none;
For thine own bowels, which do call thee sire,
The mere effusion of thy proper loins,
Do curse the gout, serpigo, and the rheum,
For ending thee no sooner. Thou hast nor youth nor age,
But, as it were, an after-dinner's sleep,
Dreaming on both; for all thy blessed youth
Becomes as aged, and doth beg the alms
Of palsied eld; and when thou art old and rich,
Thou hast neither heat, affection, limb, nor beauty,
To make thy riches pleasant. What's yet in this
That bears the name of life? Yet in this life
Lie hid more thousand deaths: yet death we fear,
That makes these odds all even."—*A*. III. s. 1.

Do we wish for a monitor to display the evil effects which follow the subordination of man to his animal propensities, and to find a check or safeguard for ourselves, we can perceive it imaged forth in his pages, with such power, that it would tend, were he has universally read as he ultimately will be, to check that desolating blight, intemperance, throughout our land: for

"As surfeit is the father of much fast,
So every scope by the immoderate use
Turns to restraint. Our natures do pursue
Like rats that ravin down their proper bane,
A thirsty evil; and when we drink we die."
*Measure for Measure, A.* 1, s. 2.

"Boundless intemperance
In nature is a tyranny; it hath been
The untimely emptying of the happy throne,
And fall of many kings."—*Macbeth, A.* 4. s. IV.

Throughout the whole of his works, Shakspere seeks to implant and engraft upon the reader's brain thoughts of the highest and most ennobling character. He seeks to teach a love of the beautiful, on account of its beauty, and to show that even in that which is externally deformed, there is a trace of the beautiful to be discovered. How unassuming, yet how winning, doth he advise us, and, ever alive to the importance of man's welfare, strives to restrain our excesses, by language like the following:

"Violent fires soon burn out themselves:
Small showers last long, but sudden storms are short;
He tires betimes, that spurs too fast betimes;
With eager feeding, food doth choke the feeder:
Light vanity, insatiate cormorant,
Consuming means, soon preys upon itself."
*Richard II. A.* ii. s. 1.

"Heat not a furnace for your foe so hot
That it do singe yourself; we may outrun,
By violent swiftness, that which we run at,
And lose by over-running. Know you not
The fire that mounts the liquor till't run o'er,
In seeming to augment it, wastes it."
*Henry VIII., A.* i. s. 1.

The good and true under all circumstances he strives to elevate; loving virtue for virtue's sake, and detesting vice for her deformity. How faithfully doth he pourtray all the phases of human character, from the noble to the ignoble, the base, the good, the vicious and the virtuous. His kings are not individual kings, but are legible types of their class, as are the whole of his characters; for in none doth the individuality of the author betray itself. By the power of his pen, he unravels the threads which connect and bind man to his fellow man. By the magic of his genius, he holds, "as 'twere, a mirror up to nature;" showing the passions and desires of men, depicting them with all their petty vices and frailties as they exist, and shows

> "Men's judgments are
> A parcel of their fortunes, and things outward
> Do draw the inward quality after them
> To suffer all alike."—*Ant. & Cleo. A.* III. s. 13.

Shakspere wrote with no special moral purpose, though his plays abound with true moral passages. He did not seek to bend everything towards a moral end, like some moral story-tellers, who never effect their purpose, from the simple fact they are never true. Shakspere wrote of life, he sought to pourtray life, and life is presented in his pages—life in its relation to nature and to man. The pointing of a moral formed no part of Shakspere's calculations. He has made his ignoble characters talk and act ignobly, because such is their nature. He has not always allowed virtue to be triumphant, and vice defeated. His great knowledge taught him that such a mode of writing would not be true; he has therefore in some instances, involved both innocent and guilty in one common ruin, totally uncaring whether such conclusion would point a moral, but determining the result should be so, for so it is often found in life.

The hand of Shakspere, like that of the great master Raphael, was unerring in its drawing. He never fails; his was the genius that grasps at a glance the whole of Nature, undivided and unbroken. What other men learn in detail and slowly attain, he comprehended in a moment, and with a dash of his mighty pen embodied thoughts and ideas which were left to future ages to develope. He has given a life to our literature, and endowed it with a vitality, which time cannot subdue, but only serve to render the more valuable. He hath imparted an importance to our language, which but for him it would not have possessed. "His noble hand" and brain hath wrought much to the advantage of our people, for he has breathed "an untirable and continuate goodness." "His fame unparalled," "the spacious world cannot again afford" one so "framed in the prodigality of nature." "Enchantingly beloved," his "desert speaks loud" "and 'gainst the tooth of time" is made secure. The whole world hath acknowledged his power, for to the supremacy of the bard of Stratford, the sons of poesy of the various nations of the earth have bowed their heads in silent awe and admiration.* The shadow of his genius has flung over our land a halo, which increaseth its intensity and burneth the brighter, the more his works are diffused and read. "Like a Colossus, he doth bestride this narrow world of ours." Shakspere is truly the poet of humanity, he knows no bounds, no country, no kindred but the whole great human family. He has written for all time and all peoples, for looking upon the human race as one great family, in which all have an equal right to share its pleasures and its woes, his language is singularly applicable to all; applicable on account of its wisdom and the inherent truth which it manifests. Shakspere, as all other great poets have been, (and it is in this respect only he has anything in common with other poets,) was a sincere lover of freedom, not the turbulent freedom of a wild, impassioned, uneducated

---

\* "Triumph, my Britain, thou hast one to show,
To whom all scenes of Europe homage owe."
*To the Memory of Shakspere.*

mob, but true freedom, such as can only be found where all have a knowledge of the laws and have a voice in the making thereof. Shakspere doth not seek to cloak a wrong, he never fails to apply the lash with vigour, where necessity calls for it, in exposing corruption and profligacy, the too frequent adjuncts of a court. What worldly knowledge he doth display, when he sayeth

"Through tatter'd clothes small vices do appear;
Robes and furr'd gowns hide all. Plate sin with gold,
And the strong lance of justice hurtless breaks;
Arm it in rags a pigmy's straw does pierce it."
*King Lear, A.* IV. s. 6.

How magnificently he inveighs against such damning sin as he hath here pourtrayed, and which, unfortunately for our country, is yet prevalent, though not so much as it was during the lifetime of our bard.

Shakspere, when describing Nature under her manifold phases, and depicting the passions which animate and pervade humanity, is lofty indeed. His descriptions never tire, they pall not, for they are always fresh and varied, and always true. He is as accurate as nature herself. His lines are not blurred nor feeble,—he lacks not colour nor breadth,—his work is ever true, for above all rises the feeling, that "truth is truest poetry." The "soft stillness" of "night," the grey eye of morning whose "golden gates" opened to "the glorious sun," turns our "cloddy earth to glittering gold." The "all shaking thunder," "the ambitious ocean swell," the "rage and foam" of "threatening clouds," the "meteors" that "fright the fixed stars of heaven," "the violets that shew the green lap of the new come spring," the "daffodils that come before the swallow dares," the "pale primroses," the "bold oxlips," with "lilies of all kinds," the "woodbine," "eglantine," "musk-roses" and "harebells" blue were storied within his wondrous brain which was exhaustless in its wealth and unrivalled in its application. "He was familiar with all beautiful forms and images, with all that is sweet or majestic in the simple aspects of nature; of that indestructible love of flowers and odours, and dews, and of clear waters—and soft air and sounds, and bright skies and woodland solitudes, and moonlight bowers, which are the material elements of poetry,—and with that fine sense of the undefinable relation to mental emotion, which is its essence and vivifying soul, and which, in the midst of his most busy and atrocious scenes, fall like gleams of sunshine on rocks and ruins—contrasting with all that is rugged and repulsive, and reminding us of the existence of purer and brighter elements."*

Shakspere's was a nature attuned to harmony, the notes he struck were all sterling gold; no tinselled ornaments pervade his works, for all is beautiful, thoughtful and true. In his paintings of Nature and her works, he lays on the colours so delicately, yet with such power, that the picture is complete; it wants not breadth, nor shade, nor light, so well he limns it. Like Titian, his colouring is magnificent, because it is true; like the masters of the Dutch school, he is powerful because he is minute; and like Raphael he is all ideal grace and perfection. "He gives a living picture of all the most minute and secret artifices by which a feeling steals into our souls, of all the imperceptible advantages which it there gains, of all the

* *Edinburgh Review*, Vol. 28, p. 473.

stratagems by which every other passion is made subservient to, till it becomes the sole agent of our desires and aversions." (*Lessing.*)

There is no poet in our tongue so redolent with beautiful and simple imagery. His "gracious words" revive our "drooping thoughts," and "nimbly and sweetly" do recommend themselves "unto our gentle senses." He is ever "a summer bird" which "in the haunch of winter sings," "lifting up the day," so that "base contagious clouds" do not obscure the beauty of the world. His endeavours come not too short of our desires and his aspirations "lift him from the earth" making him as "sweet as summer," so that "he enchants" and "all men's hearts are his." His descriptions of night are most varied in their character and how exquisitely they pourtray its approach, its intensity, and its departure; and how like a warrior eager for the fight, or a hunter for the chase, he leaps with ardour, and glows with gladness, at the approach of morn.

"Look how the sun begins to set;
How ugly night comes breathing at his heels :
Even with the vail and dark'ing of the sun,
To close the day up."
*Triolus and Cressida*, A. v. s. 8.

"Ugly night," what various thoughts and emotions are called up by this expression. Ugly, deformed, fiend-like, base, brutal, black, and horrible, each of which are expressed, and each of which are descriptive of night, which follows day so close, "breathing at his heels."

"The gaudy blabbing, and remorseful day
Is crept into the bosom of the sea;

> "And now loud-howling wolves arouse the jades
> That drag the tragic melancholy night;
> Who, with their drowsy, slow and flagging wings,
> Clip dead men's graves, and from their misty jaws,
> Breathe foul contagious darkness in the air."
> *Henry VI.*, Part II., A. IV. s. 1.

> "When the searching eye of heaven is hid,
> Behind the globe, that lights the lower world,
> Then thieves and robbers range abroad unseen,
> In murders and in outrage, boldly here."
> *Richard II.*, A. III. s. 2.

How the intensity of darkness is here displayed by the comparisons drawn; the connecting of thieves and robbers with the almost necessary sequence of murder—that "deed without a name," serves to show what night is, and in the mind of each, exciting a horror, that makes us almost dread "the tragic melancholy night," which in its coming, breathes "foul contagious darkness in the air." Let us leave "the night" with its tragic horrors, and revel with our poet in his splendid descriptions of "sable night's" best counterpart, the "gentle day," which

> "Before the wheels of Phœbus, round about,
> Dapples the drowsy east with spots of grey."
> *Much Ado about Nothing*, A. V. s. 3.

List to how bard as he sings,

> "Look love, what envious streaks
> Do lace the severing clouds in yonder east:
> Night's candles are burnt out, and jocund day
> Stands tiptoe on the misty mountain tops."
> *Romeo and Juliet*, A. III. s. 5.

> "Look the morn in russet mantle clad,
> Walks o'er the dew of yon high eastward hill."
> *Hamlet*, A. I. s. 1.

> "Lo here the gentle lark, weary of rest,
> From his moist cabinet mounts on high,

And wakes the morning, from whose silver breast,
The sun ariseth in his majesty;
Who doth the world so glorious behold,
That cedar tops and hills seem burnish'd gold."*

*Poems.*

How simple and homely the image, yet how expressive, "Night's candles are burnt out," how strikingly conclusive of the termination of the night with all its terrors and its calamities. The "envious streaks," "the severing clouds," all clearly pourtray Shakspere's wonderful observance of the workings of Nature, for they are the distinguishing phenomena of the opening morn. The "russet mantle" displays the homeliness of the morning's early attire; "the moist cabinet" of the lark depicts the dewy covering of our earth, and how splendidly is the beauty of the day described, when from "the silver breast" of morning,

"the sun ariseth in his majesty;
Who doth the world so glorious behold,
That cedar tops and hills seem burnish'd gold."

Shakspere did not create our drama, he regenerated it. He found it existing in a crude form, rude in its development, and from these materials he fashioned it afresh, endowing it with life and vigour, enriching it with the gems of his extensive comprehension, and enlivening it with the brilliant corruscations of his wit and fancy. What to others was "painful and laborious flight," which their pinions could not sustain, were to him the efforts of every day life. From all regions he drew, catching inspiration from everything by which he was surrounded, by that which preceded him, and to a great extent, forestalling that which was to come.

* For further examples of Shakspere's descriptions of night and morning, see note A.

Shakspere by many critics has been described as a poor scholar, but little versed in classic lore: be it so; yet was he better versed in all that appertains to true wisdom. By his productions, we find that he more thoroughly understood humanity, and the minutiæ which make up the individual and the class, and determine the actions thereof, than any of those who were so well versed in the Greek and Latin tongues, who flourished coeval with him, and had had the advantages of a collegiate education. The epithet barbarian Shakspere, was frequently applied to him, and even one of our own great poets, John Milton, has baptized "his wood notes wild," while the poet Thomson has seconded the baptism, by calling him "wild Shakspere."* These are decidedly misnomers, and ought not under any circumstances to be applied to our bard; for it was the union of the most consummate judgment, with the highest creative power in Shakspere, that refined our drama, and gave it that order and symmetry, which has rendered it so pre-eminently beautiful. Qualities such as these, cannot partake of the "wild" or savage, but belong alone to the truly learned, the wise, and the reflective.

In comparing Shakspere with any other poet, there are but three in our own tongue with whom comparison can be held. The one who flourished before, one coeval, and the one who followed him, Chaucer, Spenser, and Milton; these, excepting the name of Shakspere, stand highest in our poetic annals, and with these in comparing, it might be said, "that Chaucer excels as the poet of manners or real life; Spenser as the poet

---

* "Is not *wild* Shakspeare thine and Nature's boast."
*Thomson's Summer.*

of romance; Shakspere as the poet of Nature (in the largest use of the term); and Milton as the poet of morality. Chaucer most frequently describes things as they are: Spenser as we wish them to be; Shakspere as they would be; and Milton as they ought to be. As poets, and as great poets, imagination, that is, the power of feigning things according to nature, was common to them all: but the principal or moving power to which this faculty was most subservient in Chaucer, was habit, or inveterate prejudice; in Spenser novelty and the love of the marvellous; in Shakspere, it was the force of passion combined with every variety of possible circumstances; and in Milton, only with the highest. The characteristic of Chaucer is intensity; of Spenser, remoteness; of Milton, elevation; of Shakspere, everything."*

The three great poets of the world are Homer, the simple; Dante, the terrible; and Shakspere, the wonderful. The last named poet embraces the other two and stands alone when viewed as a whole. Shakspere had more fancy, more imagination, more philosophy, more knowledge, and a greater and deeper acquaintance with nature than Dante or Homer had, and therefore his works approach nearer to truth and nature than their's ever did. It is this which gives the student of Shakspere such a knowledge of humanity that he cannot fail to profit by his study, and it also teaches him that when reading the great master's works, he is reading the works of one who has lain his head upon the great heart of nature and heard the throbbings and beatings of her inmost pulsations.

* Hazlitt's Lectures on the Poets, p. 90.

Shakspere differs from Æschylus, Calderon and Voltaire, in the mode by which they each consider mankind to be governed. He does not, like the Father of Greek tragedy, make them the sport of fate, nor like the Spanish poet, represent the enigma of heaven and hell as the closing words of life; nor like the volatile Frenchman, doth he make the world a vehicle for the peculiar opinions which he held; but he makes the government of mankind to consist in the human heart, in that region alone doth he find and develope his fate. In his *Richard II.*, the hopes and fears, the resolutions and irresolutions, the dire confusion and complete bewilderments, prepares all for the conclusion, and teaches us to contemplate these sudden changes, these strange vicissitudes, without us being in the least degree surprised. Thus are his actors on life's puny stage, presented to the eye, and in his world of poetry, stand arrayed as the real characters of History. In the dramatic chronicle of Shakspere, we have a pourtrayal of the things of the world, all is real; for the time being, we behold the same sights and feel the same horrors, as those who moved and had their being therein. The more the poet descends into minutiæ and detail, the more forcibly are we impressed, until we are compelled by an irresistible power to acknowledge the truth and accuracy of the poet's pourtrayal.

Shakspere in the fullest development of his wondrous genius, possessed an absolute mastery over all the moods of human passion. He, alone, among dramatic poets possessed this power, and it is to the possession of this mastery, that we can account for his wonderful interpretations and illustrations of humanity. It was by this faculty that he discovered the life he has embodied in his works, and it is this faculty which gave him his great knowledge and his command of the conditions whereby his knowledge could be developed. No other poet, has like Shakspere, so truly developed the anatomy of the human heart. No other poet has so truthfully displayed the various emotions and feelings by which poor humanity is governed; and no other poet presents so animated and so brilliant a view of human life. In the pages of no other poet can we find such a varied range of human character, as those which his presents. He pourtrays all phases of human life and character, each having their idiosyncracies developed. The tenderness of Juliet, the fine frenzy of Lear, the melancholy scepticism of Hamlet, the calm contemplation of Prospero, the wit, humour, and pleasantrie of his Falstaff, Pistol, Malvolio, Dromio, Speed, Touchstone, Dogberry, Lance, Gobbo, and others; the patient, enduring Imogen, the gentle, loving Desdemona, the fiery, impetuous Hotspur, the cynical wisdom of Jaques, the physical monster Caliban, the mental and moral monster Thersites, the manly Valentine, the gallant Falconbridge, the winning Rosalind, the voluptuous Cleopatra, the fair, the graceful, tender Portia, the truthful, loving Cordelia, the terrific, fiend-like Lady Macbeth, the wrathful, passion-overwhelmed Othello, the cunning subtlety of Iago, the truly eloquent misanthrophy of a Timon, the never swerving constancy of a Hermione, and the fierce, fixed and irrevocable hate of Shylock are specimens of the master's power, which foreshadow his deep knowledge of humanity, and of the conditions necessary to the development of that knowledge.

If we wish for a view of other times and other lands,

we can learn from his pages of the courtly Alcibiades, of Pericles, and the wisdom and magnificence of the lofty Athenians. If we wish to go still further back, we can learn the manners of those, who on the plains of Troy for ten long years waged furious war; of Hector, Achilles, Ulysses, Troilus, Nestor, Ajax, Paris, Priam, Helen, Cressida, and the fierce prophetess, the wild Cassandra. Do we wish to learn of ancient Rome, with her eagles, her tribunes, and her lictors, turn we to Coriolanus and the Volsci, to Volumnia and her children, to Julius Cæsar, to Brutus, Marc Antony, to Cassius, Casca and Cinnius. Do we wish to learn of Egypt, with its pyramids, its deserts and its colossal architecture, turn we to *Antony and Cleopatra*. Do we wish to know of the days of semi-barbarism which have characterised our own tight little isle, turn we to Lear and Cymbeline. Do we wish to learn of fair Scotia's soil, and of wintry Denmark, turn we to *Macbeth* and *Hamlet*. Do we wish to learn of the dawn of human freedom in our native land, turn we to *King John* and *Richard II*. Do we wish to learn of the bloody wars with France, of the wars of the red and white roses, and of steel-clad knights, with brand, and glaive, and spear, turn we to *Henry IV., V., VI.,* and *Richard III.,* and do we wish to gather intelligence, turn we to his pages, and we shall find, that all ranks, all classes of the people are faithfully pourtrayed during a period, when the most startling innovations and changes were taking place; a period, when was being brought into operation an instrument, which paved the way for Luther and Melancthon, and gave importance and power to the hitherto despised toiling millions: a period commencing with the fifteenth, and continuing through the sixteenth and the first half of the seventeenth centuries. In his pages shall we find a faithful reflection of those who dwelt upon the Arno, the Tiber, and the Elbe; of those who had life and being in the waving forest of Ardennes; of those who lived in Mantua, Milan, Venice and fair Verona, all of whom he hath peopled with inhabitants perfectly real.

If we wish for a view of English society, of the feelings which actuated and directed Englishmen, we must look to the historical plays of Shakspere. In them shall we find English philanthrophy, English pride, English patriotism, in fact, all the germs of the English character revealed, for Shakspere was thoroughly national. He wrote and spoke only as an Englishman could write and speak in Elizabeth's time, and the incidents of that stirring period gave force to his writings and added wings to his imagination. The historical plays are the noblest history of England which has as yet been presented to the world, for they contain, not only the events, but the feelings, the aspirations which swayed and governed our heroic ancestors. They are life, real life, which from its commencement to its close, is a chequered career, the sunshine of April and the storms of December not unfrequently commingling. They contain no dry antiquarian research, they are not prolific of heroes of the closet, but they are redolent with life and nature, overflowing with discrimination of character, and abounding with the purposes and motives which move mankind. Shakspere was the historian of the feelings of the period in which he lived; the great bulk of the people only possessed the theatre as the means of their obtaining information, and there would they resort, to egotism; the great he tells greatly, the small subordinately. He is wise without emphasis or assertion; he is strong, as nature, who is strong, who lifts the land into mountain slopes without effort, and by the same rule as she floats a bubble in the air, and likes as well to do the one as the other."*

The state of the English language, just prior to the appearance of Shakspere as an author, and even at the time he did appear, was very bad. It was in a state of transition, and was looked upon as a rude and barbarous tongue, totally unfit to be used by scholars. His genius, seizing on the labours of all those that had preceded him in the world of literature, added to its strength, its sweetness, its grace, its fulness and its beauty. He gave it a vitality and a power that can never cease to be. He was the regenerator of our language, its refiner, and whatever word he uses takes its place in our literature, stamped with a mark that cannot be questioned. For copiousness of language, Shakspere hath no equal in our tongue; he, above all others, standeth pre-eminent, for with him language is truly a flame of fire ; a flame of such fierceness, that no other author hath ever handled it with the potency that he hath. The destruction of feudalism, which was accomplished by the wars of the red and white roses, and the enfranchisement of the English mind from the fetters of Rome; the work of the reformation, in a great measure completed the English character. At this period of our history, the exigences of our nation required great men, and they came. A rich array of names can be furnished, whose works have given to

* Emerson's Works, 1 vol. pp. 407, 408. Orr & Co., 1851.

our literature such grace, and bestowed on the English language such power, changing, in fact, the position of our nation in the world. To this state of things the works of Shakspere in no small degree contributed. The extension of our commerce, our wars with Spain, the acquirement of fresh geographical knowledge, all served to expand our notions of humanity, the philosophical conception of which, in Shakspere's time "was immensely enlarged, diversified, and enriched. The myriad-minded Shakspere—as, by an application of a term borrowed from one of the Greek fathers, Coleridge has so appropriately called him—took in this vast conception in all its breadth, and was endowed with a faculty of self-transformation into all the shapes in which the nature of man has been incarnated. He hence required a variety of phraseologies—words and combinations of words—as great as the varieties of humanity itself are numerous."*

Shakspere's personality is never displayed by any of his characters. His own personality was too plastic, looking not within, but on the infinite world without, and it readily passed into the character he sought to develope. This is one of the chief characteristics by which he is distinguished from the rest of his dramatic brethren, who frequently failed to lose their own personality in the individual they sought to pourtray. In the language of his characters, the individuality of Shakspere is never discoverable. They each speak in their true relation to the other characters of the drama, and they are constantly revealing thoughts and feelings which are common to all humanity. Each of the

* Marsh's Origin and History of the English Language, p. 566.

characters work upon each other, they are made mutually dependant, and in this consists Shakspere's observance of the true law of unity, the unity of feeling. Throughout the whole of his dramas is Shakspere self-oblivious, for they require him to be so, and "he was one of the least self-conscious men, and so he is the least personally visible in his writings. This was the condition of his greatness. He was to be so unconscious of self as to be purely reflective of all passing forms. If he had been a lesser man, he would have shown us more of himself. If more imperfect, he would have revealed more idiosyncracy. We should have caught him taking a peep at himself in the dramatic mirror. But Shakspeare's nature is all mirror to the world around him. A more conscious man would have managed to make the darkness that hides him from us a sort of lamp-shade which should concentrate the light on his own features, when he looked up in some self-complaisant pause. Not so Shakspeare; he throws all the light on his work, and bends over it so intently that it is most difficult to get a glimpse of his face. Our sole chance is to watch him at his work, and not his human leanings and personal relationship."*

Neither, is it alone, as a dramatic writer, that Shakspere is to be considered. His "sugared Sonnets," the sweet songs interspersed throughout his plays and his minor poems are among the best in our tongue. His plays transcend all others that have been written, and just in the same proportion his sonnets transcend all others. They are thoroughly natural and intensely human, full of life, moral worth and manliness. The

* Massey's Shakspeare's Sonnets, p. 533.

"myriad-minded" Shakspere, "apart from dramatic power, is the greatest poet that ever lived. His sympathy is the most universal, his imagination the most plastic, his diction the most expressive ever given to any writer. His poetry has in itself the power and varied excellencies of all other poetry. While in grandeur and beauty and passion, and sweetest music, and all the other higher gifts of song, he may be ranked with the greatest,—with Spencer, and Chaucer, and Milton, and Dante, and Homer,—he is at the same time more nervous than Dryden, and more sententious than Pope, and more sparkling and of more abounding conceit when he chooses, than Donne, or Cowley, or Butler."*

What author can be compared with Shakspere for capacity of heart; what author so redolent with universal love, that like the waters in high places it is continually gushing forth and welling up. His thorough knowledge of all, taught him a love for all; not the mawkish sentimentality which passes current in the fashionable world for that feeling, but a hearty, genuine love for the species to which he belonged, and an earnest desire to promote the wellbeing of humanity; for truly, as Ben Jonson, one of his worthiest compeers, observed,

"He was not for an age, but—FOR ALL TIME."

That Shakspere was perfect, I am not going to avow, because it would be more than we can expect from poor imperfect humanity; but that his errors are so few it would be the height of fastidiousness and false delicacy to parade them, I boldly aver. Such

* Craik's *English Literature*, Vol. 1. p. 563.

a course of judgment is a false one; it betrays a meanness incompatible with the subject, is entirely apart from the manner by which he should be judged, for it is by that which he has done, and done so well, his equal not being known, that his capabilities should be tested. "It is by the imagination, displayed in a thousand varieties of character, by his subtle and delicate fancies, his grand thoughts, his boundless charity,—nay, even by the music that steals in our souls, with the countless changes and fluctuations, from strength to sweetness, of his charming verse, that we must learn to regard him truly. But all this eulogy would be superfluous, except for a limited class of thinkers; for Shakspere is now making his way through foreign countries and distant regions; vanquishing race after race, like the great conquerors of old, in spite of ignorance and prejudice, and imperfect teachers; and in the midst of dim and obscure interpretations, that would check the progress of any spirit less potent and catholic than his own."

"In the summer time, when the world is cheerful and full of life, let us regale ourselves with the laughing scenes and merry songs of Shakspere. In the winter evenings, when sadder thoughts come forth, let us rest upon his grave, philosophic page, and try to gather comfort as well as wisdom from the deep speculations which may be found there. At *all* times let his 'Book of Miracles' be near at hand; for, be sure that the more we read therein the greater must our reverence be. And if any intruder should tell us that all we ponder on and admire is mere matter of imagination and fancy; is shadowy, unreal, without profit; and that the end is nought: bid him shew you the thing that is eternal,—or any effort of the human mind that has outlasted the dreams of poetry. Have I said that they are dreams? Alas! what is there here that is so far beyond a dream? We ourselves (so our great poet says)—

> "'Are of such stuff
> As dreams are made on: and our little life
> Is rounded by a sleep.'"*—*Tempest*, A. IV. s. 4.

---

* Barry Cornwall's Essay on the Genius of Shakspere, Tyas' edition, pp. 27, 28.

## NOTE A.

"The west yet glimmers with some streaks of day;
Now spurs the lated traveller apace,
To gain the timely inn."—*Macbeth*, A. III. s. 4.

"Sable night, mother of dread and fear,
Upon the world dim darkness doth display,
And in her vaulty prison stows the day."—*Poems*.

"The cricket sings, and man's o'er-labour'd sense
Repairs itself by rest."—*Cymbeline*, A. II. s. 2.

"Civil night,
Thou sober-suited matron, all in black."
*Romeo and Juliet*, A. III. s. 2.

"The dragon wing of night o'erspreads the earth."
*Troilus and Cressida*, A. V. s. 9.

"Good things of day begin to droop and drowse,
While night's black agents to their preys do rouse."
*Macbeth*, A. III. s. 2.

"Now the wasted brands do glow,
Whilst the scritch-owl, scritching loud,
Puts the wretch, that lies in woe,
In remembrance of a shroud.
Now it is the time of night,
That the graves all gaping wide,
Every one lets forth his sprite
In the churchyard paths to glide."
*Midsummer Night's Dream*, A. V. s. 2.

"Look, the gentle day,
Before the wheels of Phœbus, round about,
Dapples the drowsy east with spots of grey."
*Much ado about Nothing*, A. V. s. 3.

"Hark! hark the lark at heaven's gate sings,
And Phœbus 'gins arise,
His steed to water at those springs,
On chaliced flowers that lies;
And winking Marybuds begin
To ope their golden eyes."—*Cymbeline*, A. II. s. 3.

c

"Yon grey lines
  That fret the clouds, are messengers of the day."
                              *Julius Cæsar, A.* II. s. 1.

"The silent hours steal on,
  And flaky darkness breaks within the east."
                              *Richard III., A.* v. s. 3.

"The glow-worm shews the matin to be near,
  And 'gins to pale his ineffectual fire."
                              *Hamlet, A.* I. s. 5.

"See how the morning opes her golden gates,
  And takes her farewell of the glorious sun."
                              *Henry VI., pt.* 3. *A.* II. s. 1.

"The morning steals upon the night,
  Melting the darkness."
                              *The Tempest, A.* v. s. 1.

"The cock, that is the trumpet to the morn,
  Doth with his lofty and shrill-sounding throat
  Awake the god of day."
                              *Hamlet, A.* I. s. 1.

"The day begins to break, and night is fled,
  Whose pitchy mantle over-veil'd the earth."
                              *Henry VI., pt.* I. *A.* II. s. 2.

"Night's swift dragons cut the clouds full fast
  And yonder shines Aurora's harbingers."
                              *Midsummer Night's Dream, A.* III. s. 2.

"O comfort-killing night, image of hell!
  Dim register and notary of shame!
  Black stage for tragedies and murders fell!
  Vast sin-concealing chaos! nurse of blame!
  Blind, muffled bawd! dark harbour for defame!
  Grim cave of death; whispering conspirator.
  With close tongued treason and ravisher!

"O night, thou furnace of foul-reeking smoke,
  Let not the jealous day behold that face
  Which, underneath thy black, all-hiding cloak,
  Immodestly lies martyred with disgrace."
                              *The Rape of Lucrece.*

# HAMLET.

THERE have been two *Hamlets*, though but one Shakspere; the first being an early effort of the wondrous man of Stratford, the second being an elaboration of the play; and, to such an extent did the author proceed, that some have supposed the first was not written by Shakspere, but that he had merely engrafted upon the anonymous *Hamlet* his own emendations, the creation of the parts being the work of another genius. This opinion, owing to the searching enquiry which has been instituted, turns out to be a fallacy, and both the "Hamlets" have been proved to be the productions of the one great dramatist, William Shakspere. The date of the first production of *Hamlet* is the year 1600.

The earliest printed copy of *Hamlet* known, is the edition of 1603, the title of which runs as follows: "The Tragical Historie of Hamlet, Prince of Denmark, by William Shakspere, As it hath been diverse times Acted by His Highnesse servants in the Cittie of London; as also in the two Universities of Cambridge and Oxford, and elsewhere. At London, printed for N. L. and John Trundell, 1603." There are only two known copies of this edition, one being in the library of the Duke of Devonshire, and the other which was lately discovered. This copy fell into the hands of an Irish bookseller, Mr. Rooney of Dublin, who sold it in London, and it was ultimately purchased by Mr. Halliwell, in whose possession it now remains. In the last page of this copy are several different readings to the one hitherto known. In 1604 a second edition of *Hamlet* appeared, considerably enlarged and improved; the number of lines being considerably augmented, while the language is more polished and majestic in its character. It is said that the first edition was a pirated one, the words being taken down in short-hand from the mouths of the actors, while the second was published under the sanction of the author. In 1605 another edition was published, and the play was again reprinted in 1607, 1609, and 1611. It is included in the first folio edition of Shakspere's works, 1623, and another edition in 4to. was published in 1637.

After it was shown that the editions of 1603 and 1604 were the work of one genius, William Shakspere, another form of disbelief of his authorship arose, and it was contended, that, owing to a play called *Hamlet*, being played either in 1589 or 1590, thirteen years prior to the publication in 1603, that he had merely added to the work of another author. The researches, however, of modern commentators, have shown most unquestionably, that the piece which was played, and the one that was published in 1603, are identical with each other, and that the authorship belongeth solely to William Shakspere, who completed the play as we possess it now, between the years 1604 and 1607.

The history of Hamlet is found in a work of the Danish historian, Saxo Grammaticus, who died 1204. It was translated into English and published in a separate quarto tract, under the title of "The Historie of Hamlet, Prince of Denmark." The history and the play coincides to the end of the fourth chapter, but in the second, the most traces are to be found of the use Shakspere made of the story of the chronicler. It does not appear that he has borrowed scarcely an expression from the history, with the exception of the exclamation "A rat, a rat," when Polonius is slain behind the arras; and the conclusion of the play is vastly different to the history, for in that, after Hamlet's return from England, he slays his uncle, wins the affections of the Danes, is elected king, goes back again to England, slays the English king, marries two English ladies, and through the treachery of one of these ladies on his return home, he is himself slain. Such is the history, and vast is the improvement the story has received at the hands of Shakspere. He there saw a tale of rapine, murder, and adultery, the usual characteristics of a state of barbarism, and he has wedded to it a character with which the world is charmed; a character in which mankind delight, simply from the fact, of its being a reflex of themselves. The intense intellectual grandeur which Shakspere has shadowed forth in his tragedy of *Hamlet*, is as infinitely superior to the history of the chronicler, as are the temples of Greece to the wigwams of the Indians, or the statues of Phidias, to the hideous and distorted deities of the South Sea islander.

The great feature in the character of Hamlet is irresolution: opportunities present themselves, yet he does not avail himself thereof; he plays with his purposes, one moment resolving to do, the next not to do. He dreads the result of his actions, at the same time he is firmly persuaded he must perform them; for to him alone is given the power to avenge his father's murder. The killing of Polonius is made the result of accident, for on his crying for help, Hamlet thrusts his sword through the arras, exclaiming "Dead, for a ducat, dead." And on the Queen asking him, "What hast thou done?" the wish and desire that it may prove his uncle, is shown in Hamlet's answer:

"Nay, I know not: Is it the king?"—*A.* III. s. 4.

Hamlet is the representative of thought, not action: he is the child of doubt, he has no firm belief in himself, nor in those by whom he is surrounded. This doubting, the result of great thinking, is the chief cause of his non-acting; for all the results are calculated beforehand—the means whereby they are to be arrived at—and yet these calculations are not fulfilled, simply, because they serve to cripple action. This view is beautifully expressed by Hamlet himself:

"And thus the native hue of resolution
Is sicklied o'er with the pale cast of thought;
And enterprises of great pith and moment,
With this regard, their currents turn awry,
And lose the name of action."—*A.* III. s. 1.

Hamlet, though highly educated, possessing a larger share of world knowledge than any of his compeers, is morally and physically weak; a weakness which is made very apparent in the various resolutions which he adopts and never acts upon. The physical comparison which he institutes between himself and Hercules, when he exclaims "than I to Hercules," is beautifully descriptive of himself; the one all action, the other all doubt and passiveness. When Hamlet does act, it is the result of impulse, not resolve of action; he slays the garrulous Polonius, but it is only when the fit is on him. His impulses after his first interview with the ghost are to revenge his father's murder, but he does not do it. He swears by heaven that he will fulfil the commands of the ghost, that "from the table of his memory," "he will "wipe away all trivial fond records," that "with wings as swift as meditation, or the thoughts of love," he will rush to his revenge; but he does not, for he commences to think, and when his thought becomes awakened,

"Purpose is but the slave of memory,"

and he fully illustrates his own lines,

"What to ourselves in passion we propose,
The passion ending, doth the purpose lose."

The influence of the ghost leaves him, and he begins to doubt whether or no he is not the prey of an illusion. He is weak and melancholy and this latter may have over-ruled his true judgment. He is a "John a dreams, a dull and muddy-mettled rascal," and he fears the consequences of his taking action, for "the spirit," he has seen

"May be the devil; and the devil hath power
To assume a pleasing shape; yea, and, perhaps,
Out of my weakness and my melancholy
(As he is very potent with such spirits)
Abuses me to damn me. I'll have grounds
More relative than this."—*A.* ii. s. 2.

Upon the introduction of the players he determines to settle his doubts, and he conceives the idea of having presented a play, in which shall occur a scene of a similar nature to the one in which his father died; and to be more certain of the effect, he writes several speeches based upon the supposed fact of his father being murdered, and the easy way in which the forgetting wife was won by the murderer. He says,

"I have heard
That guilty creatures, sitting at a play,
Have by the very cunning of the scene
Been struck so to the soul, that presently
They have proclaim'd their malefactions;
For murther, though it have no tongue, will speak
With most miraculous organ."—*A.* II. s. 2.

These doubts will not admit of his wholly relying upon the relation of the ghost, as he does not deem that a sufficient warranty for him to act upon; he imagines his weakness may be taken advantage of, a weakness of which he is well aware; this, coupled with his melancholy, might lead to his being abused and damned. He will have greater proof before he dares to act, the chain of evidence must be strengthened, and he exclaims,

"The play's the thing
Wherein I'll catch the conscience of the king."
*A.* II. s. 2.

His purpose is answered by the play, for the king is startled, upriseth suddenly, demanding light. This circumstance fully convinceth Hamlet of the king's guilt, yet he doth not proceed to carry out his desire, the result of that conviction. On the contrary, he still procrastinates. The ghost again appears, and Hamlet, aware of his non-action, hopeth that he doth not come to chide him,

"That laps'd in time and passion, lets go by
The important acting of your dread command."
*A.* III. s. 4.

This second appearance of the ghost doth not produce any manifestation of action on the part of Hamlet, he is not yet fully decided; other circumstances are required to produce the resolve to act, and the encountering of the army of Fortinbras on its way to the war, gives occasion to Hamlet to reflect aloud upon his position. He is perfectly convinced of his laggardness, for he depicts it in the sentence,

"How all occasions do inform against me,
And spur my dull revenge."—*A.* IV. s. 4.

Of the power to accomplish that revenge he never doubts, though at times he questions its propriety,

"Some craven scruple,
Of thinking too precisely on the event."—*A.* IV. s. 4.

But the next instant returneth his self-satisfaction and the belief in his right to revenge his father's murder; yet he cannot fully resolve, there is yet something wanting, a craving he cannot satisfy,

"I do not know
Why yet I live to say 'This thing's to do;'
Sith I have cause, and will, and strength, and means
To do't. Examples, gross as earth, exhort me."
*A.* IV. s. 4.

Again he reviews his position, and compares it with that of the ready energy and bold activity of young Fortinbras, who fiery with haste is eager for the strife, while he, is sick at heart and weary in spirit. Then he compares his position with the army of the warlike Fortinbras, and shews how little cause they have to risk their lives, yet how cheerfully they do so, being ready, willing, nay eager to expose

"What is mortal, and unsure,
To all that fortune, death, and danger dare,
Even for an egg-shell:"—*A.* IV. s. 4.

While he who has a great deed to perform, does not attempt its performance; a deed, for which he hath incentives of a far more powerful nature, for hath he not

> "A father kill'd, a mother stain'd,
> Excitements of my reason, and my blood,
> And let all sleep."

These thoughts engender grief, which oppresses and overcomes his fears, and he determines, come weal, come woe, to perform his duty to the manes of his murdered parent. Thus resolved, he quits the scene to perform the deed, exclaiming

> "O, from this time forth,
> My thoughts be bloody, or be nothing worth."—*A*. IV. s. 4.

This resolve is not carried out; the feeling gradually dies away, and Hamlet embarks for England, but returns again to Denmark, when the catastrophe is brought about, not by his direct agency, though he is the instrument whereby the king is slain. He himself falls, as doth Laertes and his mother, a general wreck, in which both innocent and guilty, the avenger and the avenged, are alike destroyed; fulfilling, not poetical justice, but what is higher, the law of humanity.

The key to Hamlet's character* is found in the line

" Of thinking too precisely on the event."

This expression displays the strength of his powers of perception, without which no high development of intellectuality can take place, for it points out the cause from whence Hamlet's non-activity proceeds; and it also serves to show the intensity of his reflective powers, for his continual " cast of thought," his " thinking too precisely," prohibits him from fulfilling

* See illustrations A and B.

his dearest hopes and wishes, and completely deters him from carrying into effect those things upon which he is constantly pondering.

He is apparently convinced of his inability to act, for before he attempts action he feels that he cannot succeed, and this feeling is thoroughly in accordance with his nature which partaketh of too much thinking. He is overwhelmed by "the pale cast" and this constant state of thought awakens moral and intellectual considerations which act as checks and ultimately prevent his power of action.

Hamlet appears to be too intellectual for action; his powers of perception are so great, that he clothes with such horror to himself the consequences of the deed, that the deed itself becomes obscured, and he fails to perform it. He shrinks from its performance, wishing it to be rather the result of accident, than, that he, should accomplish the wish of the ghost and the tenor of his own thoughts. He is continually starting to achieve the slaying of his uncle, yet as continually drawing back, alarmed by the phantoms which his ever-working brain calleth into existence. When the death of the king is accomplished, and the murder of his father is avenged, it was not by Hamlet's seeking—it was, as it were, thrust upon him by circumstances, the action drifted towards him. The catastrophe is realized by the hand of Hamlet, but not through him, for it appears not to be man that fulfils it, but destiny. Hamlet had thrust upon him a great work, a work greater than he was capable of performing, for his power lay chiefly in conceiving, not in action. It is in this lack of activity and in the causes which produce it, one of Hamlet's chief characteristics, that

Shakspere has shown his almost perfect knowledge of human character, and displayed his power to delineate it. The moral nature of Hamlet is of the most "sweet and commendable" kind, he is naturally gentle, full of conscientiousness, desirous of acting upon principle, so that he never is fully satisfied that to be revenged, is to act justly. The moral feelings of the young prince are of a very sensitive nature, and this coupled with the great intellectuality which marks his character, saw no method of activity wherewith it was satisfied, and, as the necessary consequence of dissatisfaction, non-activity was the result. The evil of not acting when we resolve to act is thoroughly understood by the crafty subtle Claudio, for he most truthfully discourses upon its results in his speech to Laertes, when he says,

"That we would do,
We should do when we would; for this world changes,
And hath abatements and delays as many
As there are tongues, are hands, are accidents,
And then this 'should' is like a spendthrift sigh,
That hurts by easing."—A. IV. s. 7.

This shows how great was the master's art, how comprehensive his genius, and what a profound knowledge he possessed of humanity, and of the motives which determine human conduct and procedure, when he could thus successfully depict its character.

Hamlet in his own thinking is but the child of destiny. He is but a weak, inactive creature who has a mission to fulfil and which he shrinks from performing. His course of action is predetermined, it is thrust upon him, he being but the instrument of destiny. He would that it were not so, his wishes and inclinations being otherwise, but he feels that he has no choice, for

"heaven hath pleas'd so,—
To punish me with this, and this with me,
That I must be their scourge and minister."
*A*. III. S. 4.

The play of Hamlet is said to contain the philosophical opinions of the author, who undeniably advocates the empire of necessity throughout the play. The will is made subservient to the circumstance, and the characters act solely as necessity doth regulate them. Hamlet is the type of a sceptic, his age is just the period when men are torn with conflicting doubts, he questions everything, believes in no one, but doubteth all. The *pros* and *cons*, the doubts and hopes are put forward more powerfully in Hamlet, than in any other of Shakspere's plays. Hamlet is rendered dissatified with this world, but still he sees no hope of a better one in the future. His first soliloquy betrays this, when he says,

"O, that this too, too solid flesh would melt,
Thaw, and resolve itself into a dew!
Or that the Everlasting had not fix'd
His canon 'gainst self-slaughter. O god! O god!
How weary, stale, flat, and unprofitable
Seems to me all the uses of this world!
Fie on't! ah fie! 't is an unweeded garden,
That grows to seed; things rank and gross in nature,
Possess it merely."—*A*. I. S. 2.

Here we have the wish for entire annihilation, the complete destruction of existence; the world is not good enough to live in, the beauty of the work of creation is questioned, and the wisdom of God is doubted in the result produced, for

"it is an unweeded garden,
That grows to seed; things rank and gross in nature,
Possess it merely."

That Hamlet is a follower of the old creed of the government of mankind by circumstances or necessity, such terms being synonymous, is most forcibly shown in his description of his countrymen. Necessity or circumstance is the guide of their conduct, upon this principle they are dependent, for

"So oft it chances in particular men,
That for some vicious mole of nature in them,
As in their birth, (wherein they are not guilty,
Since nature cannot choose his origin,)
By their o'ergrowth of some complexion,
Oft breaking down the pales and forts of reason;
Or by some habit, that too much o'erleavens
The form of plausive manners; that these men,
Carrying I say, the stamp of one defect;
Being nature's livery, or fortune's star,
Their virtues else (be they as pure as grace,
As infinite as man may undergo)
Shall in the general censure take corruption
From that particular fault: the dram of ill
Doth all the noble substance often doubt, *(to put out)*
To his own scandal."—*A.* I. s. 4.

The world-famous soliloquy, "to be or not to be," is another illustration of the same principle. Necessity, thou mother of all, is the governing power, and the conclusion arrived at, is that of non-futurity. Not only does this speech show that the thoughts of Hamlet are sceptical, but it also shows that he wishes for no future state of existence; he would that the old Sadducean doctrine were true.

"To die,—to sleep,—
No more; and, by a sleep, to say we end
The heartache, and the thousand natural shocks

That flesh is heir to—'t is a consummation
Devoutly to be wished. To die,—to sleep."—*A*. III. s. 1.

The same idea Shakspere hath pourtrayed in his play of the *Tempest*, when Prospero exclaims

"Our little life is rounded with a sleep."—*A*. IV. s. 1.

In *Measure for Measure*, the same idea is found in the speech of the Duke, who after reasoning for some length on life, says it is

"As it were an after-dinner's sleep."—*A*. III. s. 1.

The words put in the mouth of the player king, are but a development of the doctrine of necessity. The destiny of man and his will run opposite to each other; our thoughts are our own, but the end, the result of such thinking, is totally beyond our control: we are only instruments acted upon, not the actor; for

"Our wills and fates do so contrary run
That our devices still are overthrown;
Our thoughts are ours, their ends none of their own."
*A*. III. s. 2.

The scepticism of Hamlet removes much of the obscurity attending the play. On no other ground can the various inconsistences and strange vagaries of Hamlet be accounted for. He is dissatisfied with the circumstances by which he is surrounded and he is equally as dissatisfied with himself. He believes not in the truthfulness of those with whom he cometh in daily contact, and his belief in humanity is thereby destroyed. He doubts himself, he doubts his fellows, and these doubts lead him into scepticism and from thence into the broad principles of materialism. The changes of nature, her transformations are shadowed forth in the lines,

> "Imperial Cæsar, dead and turned to clay,
> Might stop a hole to keep the wind away;
> O that that earth, which kept the world in awe,
> Should patch a wall to expel the winter's flaw."—*A*.v. s. 1.

This is the basis of the philosophy of the material philosophers of ancient and modern times. This principle was not probably well understood by the multitude in the days of Shakspere, but the men of learning, the philosophers of the period, and the companions of the poet were perfectly cognizant thereof. Shelley in his *Queen Mab*, a poem, in which necessity "thou mother of the world" as he calls her, is made the governing power, dilates upon the same idea, when he says,

> "There's not one atom of yon earth
> But once was living man;
> Nor the minutest drop of rain,
> That hangeth in its thinnest cloud,
> But flowed in human veins."—*C*. II.

Of the material tendency of Hamlet's remarks on the dust of Alexander there cannot be any doubt, the reply of Horatio to Hamlet's question serves to support this,

> "Twere to consider too curiously to consider so,"

for Horatio shrinks from contemplating the abyss to which such reflections would lead; the conclusions he is not at all prepared for, nor is he willing to accept the consequences of such a creed. He is a Christian, and thinks reason is perverted from its legitimate purpose, when it is directed to such peculiar speculations; while on the other hand, the scepticism of Hamlet exults in such matters, for he exclaims in answer to Horatio, "No, faith, not a jot," and then proceeds to show the various stages the body passes through, prior to becoming loam to "stop a beer barrel." These principles have been more fully developed and to a great extent have been established by the science of modern days. The immense strides which science has taken, have placed them upon a proper basis, "and had the poet conveyed his ideas in a philosophic dissertation, in place of a dramatic composition, the language he would have used, in all probability, would have been of that character which marks the philosophy of the present day, for Hamlet's observations upon this occasion, amount to the same import which the following passage implies:—Matter is eternal! the molecules of the body merely pass from one into the other; they survive the destruction, or rather the dissolution of organic and inorganic beings, when the former ceasing to live, restore to the inexhaustible fund of nature those elements which she lends, without ever parting with them."\*

Vindictiveness is another marked point in the character of Hamlet, and one that is very strongly displayed. His slaying of Polonius, affords him an opportunity of tormenting his mother, by language of a harsh and cruel nature, and he does not forget to avail himself of the opportunity. His mother exclaims,

"O what a rash and bloody deed is this!"
*A*. III. s. 4.

To which he answers,

"A bloody deed: almost as bad, good mother,
As kill a king and marry with his brother."
*A*. III. s. 4.

\* An Essay on the Tragedy of Hamlet, by P. Macdonell, late President of the Royal Physical Society of Edinburgh, pp. 48, 49.

Not content with this, Hamlet appears to lose all love of his mother in this scene, and he is determined she shall feel the weight of his words; he tells her to

> "Leave wringing of your hands : Peace, sit you down,
> And let me wring your heart : for so I shall,
> If it be made of penetrable stuff;
> If damned custom have not braz'd it so,
> That it is proof and bulwark against sense."—*A.* III. s. 4.

Then, on being questioned by his mother,

> "What have I done that thou dar'st wag thy tongue,
> In noise so rude against me?"

He paints her conduct in the darkest colours, describing it as

> " Such an act,
> That blurs the grace and blush of modesty;
> Calls virtue, hypocrite; takes off the rose
> From the fair forehead of an innocent love,
> And sets a blister there; makes marriage vows
> As false as dicer's oaths."—*A.* III. s. 4.

The hasty marriage of his mother with his uncle, he cannot account for; from that fact, he is almost inclined to conceive her a partner in the crime; he cannot forgive her, so surprised is he at her conduct, and he is struck with astonishment and wonder, that she should have so soon forgotten his father, whom he describes as

> " A combination and a form indeed,
> Where every god did seem to set his seal
> To give the world assurance of a man."—*A.* III. s. 4.

While his uncle he paints as a

> " A murtherer and a villain,
> A slave, that is not twentieth part the tythe
> Of your precedent lord :—a vice of kings ;
> A cutpurse of the empire and the rule."—*A.* III. s. 4.

So great is the enormity of his mother's conduct in his view, that he cannot believe that natural circumstance caused his mother to marry his uncle, there must have been some agency of a supernatural character to have worked the change : he asks her
"What devil was 't,
That thus hath cozen'd you at hoodman-blind?"
*A.* III. s. 4.

And then he proceeds to denounce her in language of a very strong nature.
"O shame! where is thy blush? Rebellious hell,
If thou canst mutine in a matron's bones,
To flaming youth let virtue be as wax,
And melt in her own fire : proclaim no shame,
When the compulsive ardour gives the charge;
Since frost itself as actively doth burn,
And reason panders will."—*A.* III. s. 4.

The vindictiveness of Hamlet towards his mother is so great that he almost hates her. All love for her appears to be absorbed and swallowed up in his desire to avenge his father's death, by accomplishing his revenge upon his father's murderers. He cares not how the venom of his tongue rankles in her breast; he doth not respect the love which she holds towards him; he will not hear of any excuse for her marriage with his uncle; he admits of no extenuating circumstances, but he is resolved to keep her in hand, and tells her she
"shall not budge;
You go not, till I set you up a glass,
Where you may see the inmost part of you."

The passion so grows upon him, that he would probably have slain her, had not the ghost have commanded him not to do so; for it tells Hamlet, on its first visitation, to

"Taint not thy mind, nor let thy soul contrive
Against thy mother aught, leave her to heaven
And to those thorns that in her bosom lodge
To prick and sting her."—*A*. I. s. 5.

The remembrance of this injunction restrains the prince, and it is only by words, and not by deeds, that he severely rebukes his mother's conduct.

There is a refinement of malice, the height of vindictiveness, displayed by Hamlet in his conduct towards his uncle; in the first place, by awakening remorse in the bosom of the guilty monarch by means of the play, and secondly, when he will not revenge his father's death, because his uncle is at his prayers. Hamlet, seeing the king kneeling, thus soliloquizes

"And am I then reveng'd,
To take him in the purging of his soul,
When he is fit and season'd for his passage?
No,
Up sword, and know thou a more horrid hent;
When he is drunk, asleep, or in his rage,
Or in the incestuous pleasure of his bed;
At gaming, swearing, or about some act
That has no relish of salvation in't:
Then trip him, that his heels may kick at heaven;
And that his soul may be as damn'd, and black,
As hell, whereto it goes."—*A*. III. s. 4.

The conduct of Hamlet towards Ophelia, can only be accounted for, by the spirit of vindictiveness which he evinces. His wish to defeat the designs of Polonius and his daughter, causes him to display but little regret when they have left the stage of life. The scene with Ophelia, when he tells her to get to a nunnery, furnishes us with an example of his bitter mocking spirit. He questions her honesty, her fairness, and then tells her, if honest, she should "admit no discourse to your beauty;" taunts her with her father being a fool, and when told he is at home, tells her to "let the doors be shut upon him, that he may play the fool no where but in his own house." Upbraids her, and her sex, and says, "if thou wilt marry, marry a fool, for wise men know well enough what monsters you make them."

Hamlet could never have had much love for Ophelia or he would not have treated her in the manner that he did.* Where Shakspere has painted the true development of love, as in *Romeo and Juliet*, feuds and family quarrels all yield, nay, even life itself is surrendered to its power, and had Hamlet have loved the fair Ophelia, as ardently as she loved him, he never could so have acted towards her. That Hamlet possessed no real love for Ophelia, is evinced by his treatment of the fair girl during the acting of the play scene. The coarseness of the language, his ribald allusions, and even his ribald conduct, all point to the fact that he had no love—that the feeling had been put on, assumed, not felt: a mere show, "worn upon his sleeve;" a toy, in which he found amusement, and which being "as brief as the poesy of a ring," could be easily cast off. One who truly loved could not so have treated the object of his affections, as Hamlet treated Ophelia before the King and his court.

It is said, that Hamlet's conduct at the fair girl's funeral affords ample proof of his love, but this is much to be questioned. His language is that of a mere braggart; besides, it is not sorrow for Ophelia, but anger with her brother that causes him to leap into her grave, else why the expression in the following scene to Horatio,

* See illustration C.

> "But sure, the bravery of his grief did put me
> Into a towering passion."—*A.* v. s. 2.

His being in "a towering passion" with her brother, is presumptive proof of the truth of his own words, "I loved you not." The grief, sympathy, and sorrow of Laertes over the grave of his sister, would naturally excite similar feelings in the breast of a lover, but here to mark that no love existed, Hamlet admits that he was wrought into a "towering passion" by the "bravery" of her brother's grief. The expression which Hamlet makes use of on first learning of Ophelia's death, shows that his love was not very strong; he exclaims, "what, the fair Ophelia?" is that all an earnest lover would have said—does that sentence express the weight of woe and sorrow which a lover would feel on learning for the first time the death of the dear one? No! there would have been something different to that expression, something in which more pain, sorrow, and anguish, would have been depicted—something more than is displayed in those boastful lines he addressed to her brother:

> "Dost thou come here to whine?
> To outface me with leaping in her grave?
> Be buried quick with her, and so will I;
> And, if thou prate of mountains, let them throw
> Millions of acres on us; till our ground,
> Singeing his pate against the burning zone,
> Make Ossa like a wart!"—*A.* v. s. 1.

Such language as this doth not show that Hamlet possessed any love for "the fair Ophelia"; it is but the furious outpourings of a brain, not wrought on by sorrow and grief at the loss of the loved one, but lashed into a storm of passion, as he confesses, by the great and real grief displayed by Laertes. Again, when Hamlet has learned the fact, that through his rejection of Ophelia combined with the slaying of her father, the aberration of her brain ensues, and ultimately leads to her death, he evinces no sorrow, and after the burial scene he doth not even allude to her. This silence on the part of Shakspere throughout the rest part of the play, is highly significant; it demonstrates that he intended Hamlet's love of Ophelia, should not be of a lasting nature; it was a mere transient feeling which passed away, and left the young prince's heart totally unaffected by the result of the passion. That this is the case with Hamlet is certain: were it not, there would have been some melancholy image lingering behind, which would have betrayed itself in the outpourings of Hamlet's fancy.

The one passion in which the brain of Hamlet was absorbed, is revenge of his father's murder; to this end all his thoughts converge. It takes possession of his faculties, and all other passions are discarded; there was no room for love in Hamlet's brain, that passion must have been absorbed in the greater one, revenge. Throughout the play, from its commencement to its close, revenge, not love, is the all-absorbing passion of the Danish prince, and yet from the sensitiveness of his moral nature he is never satisfied whether it is right to act upon this passion; and when even he does act, such action is not provided for, it is not from conviction, but from impulse.

Hamlet by some writers has been represented as being really mad, but this is a supposition quite apart from the truth. Were the madness of Hamlet otherwise than assumed, the sovereignty of Hamlet, which is, his great intellectuality, would be destroyed. This assumed madness is the result of intellectual calculation, for it serves as a cloak, the better to accomplish his purposes; to lead astray the parties upon whom he wishes to be revenged; to throw them off their guard, so that they may not be prepared to counteract the power that he intends to bring to bear upon them. Hamlet is thoroughly master of himself, for he can disguise so artfully that his mask is not seen through by those by whom he is surrounded. In the art of concealment he is a thorough artist, his emotions being hidden behind a veil that is impenetrable even by his friend Horatio: and it is this power which enables him to feign himself mad so closely and to sustain so naturally the part he has undertaken. When Hamlet first appears in the play, he doth not evince any signs of madness; no show of mental aberration takes place until the second act. After the interview with his "father's ghost," and he administers the oath of secrecy to Horatio and Marcellus, Hamlet's course of action commences against the usurping king. Reasons opposed to the opinion of Hamlet being really mad, are easily to be found among his own words, which furnish several examples. The first instance occurs in *A.* I. s. 5, after the ghostly visitation, when Hamlet addressing his two friends, says

> "How strange or odd soe'er I bear myself,
> As I perchance hereafter shall think meet
> To put an antic disposition on."

Again, *A.* III. s. 4, in the scene with his mother, when the ghost appeareth to him a second time, and she surprised at her son's behaviour, exclaims

"This is the very coinage of your brain;
This bodiless creation ecstacy
Is very cunning in,"
to which he replies,
"Ecstacy! My pulse as yours doth temperately keep time,
And make as healthful music: It is not madness
That I utter'd: bring me to the test,
And I the matter will reword; which madness
Would gambol from."

In the same scene, near to the close, after cautioning his mother not to let the king become acquainted with the secret, he says

"Let him not
Make you to ravel all this matter out,
That I essentially am not in madness,
But mad in craft."

His soliloquies throughout the play are also reasons against his being really mad, for no expressions can be found in them, in the slightest degree tending to show that the prince is in a state of, or approaching to insanity. Hamlet's "wildness is never incoherent as it would have been had he been really crazed. There is always intellect behind his utterances, and he strikes his adversaries as he might have done had he been free to use no mask. Thus his mask and his face were very near being one, and in the tumult of his excitement, he must have felt it highly convenient to cover his agitation with so ready an excuse."*

Of the madness of Hamlet, the king, in conjunction with the rest of the court, does not entertain a doubt; his own guilt adding force to his conviction, he is perfectly satisfied of his nephew's lunacy. In the king's

* Weldon's Register, *Dec.* 6, 1863, p. 683.

interview with Polonius, *A*. III. s. 1, he explains to him the mental condition of the prince, and after complying with the advice of the old courtier, he exclaims,

" It shall be so,
Madness in great ones must not unwatch'd go."

The third scene in the same act furnishes still further proof, when the king addressing Rosencrantz and Guilderstein relative to Hamlet being sent to England, says

" I like him not ; nor stands it safe with us,
To let his madness range.
The terms of our estate may not endure
Hazard so dangerous, as doth hourly grow
Out of his lunacies."

The fourth act scene also furnishes another proof of the king's belief in Hamlet's madness, for when speaking to the two same courtiers, he says,

"Hamlet in madness hath Polonius slain."

Hamlet never attempts to go straight or direct to accomplish his purpose. Owing to his great thinking on the result, he becomes fearful of the consequences, and this deters him from a direct course of action. He is glad to avail himself of any subterfuge, and under the guise of madness, he is afforded more chances of wounding his enemies by "hurtling words," than he would, were he to attempt it in a state of lucidity. In the history, Hamlet assumes madness to deceive his uncle Fengon, in order to escape from his tyranny, and Shakspere in this instance closely adheres to the story of the chronicler. Another historic instance is found of madness being assumed, in the case of Lucius Junius Brutus, who adopted this course of action, in order that he might better prepare the Roman people to obtain their freedom, and which the rape of Lucrece, and her death, gave him the opportunity to achieve, by destroying the Tarquin dynasty. That Hamlet completely deceives all those with whom he is brought in contact is certain; it is first seen in *A*. II. s. 2, when he enters reading, in answer to the question of Polonius, as to his knowing him, by saying, "Excellent, excellent, well; you're a fishmonger;" then he gives him advice relative to his daughter, tells him, "If the sun breeds maggots in a dead dog, being a good-kissing carrion," not to let her "walk in the sun: conception is a blessing; but not as your daughter may conceive." The instituting of the contrast between the conception of the loving Ophelia, with the germination of animal life by the rays of the sun, in the putrified carcase of a dog, is so extravagant, that none but a madman, or he who had assumed its guise, would ever have drawn it. The expression shows to a great extent, that the madness is assumed, for it contains a philosophical opinion of the day, viz. the theory of spontaneous generation, that is generation without copulation. Through the whole of this scene, Hamlet continues to banter Polonius, and so finely is the line drawn, that after depicting the character of the old courtier, Polonius, answers, "though this be madness, there is method in it." The reception given to Rosencrantz and Guilderstein by Hamlet, and the peculiar vein of language which he applies to them, affirms the truth of his madness being assumed. It is true that the madness of Hamlet is quite different to that of another character which Shakspere has drawn in a similar position, viz. Edgar, in *Lear*. In Edgar no expression occurs that would lead to the purpose being suspected for which he has assumed madness; he makes no allusion to his wrongs, while Hamlet cannot refrain from indulging in expressions which display his knowledge of the villany of his uncle. The greater firmness of purpose which Edgar's course of action evinces, arises from his intellectuality not being so great; his brain not being overwhelmed with doubt, he has no scruples of "thinking too precisely." This is shown too, in Edgar's choosing a character which undergoes physical suffering, exposed to the war of the elements and the external vicissitudes of nature. Even his language partakes of his situation, for he exclaims, "Poor Tom's a cold, poor Tom's a cold." Polonius is fully persuaded that Hamlet's mental disease is the result of his loving Ophelia and his rejection by her, for he tells the king, speaking of his daughter's conduct

"Which done, she took the fruits of my advice;
And he repulsed (a short tale to make),
Fell into a sadness, then into a fast,
Thence to watch, thence into a weakness,
Thence to a lightness; and, by this declension,
Into the madness wherein now he raves,
And all we mourn for."—*A*. II. s. 2.

So convinced is Hamlet's mother of her son's madness, that she is ready to adopt the opinion, of the loss of Ophelia's love as the cause, and hopes—but the wish is father to the hope, that with her love will come the cure. She thus addresses Ophelia,

"I do wish,
That your good beauties be the happy cause
Of Hamlet's wildness: so shall I hope your virtues
Will bring him to his wonted way again,
To both your honours."—*A*. III. s. 1.

The scene with Hamlet and Ophelia which follows, display this wildness to its fullest extent, the bitter words, the galling jibes, and Hamlet's total denial of his gifts to the fair maiden, completely convince her of the truth of her father's supposition, for she exclaims,

"O what a noble mind is here o'erthrown."

The scene with Rosencrantz and Guilderstein in *A*. III. s. 3., clearly shows that his madness is assumed, for he perceives to what purpose they are seeking to play upon him, and by his conduct, he shows, how thoroughly conversant he is with their designs. Had his madness been real, this great power of perception could not have been displayed; madmen may be cunning, many have evinced the faculty, but none who have been really mad, have ever developed such power of perception as doth the character of Hamlet. How exquisitely doth he reveal the inmost natures of the two butterfly friends, and shows to them how futile are their efforts to blind him to their purposes. His introduction of the pipe, and his questions relative to their playing upon it—their answers, and his crushing reply—prove that it is an assumption of madness, not reality. He says, "Will you play upon this pipe?" they cannot, for they have not the skill; to which Hamlet replies, "Why, look you now, how unworthy a thing you make of me. You would play upon me; you would seem to know my stops; you would pluck out the heart of my mystery; you would sound me from my lowest note to the top of my compass: and there is much music, excellent voice, in this little organ; yet you cannot make it speak. S'blood! do you think I am easier to be played on than a pipe? Call me what instrument you will, though you can fret me, you cannot play upon me." He who could thus point out the weakness of his enemies, and display his own strength, must exist in a state of sanity, not that of insanity. There is nought disordered or raving; there is no outpouring of frenzy or despair; but there is the cool, biting sarcasm of one who had a thorough knowledge of his opponents, but whose opponents had no knowledge of him. The conclusion of the scene, when Hamlet resolves on visiting his mother, is yet further illustrative of this view. The manner he intends to act towards her, the language he shall use is determined upon before going; he would not that "the soul of Nero" should enter his "firm bosom;" he would

> " Be cruel, not unnatural:
> I will speak daggers to her, but use none;
> My tongue and soul in this be hypocrites;
> How in my words soever she be shent, [*reviled, abused*]
> To give them seals never, my soul, consent."—A. III. s. 2.

The character of Ophelia is most exquisitely drawn by Shakspere; "the fair Ophelia," the gentle rose, the bud of beauty lost in blossoming, is another triumph of the great master's skill. With a temperament highly sensuous, yet not passing into sensuality, she plays her part, moved to action by the wishes and desires of her father and the commands of her sovereign. She is perfectly pure in thought and in action; her virtue is part of herself, it does not proceed from fear of the world, but it is the result of her nature. She quarrels not with her brother, when giving his advice and exhorting her to preserve her chastity;

she passes by the reproof, for her virtue is of that nature, that it

> "suns the doubt away
> Wherewith mistrust would cloud it."*

Of her love for Hamlet there cannot be any doubt; with her the passion is a strong and holy one; she loved him with all the fervour of a woman's love, with all the passion of a first love; and when Hamlet grows cool, denying the passages which occurred between them, her reason gets unstrung, the death of her father giving the finishing stroke to the evil, commenced by the rejection of her love by Hamlet. She glows with pity, when she imagines Hamlet has lost his reason, being deceived by his assumption of madness, and her love displays itself in the brilliant description which she gives of her former lover.

> "O, what a noble mind is here o'erthrown!
> The courtier's, soldier's, scholar's, eye, tongue, sword;
> The expectancy and rose of the fair state,
> The glass of fashion and the mould of form,
> The observ'd of all observers, quite, quite, down!
> And I, of ladies most deject and wretched,
> That suck'd the honey of his music vows,
> Now see that noble and most sovereign reason,
> Like sweet bells jangled, out of tune and harsh;
> That unmatch'd form and feature of blown youth
> Blasted with ecstacy: O, woe is me!
> To have seen what I have seen, seen what I see."
>
> *A.* III. s. 1.

The real madness of Ophelia serves also to show the madness of Hamlet to be assumed, by the latent thoughts which are developed while the fair maid is in her insane mood. Hamlet thoroughly perceives the

---
\* *The Wife, A.* III. s. 4.

movements of his opponents, he is completely master of their positions, and in language of the most forcible character he does not fail to tell them so. Intellectuality being the distinguishing point of his character, the madness which he assumes partakes of the intellectual. This is the reverse of true madness, for in a real state of insanity the very opposite is the case, the most pious become blasphemous, the most pure become lewd. Ophelia in her sane state was never sensual, though sensuous; throughout her life she had struggled and wrestled, conquering her passions, but when reason was dethroned, when the brain became unshipped, she sings snatches of lewd songs, and her talk appertains to lewdness. This, by some, has been raised as an objection to the completeness of the author's skill; they, the objectors, have contended that Ophelia ought not to have known such lewdness, forgetting that the period in which the play was written and the period to which the play alludes, that many of the ballads were tainted with wantonness. The fact of the author putting such snatches of songs into the mouth of Ophelia, only proves his through knowledge of humanity. We all know things of a lewd nature, the knowledge of which is forced upon us, for we know not the means nor the manner by which it comes in our passage through the world, and which our better part, viz. our moral power, while in a state of sanity, would prevent us from putting into practice, but should we unfortunately pass from sanity into a state of insanity, then the foe which we have struggled with and subjected, becomes a master holding tyrannic sway.

Polonius is a character most masterly drawn; we find him under some circumstances a complete courtier,

full of garrulity and nonsense, squaring his notions with those of his sovereign; continually thrusting himself forward to serve the kingly interest; centering all things to advance himself in kingly favour. He would have made a most excellent diplomatist, for he turns everything towards his one thing, and seeks to divert the most opposite to support his own views. He is fond of crooked ways, he loves eaves-dropping; he never looks direct but always aside; he is full of the conceit of emptiness, whose fancied craftiness is but a "foolish prating knave." His wisdom is of that character that he arrives at his conclusions by the use of contrarieties, as when he tells Reynaldo,
"And thus we do of wisdom and of reach,
With windlasses and with assays of bias,
By indirections find directions out."—*A.* II. s. 1.
He feels and acknowledges the "divinity which doth hedge a king," and when he learns of the love-passages between his daughter and young Hamlet, he determines to prevent a continuation thereof, charges Ophelia to return the presents she has received, and prohibits her from having conversation with the young prince, until he has learned the royal will. His subservience to the court is here shown, his admiration of routine is here displayed, for he even will not have the love carried on, though fully satisfied of Hamlet's sincerity, believing, as he does, his preventing the same is the cause of the lord Hamlet's madness, until the prince's uncle knows what has taken place. Afraid of the consequences which would result to him, he says to his daughter,
"Come, go we to the king:
This must be known; which, being kept close, might move,
More grief to hide than hate to utter love."

At times, the spirit of the father, the love of his children breaks out, we find him full of wise saws and giving sound and healthy advice. His maxims to Laertes, when going on an embassy to France, are full of sound wisdom, of wisdom which shows his knowledge of the world and his peculiar belief of the manner which a man should act in it. They are precepts which he wishes his son to treasure up in his memory, precepts, which Laertes should remember simply as precepts, for the ideas which they should engender, Polonius knows not of, he has no construction in his nature, therefore the precepts are only preached: he says,

"Give thy thoughts no tongue,
Nor any unproportion'd thought his act.
Be thou familiar, but by no means vulgar.
The friends thou hast, and their adoption tried,
Grapple them to thy soul with hoops of steel;
But do not dull thy palm with entertainment
Of each new-hatch'd, unfledg'd comrade. Beware
Of entrance to a quarrel; but, being in,
Bear't, that the opposed may beware of thee.
Give every man thy ear, but few thy voice:
Take each man's censure, but reserve thy judgment.
Costly thy habit as thy purse can buy,
But not express'd in fancy; rich, not gaudy:
For the apparel oft proclaims the man;
And they in France of the best rank and station
Are most select and generous, chief in that.
Neither a borrower, nor a lender be;
For loan oft looses both itself and friend,
And borrowing dulls the edge of husbandry.
This above all,—To thine ownself be true,
And it must follow, as the night the day,
Thou canst not be false to any man."—*A.* i. s. 3.

These are precepts learnt by rote, they are but maxims*

* "A maxim is a conclusion upon observation of matter of fact, and is merely retrospective: an idea, or, if you like, a principle, carries knowledge

so doled forth; with them, as Polonius prates, there is no association of ideas, there is no weighing, no analyzation; he does not teach his son their relative value, but he only repeats them as he has learned them, simply because he is a man of maxims, not ideas. "Polonius never had an idea, and could not have one; he had maxims, beautiful and true, and laws warranted to apply to cases which he had tried; but a constructive thought—something which, carried with us, shall develope itself into a law, as circumstances demand—he had not; therefore, where experience carried, he is wise; where rule of thumb had not taken him, he is a fool."* In Polonius there is no real sincerity, except we view him under the aspect of a father; in all else, he is weak, garrulous and impotent; and his discourse to the king, relative to Hamlet's madness, is a splendid example of the folly of his talking. When viewed as a courtier, Polonius appears a tedious old fool, but when viewed as a father, he is full of love for his children and highly gifted with prudence. He was beloved by his children, for his death is the chief cause of Ophelia's insanity, and the desire of Laertes to revenge his loved father's death is so great, that he sacrifices his honour to accomplish it. A natural result in one who is devoid of thought and is but the creature of action. There is an inconsistency on first looking at the character of Polonius, but it is only an apparent one, for Shakspere, always

within itself, and is prospective. Polonius is a man of maxims. Whilst he is descanting on matters of past experience, as in that excellent speech to Laertes before he sets out on his travels, he is admirable; but when he comes to advise a project, he is a mere dotard. You see Hamlet, as the man of ideas, despises him."—*Coleridge's Table Talk*, p. 40.

* Rev. George Dawson on *Hamlet*.

true to nature, distinguishes between the understandings and the moral habits of men, and he makes Polonius to be a gossiping, time-serving man of the world, devoid of a love of the truth, a repeater of maxims, deficient in the power to construct and exemplify the ideas which should be generated by his talking.

Horatio is a most excellent foil to the character of Hamlet; he is a scholar and a gentleman, with just sufficient ability to pass the ordeal of a University examination, yet without the great genius to fully value the character of his friend. He is prosaic, belongs to the matter-of-fact world, while Hamlet is full of poetry and philosophy. Horatio represents the standstill policy of human thought and human action, for he is terribly frightened at the consequences—consequences anticipated by his own fears—at the longings and questionings of the young prince. The speculations of Hamlet, relating to a future life, he seeks to check; he is perfectly content to take things as he finds them, and implicitly to believe, solely, because he has been so taught. There is just sufficient intellectuality in the character of Horatio for Hamlet to make him his friend, but he lacks capacity, he is deficient in power of brain to interchange thought and action in the mental world with the Prince of Denmark. His friendship partakes of the outer, not the inner world, with him there is no similarity of ideas, no commingling of intellectual activity, no rendering back a phase of thought for those which he receives. Horatio is simply receptive in his capacity, in him the productive faculty does not exist. Had he have possessed this mental calibre, the play would have contained two Hamlets, but Shakspere has wisely placed him as the receiver of the outpourings of Hamlet's fancy and aspiration, withholding the power of imaging them forth.

The character of the King is essentially true to nature. In him we have the "vaulting ambition," of which Macbeth is another phase. There is not the high resolve, the daring of the Scottish chieftain, to be found in the king of Denmark, for he achieves by means more stealthy, the murder of his brother. The marriage of the widow, in fact, proceeds from a desire to posses the show of right to claim the vacant throne. He is but a petty villain;

"A murtherer,—a slave,—a vice of kings!
A cutpurse of the empire and the rule;
That from a shelf the precious diadem stole."
*A.* III. s. 4.

Had the king have possessed the hardihood of Macbeth and adopted the same mode of accomplishing his purposes, the going direct, instead, of only plotting as he does the death of Hamlet; had he himself been the perpetrator, the doer of the evil deed, he would have detracted from the all-absorbing character of the play, for the course of action with which he commenced would have been continued by him, and the young prince would have been as safely disposed of as the aged Duncan was by the murderous thane. The nature of Hamlet's uncle is too pusillanimous to adopt such a course of action; it is too weak, shrinking, from fear of the result to himself, and he simply conceives the assassination, leaving it to others to effect his hopes and desires.

The queen figures but as a subordinate in the play, yet with her, as with some of the principal characters, there is a continual struggle, a wrestling for victory between the antagonistic principles of right and wrong. In the scene with her son, she is probed to the very quick, and though pained by the sharp invectives which he applies, her maternal love rises above the pain, and she implores him, when he is wrought upon by the appearance of the ghost,

"O gentle son,
Upon the heat and flame of thy distemper
Sprinkle cool patience.—*A.* III. s. 4.

There is no allusion in the play to imply her guilty knowledge of the deeds done; she is gentle, mild, and maternal, anxious for the well-being of her only child; and even after that child "hast cleft her heart in twain," she still loves him, and when dying, exclaims with a mother's anxiety and love,

"O my dear Hamlet."—*A.* v. s. 2.

The choleric, impetuous Laertes is the opposite of Hamlet, he does not give way to thinking, he reasons not upon how, when, or where to act, but acts at once. The nature of his character presents a most striking and powerful contrast to that of the young prince. No sooner does he learn of the death of his father, than he flees from Paris to avenge it. The one thought of vengeance alone filleth his mind, and every nerve is strained to action. When he arrives in Denmark, and discovers to whom suspicion points as the murderer of his father, the king, *he* having caused Polonius to be secretly buried, thus bringing suspicion on himself, Laertes fears not, exciting the people by his wrongs, he leads them to revolt, till "rebellion looks so giant like," and backed by armed men rusheth into the kingly presence, demanding his father, and when told that he is dead, demands,

> "How came he dead? I'll not be juggled with;
> To hell, allegiance! vows, to the blackest devil!
> Conscience, and grace, to the profoundest pit!
> I dare damnation: to this point I stand,—
> That both the worlds I give to negligence,
> Let come what comes; only I'll be reveng'd
> Most thoroughly for my father."—*A.* IV. s. 5.

Satisfied with the assertions of the king that the guilt belongeth not to him, Laertes, in his intense desire to avenge his father's murder, a desire rendered yet more strong by witnessing the sad state of his dear sister, falleth readily into the kingly plot, and determines to do aught and everything, for when questioned by the king

> "What would you undertake
> To show yourself your father's son in deed
> More than in words?"

answers,

> "To cut his throat i' the church,"

and not content with this, in order that his revenge may be gratified, he will sully his knightly honor, by anointing his sword with "an unction" bought of a mountebank,

> "So mortal, that but dip a knife in it,
> Where it draws blood, no cataplasm so rare,
> Collected from all simples that have virtue
> Under the moon, can save the thing from death,
> That is scratch'd withal: I'll touch my point
> With this contagion, that if I gall him slightly
> It may be death."—*A.* IV. s. 7.

Laertes and the warlike Fortinbras, are both representatives of action, and as such furnish a most expressive contrast to the non-activity of the Danish prince.

The grave digging scene is one of the most charming in the tragedy. In it the reflective phase of Hamlet's character is most excellently developed, and his contemplative speeches afford a beautiful contrast with the rude, rugged pleasantries of the humorous sextons. The solemnity and pathos of Hamlet's musings in the churchyard are most wonderfully set off by the jests of the grave diggers. Here are two extreme aspects of the same humanity. The fellow who "hath no feeling of his trade, shall yet have acquittal, for need and custom have made him what he is; and the fastidious prince shall shrink the less from the coarse jester, since he might have been like to him, but for the chances of thought and leisure,— 'the hand of little employment hath the daintier sense.' "*

The introduction of this scene, has been condemned by some writers, but their condemnation carries with it its own refutation; for it shows how infantine was and is their knowledge of humanity, and how little they understood the author's aim. They have complained that it was vulgar, the wit of the grave-diggers low, and that the comedy which they pourtray, interfered with the harmony and destroyed the solemnity of the play. In real life, we perceive the joys and sorrows, the tragic and the comic phases mingle together; the ridiculous treading hard upon the heroic, as night followeth hard upon the day; and the poet to be true, must not forget to display this.† His work to be

* The *Athenæum*, No. 1491, January 7th, 1865.
† Gerald Massey, in one of his poems, called *Husband and Wife*, beautifully pourtrays this idea:
"The suns will shine, and the rains will fall,
On the loftiest, lowliest spot!
And there's mourning and merriment mingled for all
That inherit the human lot."

HAMLET. 73

perfect must be in harmony with nature, "and so in it there must, as in an April day, be sunshine, and cloud, and shadow, and the play of children, and the sorrows of the soul, and the house of mourning next to the wedding house, and men must go from one to the other. Thus that grave-digging scene is just and beautiful in its place—is obedient to the law of life, shows us what life truly is, makes us accept its uncertainties, and learn that great lesson—how different are the laws of the construction of this world from what they would be if made by our unlearned art. If out of life we can shake vain and unseemly jests, then out of our play we may shake the clowns and the jesters, who are always there in Shakspere's plays to teach us the lesser side of life, to show us the harmonic whole, and teach us to call nothing common or unclean."\*

Murder, adultery, deep drinking and a great want of honour and moral worth is evidenced by most of the characters by whom Halmet is surrounded. The knowledge and power of thought which the young prince possesses is not in unison with the state of society in which he is placed. It is a wild period and the manners and customs are rude and barbaric. From such a state the nature of Hamlet wholly reverts, for by his great thinking he has become more tenderly alive to the finer feelings of humanity, and thus he hath enkindled a deep sensibility and a high state of intelligence which unfits him for the physical action so necessary in such an age.

*Hamlet* is a work upon which no two writers have wholly agreed, but it is a work the most complete that

\* Rev. G. Dawson on *Hamlet*.

ever has been written. Human life with all its hopes
and aspirations, its joys and sorrows are here displayed,
and the reader or the spectator can readily embody
them as his own. The villainous king, the easy
yielding queen, the hot choleric Laertes, the cool prosaic Horatio, the rude wit of the grave-diggers, the
sententious garrulity of the worldly wise, maxim
preaching Polonius, the foppery of Osric, the fawning
sycophancy of Rosencrantz and Guilderstein, the fair
and loving Ophelia, and the warlike Fortinbras, with
the pomp and majesty of war, all form a picture of
the most varied and animated kind. A picture, in which
every shade of thought, the dark perplexities of our
being, the endless enquiries and divings in the arcana
of Nature, the restless longings, the hopes and fears
of another life, are all foreshadowed and dwelt upon.
From another world the more forcibly to paint the
picture, has Shakspere drawn one of his characters;
the grave has been called upon to surrender one of its
tenants, and in the ghost of Hamlet's father, we see
as it were an herald demanding vengeance upon those
who had been guilty of an enormity: a demand which
is complied with by accidental means only, and not
by a course of justice, which would the more solemnly
impress upon the spectators, or reader, the natural
result of unbridled passions, but innocent and guilty
are alike dragged down in one common ruin, no distinction or difference being made, between the guilty,
the less guilty, and those wholly innocent. Nor could
the poet have made that distinction, he seeks to
represent the world and those who move and have their
being therein, to depict the motives which move and
govern humanity, and thus holding up "the mirror"

to be true to nature, he could not have made the piece to finish with universal happiness, for it would have been at variance with the law of humanity.* Under all circumstances, is the poet ever faithful to this law, and though in this play, to use the words of Schlegel, "the destiny of humanity is exhibited as a gigantic sphinx, which threatens to precipitate into the abyss of scepticism, all who are unable to solve her dreadful enigmas,"† we are compelled to acknowledge that truth, fair truth, is here seated on her throne, and that a lesson of the most useful character is laid down for our instruction and admiration.‡

\* See illustration D.
† Schlegel's Dramatic Literature, p. 406.
‡ "This drama is stern. In it truth doubts, sincerity lies. Nothing can be more immense, more subtile. In it man is the world, and the world is Zero. Hamlet, even full of life, is not sure of existence. In this tragedy, which is at the same time a philosophy, everything floats, hesitates, delays, staggers, becomes discomposed, scatters, and is dispersed. Thought is a cloud, will is a vapour, resolution is a crepus cule; (broken light) the action blows each moment in an inverse direction, man is governed by the winds. Overwhelming and vertiginous, (whirling) work, in which is seen the depth of everything, in which thought oscillates only between the king murdered and Yorick buried, and in which what is best realized, is royalty represented by a ghost and mirth represented by a death's head.
Hamlet is the chef d'œuvre of the tragedy dream.—*Victor Hugo on Shakspere*, pp. 199, 200.

## ILLUSTRATIONS.

(A) "If he had been a man of action, whose firstlings of the heart are those of the hand, he would have struck in the earliest heat of his revenge. He feels while he questions, that it is not true that he is 'pigeon liver'd, and lacks gall to make oppression bitter;' but he does lack that resolution which 'makes mouths at the invisible event;' he does make, 'I would, wait upon, I will:' he does hesitate and procrastinate and examine his motives, and make sure to his own mind of his justification."—*The Psychology of Shakspere, by Dr. Bucknell*, p. 67.

"Hamlet's character is the prevalence of the abstracting and generalizing habit over the practical. He does not want courage, skill, will, or opportunity, but every incident sets him thinking; and it is curious, and at the same time strictly natural, that Hamlet, who all the play seems reason itself, should be impelled at last by mere accident to effect his object."—*Coleridge's Table Talk*, p. 40.

Hamlet "is not a character marked by strength of passion or will, but by refinement of thought and feeling. His ruling passion is to think, not to act, and any vague pretence that flatters this propensity, instantly diverts him from his previous purposes."—*Hazlitt's Shakspere Characters*, pp. 108, 111.

Hamlet's "irresolution results in no wise exclusively from weakness, but essentially also from conscientiousness and virtue: and it is just this subtle combination which renders Hamlet such an essentially tragic character. His doubts as to the certainty of the fact and the legitimacy of revenge, the gentleness of his soul, which unconsciously struggles against the means of vengeance, the bent of his mind to reflect upon the nature and consequences of his deed, and by this means to paralyse his active powers, all these scruples 'of thinking too precisely on the event,' he himself calls in the warmth of self-blame,

"A thought which quartered, hath but one part wisdom,
And ever, three parts coward."
*Gervinius's Shakspere Commentaries*, vol. II. p. 133.

"The chief thing which strikes us in the character of Hamlet is his irresolution; everything he does is 'sicklied o'er' with doubt and uncertainty; he occupies himself with constant and unsatisfactory meditations upon the great mysteries of life and death; he is in all things sceptical, and in losing his faith in nature, he loses much of his love of it also."—*Essay on Hamlet, Shakspere Gallery.*

"The character of Hamlet embodies the predominance of the contemplative element over the practical in a mind of the highest order, both intellectually and morally."—*W. W. Lloyd's Essay on Hamlet.*

"The rise, progress, and consummation of the whole plot of the tragedy of Hamlet, is a consistent theme upon the conflict between determination and irresolution, arising from over reflection; and in nothing throughout the whole scheme of the play is the art of the poet more grandly developed, than in making the vacillation of the hero to turn solely upon that over-reflectiveness of his nature."—*Shakspere's Characters, by C. C. Clarke*, p. 91.

(B) "Captured by pirates, he is set on shore in Denmark against his will, and although he seems at last to make up his mind to act, nevertheless, no one of the subsequent events is brought about by his own free volition, or according to his own intention."—*Ulrici on Shakspere's Dramatic Art*, p. 220.

"To me it is clear that Shakspere meant in the present case to represent the effects of a great action laid upon a soul unfit for the performance of it. In this view, the whole piece seems to me to be composed."—*Goethe's Wilheim Meister*, vol. I. p. 200.

Hamlet "is eaten up with a great woe, which shuts out all sympathy with others, and wanders about on the stage of life like a man who has some task to do greater than he can perform. Destiny has proposed to him a riddle which he cannot solve; and because he cannot, like the Sphinx of old, it devours him."—*H. T. Essay on Hamlet, Shakspere's Gallery.*

(C)  "Even if we exclude the scene of his excited violence towards her, and forget the dumb-show mummery that she relates, there still remains a frigidness in all his allusions to her, and in the rarity of these allusions also, that impeaches the sincerity of the passion that he once professed for her, and even the ordinary considerations and delicacy that were due to her misfortunes, tho' they had not originated with himself."— *W. W. Lloyd, Essay on Hamlet.*

(D)  "Here we have no villain punished on some self-conceived and rigidly accomplished scheme of vengeance: a horrid deed occurs; it rolls itself along with all its consequences, dragging guiltless persons also in its course; the perpetrator seems as if he would evade the abyss which is made ready for him; yet he plunges in, at the very point by which he thinks he shall escape and happily complete his course.

"For it is the property of crime to extend its mischief over innocence, as it is of virtue to extend its blessings over many that deserve them not; while frequently the author of the one or of the other is not punished or rewarded at all. Here in this play of ours, how strange! The pit of darkness sends its spirit and demands revenge; in vain! Neither earthly nor infernal thing may bring about what is reserved for Fate alone. The hour of judgement comes: the wicked fall with the good; one race is moved away that another may spring up."—*Goethe's Wilhelm Meister,* vol. I., p. 206.

# THE
# MERCHANT OF VENICE.

This Comedy was probably produced in 1594, for there is an allusion in Henslowe's Diary which serves to support this view. It records the performance of "The Venesyon Comedy," on the 26th of August, 1594, at which date the company to which Shakspere belonged, was playing conjointly with Henslowe's, at Newington Butts. It is mentioned by Francis Meres, in his *Wit's Commonwealth*, published in 1598. The earliest printed edition was in 1600, the title of which ran as follows: "The most excellent Historie of the Merchant of Venice, with the extreame crueltie of Shylocke the Iewe towards the sayd Merchant, in cutting a just pound of his flesh: and the obtayning of Portia by the choyse of the three chests. As it hath beene diuers times acted by the Lord Chamberlaine his Seruants. Written by William Shakspere. At London, printed by J. R., for Thomas Heyes, and are to be sold in Paules Churchyard, at the signe of the Greene Dragon." Another edition was published in the same year, printed by J. Roberts. *The Merchant of Venice* is among the plays contained in the folio of 1623. In 1637 an edition in 4to. was published, and another in 1652.

It has been thought by some that Shakspere derived his plot from a ballad called *Gernutus, the Jew*, printed by Percy, in his *Reliques* of Antient English Poetry, but the earliest date assigned to the publication of the ballad is 1598, and the comedy being produced about 1594, four years prior to the ballad, the plot or idea could not possibly have been borrowed from it. The allusion in Gosson's *School of Abuse*, is of too vague a nature to conclude that an elder play existed prior to Shakspere's, upon which he grafted his own conception. A collection of tales under the title of *Gesta Romanorum*, was probably the source from whence the incidents of the comedy were drawn, the incidents being founded upon two separate narratives of the action of the pound of flesh and of the three caskets contained in that work, but the characters, the language, and the poetry and sentiment, alone belong to William Shakspere, who has produced a play full of the deepest worldly wisdom, fraught with lessons to the human race, for it is a reflection of the realities of ordinary life, in which the qualities and passions of human nature are investigated.

Shakspere in this comedy as well as in his tragedy of Othello, seems thoroughly to understand the nature and state of Venice and the Venetians. "It is impossible not to feel the truth of atmosphere in the whole movement and tone of the plays themselves. The moment we look behind Shylock or Othello we see Venice, the glare of its torches, the noise of its revels, the endless warfare of lazzi and badinage, its easy morals, its cynical proverbs, its quick, secret rivalries and passions, the silence and order of its streets, the proud gravity of its nobles, the wise whispers of its council chamber, the hum of its Rialto, the strange medley of East and West on its piazza." It was the only state in which the confusion of tongues could be heard, and in which the turban of the Turk and the gaberdine of the Jew could be seen in contact with each other. On its lagunes and canals, within its palaces and squares, beneath its piazzas, the representatives of many nations were gathered together, and Venice was the only city in Europe at that time, in which a dream of our common humanity could be indulged in with any degree of dramatic truth. Shakspere has seized upon this advantage and here reproduces with wonderful fulness and completeness, the Venice of the 16th century.

In this comedy Shakspere depicts the wrongs which the Jews suffered because of their religious opinions; and points out the intense hatred in which the Jews were held by the Christian inhabitants of the European continent, at the period of the play, which may be put down as the early part of the author's life. All the characters are tainted with this vice. They all indulge in sneering remarks upon the Jewish people, and under every and all circumstances treat them with contempt. This intense hatred of the Jews is first shown when Shylock describes the wrongs he has undergone at Antonio's hands. It is shown again in the conduct of the clown Gobbo, who will not let his father make a present to his master Shylock, because he is a Jew. "Give him a halter," he exclaims; inferring that anything but hanging is too good for a Jew.

The speeches which Shakspere hath put in the mouth of Shylock show that he lived before his age. The intense dislike which was felt and held by the majority of mankind relative to the Jewish people had not died out. Everywhere they were held up to scorn and execration. But Shakspere's great love of humanity,—that golden link which binds and connects him with all ages,—prevented him from indulging in the common feeling against the Jews, and was the one great cause of the fairness of his view and portraiture of Shylock. Though probably not wholly exempt from the taint of dislike to the Jewish people, yet with what infinite wisdom has he in this comedy inculcated that great law of humanity, which owns the wickedness, as well as shows the folly of revenge. To both Christian and Jew he deals out the same vigorous blows; to both he points out with unerring hand, the evil results which flow from indulgence in "unbridled revenge," and that under no circumstances can such a course of action be right, for its basis is wrong, and all the results which flow, must be wrong also.

The tragic interest turns upon the contumely with which the Jews are treated. From this cause, in conjunction with Antonio's lending "out money gratis," arises the intense hatred which Shylock bears him. The railing of Antonio against Shylock's "sacred nation," his mocking "at his gains," his thwarting of his bargains, and his laughing at his losses, because he is a Jew, awakens that fierce hate which leads to the desire of Shylock to accomplish Antonio's death, by demanding the fulfilment of his bond, and thus "the ancient grudge" which Shylock holds, will be fatly fed.

The character of Shylock is a compound of money-loving and hatred of Christians. This can in no way be wondered at; it is the natural result of what he and his nation have suffered at the hands of the so-called followers of Christ. The hate of Shylock to Christians displays itself almost as soon as he enters. In reply to Bassanio's invitation, he breaks out into invectives, sneers at Jesus, and says he will do anything but eat, drink, and pray with a Christian. His deep hatred of Antonio in particular, is most forcibly displayed, and his reasons are made most apparent,—firstly, because of his lending "out money gratis;" secondly, because "he is a Christian;" and thirdly, because Antonio hates his "sacred nation;" and he rails

"Even there where merchants most do congregate,
On me, my bargains, and my well-won thrift,
Which he calls interest. Cursed be my tribe,
If I forgive him."—*A*. I. s. 3.

Shylock's enumeration of the insults which he has received, both in word and deed, awakens most strongly his desire of revenge; and should he "catch him once upon the hip," he will "feed fat the ancient grudge" he bears him. His willingness to lend the money, not for interest, but simply for the bond "of a pound of flesh," betrays his anxiety to have Antonio in his power, for he calculates the probability and possibility of the merchant's ventures on the main being swallowed up by the "yesty waves that confound navigation," and then, true to his hatred, he will have his bond and his bond alone.

In the scene with Jessica, *A*. II. s. 5, the same feeling breaks forth in Shylock, when telling her he is

"Bid forth to supper.
There are my keys. But wherefore should I go?
I am not bid for love; they flatter me:
But yet I'll go in *hate*, to feed upon
The prodigal Christian."

No fear of consequences can overcome this feeling. Above all others it is paramount; the portents which affect him, do not so, sufficiently, to rule him. He is "right loth to go," but go he will, though

"There is some ill a-brewing towards his rest."

His dreaming "of money bags" will not deter him, so strong is his hatred of Christians; and this feeling is also the cause of his parting with the fool, because he parts with him

"To one that I would have him help to waste
His borrowed purse."

The money-loving side of Shylock's character is most masterly shown in the speeches of Salanio when describing the Jew. Shylock in money matters is cautiously circumspect and full of meanness. He loves his money for the results which flow from its possession and for the importance which it adds to his position on the Rialto where "merchants most do congregate." He is the very opposite of Antonio in matters of wealth, for the princely merchant values it, chiefly for the sake of his friends and is therefore disinterested, while the Jew loveth it for its own sake and for the good bargains it enables him to drive. His love of money, and his less love of his daughter, are truthfully displayed in his exclamations,

"My daughter! O my ducats! O my daughter!
Fled with a Christian! O my Christian ducats!
Justice! the law! my ducats, and my daughter!
A sealed bag, two sealed bags of ducats,
O double ducats, stolen from me by my daughter!
And jewels, two stones, two rich and precious stones,
Stolen by my daughter! Justice! find the girl!
She hath the stones upon her, and the ducats!"

*A.* II. s. 8.

In the opening part of scene 1, *A*. 3, above all things rises the loss of his ducats. His money to him is of more consequence than the loss of his daughter. He cares not so much for her, it is not the loss of her that makes him furious, it is the ducats she has taken,—the ducats it hath cost him to pursue her. If she were dead at his feet, he would not care, so long as she had the jewels in her ears, or "the ducats in her coffin." It is the loss of the jewels and the ducats which preys upon him, for there is no spark of humanity left in his nature, it is completely absorbed. swallowed up in his love of money and his hatred of the Christian world.

In this scene, the hate which Shylock bears Antonio, wells up till it bubbles over. Every insult, every wrong, whether real or imaginary—he remembers, and upon the head of Antonio will he pour out the vial of his wrath. He is determined not to spare him,—he will have his "pound of flesh," if only to "bait fish withal." His appeal to Salarino relative to the hopes, desires, and feelings of a Jew being equally the same as those of a Christian, only serves to whet his appetite, and make him the more resolved to vent the whole of his hatred of the Christian race upon the person of the "royal merchant," Antonio. This hatred rises to the topmost height, when Shylock learns from Tubal the intelligence relative to Antonio. His present losses he recks not of; all those losses can be made up again, for by working out his revenge on the merchant, in compelling him to fulfil his bond, he "will have the heart of him, for were he out of Venice, I can make what merchandize I will." This sordid feeling which is one of the great features in the Jewish character, in conjunction with his hatred of the Christian world, wholly destroys all love for his child, and he leaves the scene, directing Tubal to fee him "an officer," without reverting to her who had rebelled against him, who had forsaken his house and left him a childless man; for childless he must become, his daughter being compelled to abjure her father's creed and accept the Christian one, before she could be married.

In scene 3, A. III. the hatred of Shylock is still further developed. He is solely intent upon his bond. No tears shall move him from his purpose. He will not be told of mercy; he is sworn against it. His solemn oath, the oath of his nation, is pledged to have his bond, and have it he will: he'll

"not be made a soft and dull-eyed fool,
To shake the head, relent, and sigh, and yield
To Christian intercessors."

His passionate exclamation of "Follow not," shows that he is determined not to be moved from his purpose; he will not listen any longer, for he leaves, saying,

"I'll have no speaking: I will have my bond."

The trial scene is one of the finest in the comedy, and throughout this scene Shylock has the best of the argument. The law is in his favour. He has both that and justice on his side, for the signing of the bond is the voluntary act of Antonio, an act, the result of which was foretold him before he signed it, and of which he himself was perfectly cognizant. In the law lieth Shylock's power,—to that he appeals, the law in its letter not in relation to its spirit. He discards all feelings of humanity, and demands the fulfilment of the letter of the law. In this scene the coolness and firmness of Shylock is magnificently pourtrayed. His coolness, by the excellent manner in which he answers both the Duke, Bassanio and the others who seek to drive him from his purpose; and he displays his firmness, by his positive expressions of standing by the law and the law only. His intense hatred of Antonio, because he is a Christian, and also because he has injured him in trade, so bind up Shylock, that all feeling for human-kind is dried up within him, and he desires nought, and will accept nought less, than the "penalty and forfeit of his bond." When by an evasion, owing to an omission in the wording of the bond, his desires are overthrown and his purpose defeated, his firmness giveth not way; it does not yield until the means whereby he lives are taken from him, when his whole wealth is wrested from him and given partly to his foe, and partly to his daughter and her husband, then his physical—not mental—nature yields, and he asketh for

" Leave to go from hence ;
I am not well : send the deed after me,
And I will sign it."

This physical prostration lasts but an instant, for when he is leaving the stage, the taunts of Gratiano awaken once more his fierce hatred of the Christian race, and he gathers himself together, and turning round upon his tormentor, fixes upon him a look of intense hate and ineffable scorn, and thus leaves the busy scene to be seen no more.

Antonio, the sad, here used in the sense of grave, yet gentle merchant, is most firmly and truthfully drawn by the master's hand. He is no mere trader, no " petty trafficker," he is truly of that great merchant class, whose commercial spirit and enterprise effected changes of such a character as to influence, direct and rule the destinies of nations. His dealings with the world are of the most honorable kind. His charity, his real love for his friend, which even the dread of death can not destroy, all serve to mark him as a character which winneth the esteem of those with whom he cometh in contact. He is generous to a fault, and his openness of nature will not permit him to tell a falsehood. He has no care for wealth, but as it will serve to administer to the wants of his friends, for when appealed to by Bassanio, he says,

> "My extremest means,
> Lie all unlock'd to your occasions."

He is "the dearest friend," full of kindness and goodness, an "unwearied spirit."

> "In doing courtesies; and one in whom
> The ancient Roman honour more appears
> Than any that draws breath in Italy."
>
> A. 3. s. 2.

When charged by Shylock with having reviled his "sacred nation," and "spat upon" his "Jewish gaberdine," he at once admits the truth of the charge in his answer, and candidly confesses he should do the same again. He says,

> "I am as like to call thee so again,
> To spit on thee again, to spurn thee too."—A. 1. s. 3.

This scoffing of the Jew, this reviling and spitting upon Shylock, was the characteristic of the age, rather than of the individual; for the nature of Antonio is gentleness and honesty. His bigotry and intolerance result from the state of society, which collectively looked upon the Jewish people as an inferior portion of mankind. In the like manner in the Northern States of America, although the negroes are legally held to be free, yet are they still held up to scorn and looked upon as an inferior race to the white population. No posts of honour or of emolument in the state, however great their ability, are they allowed to occupy, and even when serving in the ranks of the Northern army, however great the skill and bravery they may display, they are not allowed to rise above the rank of a non-commissioned officer. Such too was the condition of the Jewish people on the continent at the time of the play, and the estimation they were held in was of no higher character. Even in their dress, the law interfered, and they were compelled to wear an orange coloured bonnet, nor were they allowed to appear in any other colour on the head, orange or yellow being considered an infamous colour.

Antonio's friendship for Bassanio is of the finest description, it in fact passes into love,—a love not of the character which is found existing between the sexes, but a love which rises above the fear of consequences and which nought on earth can subdue or destroy. Whatever comes "within the eye of honour," he is willing and ready to do for Bassanio. His purse, his person, his "extremest means," are "all unlocked" for Bassanio's use. He even would not that Bassanio should spend the time "to wind about" his "love with circumstance." It is this love which sustains him in the trying hour, and which causes him to exhort Bassanio thus:

"Repent not you, that you should lose your friend,
And he repents not that he pays your debt."—*A.* IV. s. 1.

The approach of death,—for death must be the result of the carrying out of Shylock's bond, in nowise intimidates Antonio. He preserves the same gravity which he displays in the earlier scenes, nor does he complain of the strait that he has fallen into by being bound for his friend. On the other hand, he wishes

Bassanio to commend him to his "honourable wife," to tell her how he loved him, and when she knows all

"bid her be judge
Whether Bassanio had not once a love."—*A.* IV. s. 1.

When released from his state of peril, he seeketh not to have his revenge upon the Jew. His gentleness breaks forth—the gentleness of his nature overcoming the harshness of his religious training—and he displays no desire to become possessed of the half of the Jew's fortune which the state awards him,

"So please my lord, the duke, and all the court,
To quit the fine for one half of his goods,
I am content; so he will let me have
The other half in use, to render it,
Upon his death, unto the gentleman
That lately stole his daughter."

He then relapses slightly into the bigotry of the age, when he demands

"Two things provided more, that, for this favour,
He presently become a Christian."

But it passes away in the next breath, for he proceeds on Jessica and Lorenzo's behalf, when he asks,

"The other, that he do record a gift,
Here in the court, of all he dies possess'd,
Unto his son Lorenzo and his daughter."

The gentleness of Antonio and the strength of his love for his friend, are yet made more apparent in the last scene, which ends this charming comedy, when he becomes the peacemaker between Bassanio and his wife. In the playful quarrel which ensues between Portia and her husband, relative to the giving of the ring, he says,

"I once did lend my body for thy wealth;
Which, but for him that had your husband's ring,
Had quite miscarried: I dare be bound again,

My soul upon the forfeit, that your lord,
Will never more break faith advisedly."—*A.* v. s. 1.

Bassanio is most skilfully depicted. He is an adventurer, whose means have been dissipated in externals, whose estate hath been disabled

"By something showing a more swelling port"
than his
"faint means would grant continuance."

His form and features are most excellent, his nature is open, brave and generous, and this combination winneth the love of Portia. His openness and generosity form the chief connecting link between him and Antonio. They are each ready to make sacrifices for each other; Antonio places himself and his life in peril to serve his friend, and Bassanio in return, is willing to "pay twice the sum" of Shylock's bond, and "if that will not suffice," "to pay it ten times o'er," on forfeit of his hands, his head, his heart.

Bassanio's love of dress, both for himself and his followers is displayed, when he accepts the services of Lancelot, and directs his steward, Leonardo, to

"Give him a livery
More guarded than his fellows."—*A.* II. s. 2.

He is a "Venetian, a soldier and a gentleman," incapable of meanness, or any of the petty vices which infect humanity; for were he possessed of those and guilty of their practice, he would not be a fit compeer for the "royal merchant" Antonio, who, evidently holds him in the highest esteem, placing him first upon the list of his friends, as he is already first in his heart. Believing, as Antonio does, that it is to Portia's advantage that she becomes possessed of Bassanio, he fails not to tell her, that it was for her "wealth," (wealth being here used in the sense of advantage) that he "did lend his body" and become security for his friend.

Bassanio is also possessed of no mean share of scholastic attainments, and his powers of perception have been well cultured in his passage through the world. He displays those powers in the scene with Shylock and Antonio, when the Jew proposes the terms of his bond as security for the loan advanced. The fear of consequences, resulting from such a bond, is foreshadowed by his active intellect, which at once perceives the risks to which Antonio's merchandise is exposed, the possibility of a total loss, and he shrinks with dread from his friend being bound for him in such a bond. Instinctively he feels and knows the hate of Shylock to Antonio, and this knowledge prompts him to advise his friend not to sign such a deed, declaring

"You shall not seal to such a bond for me:
I'll rather dwell in my necessity."

This fear, this dread, is not removed by Antonio's answer, and Bassanio, even after the merchant has declared his intention of signing, still remains affected. He cannot conceive of Shylock being kind; he believeth not in the Hebrew, as evidenced by his expression,

"I like not fair terms and a villain's mind."

The praise bestowed upon Bassanio, by the messenger, is of no mean character, and fitly pourtrays one that should be compeer to such a one as Antonio. Speaking of the "young Venetian," that comes to announce his lord Bassanio's approach, he says,

"I have not seen
So likely an ambassador of love;"

and the comparison he institutes between him and Bassanio is most beautiful,

"A day in April never came so sweet,
To show how costly summer was at hand,
As this fore-spurrer comes before his lord."—*A.* II. s. 9.

Bassanio possesses all the qualities to win a woman's sympathy and love, and it is these self-same qualities that endears him to the feelings of Antonio, who becometh security to supply his wants; and it is through these wants Shylock gets connected with Antonio and the action of the piece goeth on.

Gratanio is the gentleman wit of the comedy, and presents a forcible contrast to the clown Lancelot Gobbo. He makes no attempt to "try confusions," he plays not upon words; he transposes no sentences, but he speaks "an infinite deal of nothing." He is a mere utterer of words which convey no meaning and are only pregnant with sound. He hath but little thought in his composition, and his expressions evoke but little thought in others. Reason with him is almost a stranger, for though he talks "more than any man in all Venice, his reasons are as two grains of wheat hid in two bushels of chaff; you shall seek all day ere you find them: and when you have them, they are not worth the search." He would play

"the fool,
With mirth and laughter let old wrinkles come;
And let my liver rather heat with wine,
Than my heart cool with mortifying groans."

He is all life and animal spirits. Sadness and he have parted acquaintance; he is full of bantering; each and all come in for their share of his lively rattle. He is the prototype of a fast man of the modern time.

Bassanio's fears arise that the purpose of his visit to Belmont may be spoiled by Gratiano's exuberance; his "wild behaviour" may be misunderstood. He is not willing that he should go, and when Gratiano exclaims,
"I must go with you to Belmont,"
Bassanio answers,
"Why, then you must:—But hear thee, Gratiano:
Thou art too wild, too rude, and bold of voice;
Parts that become thee happily enough,
And in such eyes as ours appear not faults;
But where they are not known, why there they show
Something too liberal. Pray thee, take pain
To allay with some cold drops of modesty
Thy skipping spirit; lest, through thy wild behaviour,
I be misconstrued in the place I go to,
And lose my hopes."—*A.* II. s. 2.

The reply of Gratiano is a quiet, yet highly effective sarcasm upon the hypocrisy, not only of Shakspere's time but all other times. Its beauty consists in its truthfulness and in its universal applicability, for the putting "on a sober habit," looking "demurely," "grace saying," sighing, &c. are still adopted, if not to please "a grandam," to please the world, the better to promote one's prospects therein. The serious side of Gratiano's character is shewn in the trial scene; he there loses all his folly, when he perceives the danger in which Antonio stands, for he quickly apprehends that the merchant's life must be lost if the tenor of the bond be fulfilled. He thoroughly knows the harshness of the Jew's nature, his own prejudices strengthening his belief in that harshness. He sees through the guise of Shylock, who in simply standing by the law will obtain the life of the merchant, and thus consummate the revenge he has long been seeking.

Shakspere, true as he ever is, puts not in Gratiano's mouth, even in his graver moments, language of a persuasive nature. In such a boisterous youth, one "so rude and bold of voice," it would have been out of place and totally inconsistent. He has therefore given him language, in which invectives of the strongest character are found, but all of which fail to move the Jew from his point, the "bond," for Shylock somewhat tauntingly replies,

"Till thou canst rail the seal from off my bond,
Thou but offend'st thy lungs to speak so loud:
Repair thy wit, good youth, or it will fall
To cureless ruin."

Gratiano's mocking spirit returns to him when Shylock is overcome by the subtlety of Portia, and when the Jew is broken in fortune and in mind, compelled to become a Christian, he tells him

"In christening shalt thou have two godfathers:
Had I been judge, thou shouldst have had ten more,
To bring thee to the gallows, not the font."

There is not much to mark the character of Lorenzo, yet there is sufficient to make him of interest and a necessity to the development of the plot of the comedy. His love for Shylock's daughter, her love for him and their elopement are necessary to the action of the piece. In worldly knowledge Lorenzo is weak; of the value of money he hath scarcely any knowledge. Like Jessica, he squanders it away upon any frivolity. This is the result of his training, and this weakness is well known to Antonio, who wishes, and the wish is granted, to have the half of old Shylock's money to use for the benefit of Lorenzo and his wife. Lorenzo is another of the trio of friends whose adventure upon the sea of matrimony has had a successful issue. He is a little in advance of the period; his prejudices against the Jewish people not being so strong as those of Antonio and the rest of the characters. There is more poetry in his nature than in any other of the male characters, and wherever the poetic faculty exists, a corresponding expansion of ideas is found. That he truly loveth Jessica is evidenced by his language. He says, speaking to Gratiano,

"Beshrew me, but I love her heartily;
For she is wise, if I can judge of her;
And fair she is, if that mine eyes be true;
And true she is, as she hath prov'd herself;
And therefore, like herself, wise, fair, and true,
Shall she be placed in my constant soul."—*A*. II. s. 6.

This speech is most beautiful, and it shows the earnestness of his love for the pretty Jewess, despite the difference of their religious creeds,—a difference that does not in any way affect his passion, nor prevent him from fulfilling "the crown of his heart's desire," the marrying of the Jewish maiden. This is but another phase of the power of love,

"Sole monarch of the universal earth,"

which the great master has so frequently and so skilfully shown.

The opening of the last act of the comedy is full of splendid language, and the speeches which fall to the lot of Lorenzo, are full of classic allusions and beautiful ideas, developing the poetic side of his character, for it is this poetic feeling, that first fixes his affection upon the pretty Jewess, and which finally resolves him to consummate his love by the bond of marriage.

Solanio and Salarino are specimens of the gay young men of Venice,—lads for feasting, fun, and revelry.

They are of a class that were numerous in the city of the sea, who were unfitted for trade by the volatility of their dispositions, nor did they possess a sufficiency of ballast to be marked for embassies or other matters pertaining to the state. They are precursors of a class that are to be found numerous in our own country, possessing neither gentle manners nor great intellectual acquirements. Both Solanio and Salarino are tainted with the vice of the age, uncharitableness; both scoff and flout the Jew, sneering at the passion into which Shylock is thrown by the loss of his ducats and his daughter. Both taunt him and upbraid him, and both rejoice in the part they have played in assisting Lorenzo in his elopement with Jessica. Their conduct to the Jew is apt to raise our disgust, and it is only kept down by the high admiration in which they hold the "royal merchant." They are all feeling for Antonio, than whom "a kinder gentleman treads not the earth." They are apprehensive for his means and they would not cause him any pain by the relation of his losses, for when Salarino learns from the Frenchman, that

"in the narrow seas that part
The French and English, there miscarried
A vessel of our country, richly fraught:
I thought upon Antonio when he told me;
And wish'd in silence that it were not his.
*Solan.*—You were best to tell Antonio what you hear;
Yet do not suddenly, for it may grieve him.
*A.* II. s. 7.

Launcelot Gobbo, "young master Launcelot" as he would be called, is one of the pleasantest among the quaint clowns of Shakspere. He is a worthy compeer of Launce and Speed, and he is equally at home as either of those worthies in playing, twisting and contorting his mother tongue. He is full of misinterpretations, loving to "try confusions" with all and any with whom he may come in contact; and so strongly does this feeling abound with him, that he will play upon his own father with as much readiness as he would upon a stranger. He is redolent with mirth and the means of mirth-making; "a merry devil," robbing the house of some taste of its tediousness, for his memory is "planted" with "an army of good words," and

> "Many fools, that stand in better place,
> Garnish'd like him, that for a tricksy word
> Defy the matter."—*A.* III. s. 5.

The pride, the haughtiness, and the punctilio of the Prince of Arragon is no caricature, as drawn in this comedy, of the Spanish character. Like the whole of Shakspere's works, it is in unison with truth, and the language so aptly fits the character that none can question its veracity. The Spanish prince will not "jump," herd, agree "with common spirits;" his pride of blood will not admit of that. Standing upon his hidalgo extraction, he wishes to have the old proverb applied to him, "eagles fly alone, sparrows herd together." The vauntings of the blood-proud prince meet with their just reward, for seeking to advance his own merits by lowering the merits of others, thus raising his own deserts in his own opinion, and fully believing, puffed up with his own vanity, that *he*, and he alone deserves the lady,—he chooseth the silver casket for the reason, that he who chooseth that, gets "as much as he deserves; forgetting that he has to take another's measure of his standard and not his own. This he soon discovers when unlocking the casket, he perceives "a fool's head," being just as much as he truly deserves; and he quits the scene, muttering

> "With one fool's head I came to woo,
> But I go away with two.
> Sweet, adieu. I'll keep my oath,
> Patiently to bear my wroth."—*A.* ii. s. 9.

The Prince of Morocco is seldom placed upon the stage, is hardly ever included in the *dramatis personæ;* but why he should be left out no real reason has been assigned. Both he and the Prince of Arragon, as a rule, are not represented; but Messrs. Phelps and Kean, with that love of Shakspere which they have ever evinced, have restored them both to the stage. The language used by the Moor affords a strong contrast with that of the Spanish prince. The one boasts of his birth, blood, and breeding; and the other of his deeds, and what he would accomplish to win fair Portia. He regrets that it is left to "blind fortune." He would that it were dependent, not upon chance, but upon some deed—no matter what, he would attempt its accomplishment. He swears by his scimetar,

> "That slew the Sophy and a Persian prince,
> That won three fields of the Sultan Solyman,
> I would out-stare the sternest eyes that look,
> Outbrave the heart most daring on the earth,
> Pluck the young sucking cubs from the she-bear,
> Yea, mock the lion when he roars for prey,
> To win thee, lady."—*A.* ii. s. 1.

He is afraid to choose for fear, "blind fortune" leading him, that he

> "Miss that which one unworthier may attain,
> And die with grieving."

Ultimately he resolves to choose, and he leaves the scene exclaiming,

> "Good fortune then!
> To make me bless'd or cursed'st among men."

What shall be said of Portia! of her, whom Jessica describes as one of the noblest of women, in reality, the noblest, for she says,

> "the poor rude world
> Hath not her fellow."—*A.* III. s. 5.

She is a character most exquisitely drawn;—one among the most beautiful ever limned by Shakspere. Each and all of the Venetians describe her as a paragon, and Bassanio, when speaking to Antonio, says,

> "In Belmont is a lady, richly left,
> And she is fair, and fairer than that word
> Of wond'rous virtues.
> Her name is Portia; nothing undervalued
> To Cato's daughter, Brutus' Portia."—*A.* I. s. 1.

Portia is all knowledge, worth and gentleness. In her the intellect is highly cultivated and aided in its result by a strong poetic imagination. There is nothing of the blue stocking in her character, nothing of cleverness, but there is a union of the perceptive and the reflective faculties, and these are so harmoniously blended, so closely interwoven with each other, that they give to her that sweetness, and dignity, and tenderness, so characteristic of such a woman. In her first scene, which is a most charming one, she displays her culture, by the complete manner in which she describes her numerous suitors. The way she dwells upon their defects, dissecting each and pointing out why she dislikes them, most plainly shows, that with none of those her heart is touched; but when Nerissa mentions the "Venetian, a scholar and a soldier," she remembers him and his name Bassanio, and also, that he was worthy of praise, thus displaying symptoms, which prove, that within her heart he hath effected a lodgment.

In the two scenes, with the caskets, prior to the one in which Bassanio chooses, her world knowledge is again pourtrayed, and in the scene after the result of the Spanish prince's choice, it is still further shown, when she exclaims,

"Thus hath the candle singed the moth.
O, these deliberate fools! when they do choose,
They have their wisdom by their wit to loose."—*A.* II. s. 9.

In the scene while Bassanio's choice is being made, Portia is swayed alternately by hope and fear. She evidently loveth Bassanio by the anxiety she displays, and she can scarcely control her feelings when he has made his selection, so apparent is her wish, that the selection he hath made should be the right one. She is on "the tip-toe of expectation" and exclaims,

"How all the other passions fleet to air,
As doubtful thoughts, and rash-embraced despair,
And shuddering fear, and green-eyed jealousy!
O love, be moderate; allay thy ecstacy;
In measure rein thy joy; scant this excess;
I feel too much thy blessing—make it less,
For fear I surfeit!"—*A.* III. s. 2.

Her worth is seen when she learns that her husband's dearest friend is in trouble. She will have everything give way, so that Bassanio may start, and that promptly, to his friend's relief. Neither money, or any other means are to be wanting, and she will that Bassanio shall only go with her to church, to call her wife,

"And then away to Venice to your friend;
For never shall you lie by Portia's side
With an unquiet soul. You shall have gold

To pay the petty debt twenty times over;
When it is paid, bring your friend along.
My maid Nerissa, and myself, meantime,
Will live as maids and widows.  Come, away!
For you shall hence upon your wedding day:
Bid your friends welcome, show a merry cheer:
Since you are dear bought, I will love you dear."

In the following scene, Portia adds to her worth, by the idea she seeks to convey relative to Antonio. She believes her lord to be all that a man should be, and she naturally concludes that his bosom friend, his Damon, should be the counterpart of himself. She thinks it impossible to be otherwise, for where

"Souls do bear an equal yoke of love,
There *must* be needs a like proportion
Of lineaments, of manners and of spirit;
Which makes me think, that this Antonio,
Being the bosom lover of my lord,
*Must* needs be like my lord."—A. III. s. 4.

Her tenderness is characteristically shown, when appearing as the young advocate. She would have the Jew merciful, because mercy is above all other things,

"It is the mightiest in the mightiest."

She knows that she can save the merchant by the wording of the bond, and that the Jew can be brought within the jurisdiction of the law, but her tenderness first appeals to his humanity. The appeal is in vain, for Shylock's humanity is absorbed and taken up in his desire for revenge. She then appeals to Shylock's avarice,

"Shylock, there's *thrice* thy money offered thee,"

but this like her former appeal meets with no success.

Not satisfied, she again appeals to his pity in combination with his avarice,

"Be merciful!
Take *thrice* thy money,"

but the Jew is not moved. Her own tenderness and sweetness of character is so strong, that she remains unwilling to accept Shylock's inhumanity; she can scarcely credit the firmness of the Jew. She would that Antonio should appeal to him, and it is only after the failure of the merchant to move Shylock from his purpose, that she resolves the law shall have its course, knowing full well, that her husband's friend will be saved and the Jew will be ruined in reputation and in fortune. Portia is a true woman, one worthy of being loved, and one, who having chose her idol, would bestow upon it the whole of her affections.

Nerissa, Portia's fair attendant is but a subordinate part in the comedy, yet she serves to complete the picture. She is witty, playful, and charming, copying a part of her mistress' elegance, affecting a portion of her mental culture, and naturally, is not devoid of grace and good manners. She is quick in discrimination, fails not in the use of her tongue, and is in all respects an excellent match for Gratiano, for though not so boisterous in her manner, she is equally as playful and as ready for fun as he is.

Jessica, the pretty Jewess and Lorenzo's love, serves to work out the sunny side of the comedy. Her love for Lorenzo destroys her filial feeling, which is not of the strongest nature; a result which arises from her father valuing her less than the ducats and jewels he possessed. The light manner in which he held his daughter, is the only justification that can be pleaded for her leaving him and taking away his property. The manner in which her father has secluded her from the world, his harshness and constant inveighing against the Christian race, causes her to act with duplicity. Her duplicity is made manifest in the scene when Shylock is going out to supper, and bids her not to thrust her

> "head into the public street
> To gaze on Christian fools with varnish'd faces;"

for in answer to her father's question,

> "What says that fool of Hagar's offspring? ha!"

she replies knowing full well that the reply is not truthful

> "His words were, Farewell, mistress; *nothing else.*"

This deceiveth the old man and awakens a little of his humanity, for it extracts from him an acknowledgment,

> "The patch is kind enough."

In this same scene she hath already agreed to elope; the time and means are arranged, and her answer to her father's proverb of

> "Fast bind, fast find,"

is,

> "Farewell; and if my fortune be not crost,
> I have a father, you a daughter, lost."—*A.* II. s. 5.

It is not to be wondered at that Jessica should act in the manner that she does, when we consider the circumstances in which she is placed. We feel that it is not right for children to revolt against their parents, but what are we to expect from children when parents forget to perform their duties towards their offspring. That Shylock failed to perform his parental duties is evident, and Shakspere with his usual truthfulness, in

## THE MERCHANT OF VENICE. 105

the conduct of Jessica, shows the result of such a failure. In all things, irrespective of her conduct to her father, Shakspere has made Jessica good, kind and chaste. Her chastity cannot be questioned, and her modesty is shown in the elopement scene, when she is dressed in a page's garb, in her words,

"I am glad 'tis night, you do not look on me,
For I am much asham'd of my exchange."

Shakspere in his *Romeo and Juliet* has pourtrayed the same feeling in the famous balcony scene, when Juliet exclaims,

"The mask of night is on my face,
Else would a maiden blush bepaint my cheek."

The pretty Jewess, despite her want of deep filial feeling, is one of the most beautiful characters Shakspere has drawn. Her simplicity is so child-like and winning, her firm reliance upon her lover and her strong belief in his truthfulness, the romance of her position, and the veil of poetry with which both she and her husband are enveloped, all serve to win our sympathies, and to render her, if not a principal figure, at least a charming one in this most charming comedy.

Among the whole of Shakspere's productions there is none more perfect than this comedy, and there is none that keeps its hold upon the stage and is more frequently represented than this. It is full of interest. The reader and the spectator, until the trial scene is nearly ended, are full of anxiety and are kept in a state of great suspense, happily relieved by the defeat of the Jew's intent. The interest never flags, the action never stands still, all goes on, gradually accumulating in intensity until the climax is reached in the speech prior to the evasion set forth by Portia, and which evasion relieves the feelings, and carries them from a state of doubt, despondency and despair into one of pleasure, joy and happiness.

A great absurdity is frequently committed by managers and *star* actors (?) finishing this comedy with the trial scene. Shylock, no more appearing among the *dramatis personæ*, they have conceived the idea, that the piece should terminate with the fourth act, losing sight entirely of the underplot, so necessary to be developed to complete the chief character, Portia, and the characters of Antonio, Bassanio, Gratiano and the rest. By leaving out the fifth act, they also leave out some of the finest poetry of the comedy, for the language of Portia and Lorenzo overflows with poetic imagery and beautiful ideas. The playfulness evinced by Lorenzo and Jessica in their allusions to classic love stories, and their seeking to outvie each other in their protestations of love,—Lorenzo's apostrophe to music,—the fictitious quarrel of Bassanio and Portia, Gratiano and Nerissa relative to their rings,—and the news which Portia gives Antonio

"of three of your argosies,
Are richly come to harbour suddenly."

aptly finish a comedy, one of the highest among our bard's productions,—a comedy which abounds in incident, interest and humour, enthralling, and keeping enthralled both reader and spectator.

# TIMON OF ATHENS.

"THE Life of Timon of Athens," was first printed in the folio of 1623, and the date of its production is assigned to the year 1610. There is but little external evidence so to affix the date, but the internal evidence will well serve this purpose, for it is written in the same elliptical condensation of style which distinguishes the plays of Henry VIII., Coriolanus, and The Winter's Tale. These plays are all characterised by peculiar contractions and they all belong to one period of writing. The twenty-eighth novel in Painter's Palace of Pleasure, is said to be one of the sources from whence this tragedy was derived, while an early play* in which the character of Timon appears, has been supposed to be another source, and a passage in North's translation of Plutarch's Lives, serves for another. In neither the novel by Painter, nor in the early play, nor in North's translation, can we, however, find the Timon of Shakspere. Skottowe in his life of Shakspere, traces some remarkable coincidences between Shakspere's Timon and Lucian's Timon, or the Misanthrope; but they are accidental coincidences which have arisen irrespectively, for

* This play, which is a wretchedly poor production, was edited by the Rev. W. Dyce, for the Shakspere Society, and published in 1842.

Shakspere could not have borrowed any incidents from Lucian, no translation of Lucian's dialogue being known at the date of the production of Shakspere's play.

There is none among the plays of Shakspere about which a greater variety of opinions have been expressed than about Timon of Athens. Coleridge thought that much of the text had been mutilated and spoiled by the actors, who frequently indulged in such alterations for the purpose of making points. Charles Knight says, that it is not wholly a work of Shakspere's, but that he simply remodelled an elder play, which he found existing ready for his hand. By some the play has been looked upon as an unfinished work, a mere outline left incomplete for representation, and in this opinion Delius concurs. Others have ascribed its origin to the peculiar state of the poet's mind at this period, and give this as the only true solution which can be found for the irregularities of the versification and the careless manner in which some of the parts are developed, although the unity of idea in the composition of the play is most carefully attended to and carried out. By Hallam it was said, "There seems to have been a period of Shakspere's life when his heart was ill at ease, and ill content with the world or his own conscience ; the memory of hours mis-spent, the pang of affection misplaced or unrequited, the experience of man's worser nature which intercourse with unworthy associates, by choice or circumstance, peculiarly teaches ;—these, as they sank down into the depths of his great mind, seem not only to have inspired into it the conception of 'Lear' and 'Timon,' but that of one primary character, the censurer of mankind." * This phase of opinion is endorsed by Ulrici, who alludes to the latter period of Shakspere's life being embittered by "outward causes," and it is also endorsed by Gervinus, who says that "the carelessness in a number of the plays of this date," is attributable "to one common, though unfathomable cause,—the state of the poet's mind."† The choosing for the subject of the play, "misanthropy," partly shows a brain somewhat vexed with the circumstances and with the specimens of humanity with which the poet had come in contact. This is a view evidently inconsistent with the character of Shakspere, who above all other writers expresses his untiring love and belief in humanity. He was filled with charity and his works abound with the manifestations of its spirit. On all classes, like the beams of the morning sun, it falls, diffusing joy and pleasure, on human kind. To infer that our gentle bard had thoughts and was guilty of acts of which he was thoroughly ashamed, and to prove that he was repentant, he manifested his knowledge and regret of such thoughts and acts by the production of this and other plays of the same class, is entirely incompatible with the whole tenour of his works. This question has, however, received its *coup-de-grace* from the work of Mr. G. Massey, on the Sonnets of Shakspere, in which work this opinion is most successfully combatted. The propagation of such an opinion must have proceeded from a forgetfulness of the great powers of Shakspere, who myriad-minded as he was, none other possessing "such strength at once, and such variety of imagination," it was just as easy for him to develope the

\* Literary History, Vol. 3, page 309.
† Gervinus on *Shakspere*, Vol. 2, p. 422.

worst phases of human character as it was the best, for all phases were by him thoroughly understood, and this play must be looked upon as a simple manifestation of his wonderful powers.

In this tragedy, the lower classes are most favourably contrasted with the upper, for the servants of Timon display an amount of incorruptibility which is altogether wanting in most of the characters who belong to the upper classes. The flame of humanity is partially rekindled in the brain of Timon by the prudence and fidelity of his frugal steward, who is as true to Timon as was Kent to Lear, and who despite all misfortunes, remains constantly true to his master, being willing to share his last coin in seeking to improve that master's condition. It has been wisely said, that all extremes are hurtful to the individual and also hurtful to society. This is fully evidenced in this tragedy, by the profuse prodigality of Timon, for the practice of such prodigality destroys the innate goodness of Timon's character. The Merchant of Venice also furnishes an example, for there the excessive greed and avarice of Shylock defeats his own desires and completely destroys his feelings of humanity.

Timon is the representative of a true prodigal, for he is equally as lavish with his love as with his fortune. If "the world" were his he would "give it in a breath," nor care "how quickly were it gone." He is untiring in his kindness, devoid of assumption, and moved by disinterested and unselfish motives. From a strict sense of duty he is impressed with the belief that we are "born to do benefits," and most faithfully he sought to carry out his ideal, which was composed of all the social virtues and the truest friendship. He thoroughly believes in the goodness of humanity, and knowing his own goodness, and the liberalness of his own thoughts and acts, he judges that others are the same. When the hour of misfortune comes upon him he still cherishes this belief, nor does he yield it, when he receives his first check by the act of the senators, who decline to assist him in the hour of his adversity. Experience, that bitter mistress, soon undeceives Timon, and he quickly learns the sorrowful fact, that all those whom he had fed by his liberal bounty, will not feed him when he is in want. Ventidus, who ransomed from slavery by the wealth of Timon and who hath become one of the wealthy few who fatten upon the needs of others, even he, will not lend the sum to Timon that he had formerly received as a gift. Lucullus, Sempronius and Lucius, all of whom have been greatly benefitted by Timon's generosity, all decline to aid him in the time of his difficulties and evince a callousness of disposition, demonstrating their perfect inhumanity. These ungrateful acts overwhelm Timon and strike him prostrate. He becomes aware of the folly he has committed, and the unpleasant truth is forced upon him that he has bartered wealth for avarice, friendship for falsehood, and all the nobler feelings of his nature are wrecked, "one winter's brush has shaken the leaves from the boughs and left him open, bare for every storm that blows."

Discarding his thorough belief in the goodness of man, he loses his "alacrity of spirit," his "cheer of mind," and he passes into the other extreme. Instead of being a philanthropist, loving mankind and seeking to promote the happiness and well being of his fellows, he becomes a misanthrope, a hater of his race, for "man delights him not:" From being a practiser of the social virtues, he seeks in the solitude of nature for solace to his withered hopes. The cherished dreams of his life are for ever dispelled by the talisman of fact. So marvellous is the transformation which he undergoes, that even in his tastes and desires he is altogether changed, and so wondrous is the effect produced by the base ingratitude of those for whom he had smoothed life's thorny path, that mentally, morally and physically, he is different both in kind and in degree. There is no pain too severe, no punishment too harsh for those to undergo who have deceived him, and he invokes the aid of "infectious fevers," "cold sciatica," "general leprosy," of fire and all the other evils which affect poor humanity to punish and destroy the "knot of mouth-friends," "detested parasites," and coveteous destroyers," whom he hath proved to be false as "dicer's oaths."

When Timon again becomes possessed of wealth he gives it away that society may be punished, for he would sow discord among the human race. To Alcibiades he giveth gold "to pay his soldiers," conditionally, they "spare not the babe," "the virgin's cheek," the "white beard" of age, nor the "yells of mothers." He giveth gold to the courtesans, with the hope that they will "consumptions sow in the hollow bones of men," and he will share a portion of his wealth with the faithful Flavius, on the harsh condition, that he shall
"build from men;
Hate all, curse all; show charity to none;
But let the famish'd flesh slide from the bone,
Ere thou relieve the beggar."

Despite the intensity of his hatred the warm fidelity displayed by his steward partially overcomes him, awakening nobler feelings, developing the better part of his nature, and forcing him to admit the uprightness and truthfulness of "one honest man," and he prays the gods to forgive him for his "general and exceptless rashness." In this mood he doth not long remain, it is but a transient feeling, and he quickly reverts again to his fierce hatred of humankind, at whom he hurls his harsh invectives, and the more powerfully to strengthen the consistency of this feeling, he quits the scene, not to die of a broken heart, but seeking his rest in the great bosom of nature, by the committal of suicide, and thus "Timon hath done his reign."

Apemantus is a cynic, "native and to the manner born," "opposite to humanity," charged with disgust and exaggeration, representing the other extreme to Timon. Apemantus despises all social virtues and pleasures, refuses belief in the goodness of humanity, for he looks upon the human race as degraded and brutish, a natural result, when we remember that he erects himself as the standard by which they should be judged. He is a thorough "churl," who is ever angry, filled with pride as great as his master Diogenes and prouder than Timon, for he constantly flaunts his poverty, his rags and his brutality. He is always parading his plain speaking, this latter qualification being the result of his base, envious and malicious nature, which delights in scurrility, and which conceives that to indulge in coarse retorts and harsh and crabbed answers is to speak plain. He refuses to see good in anything except in "honest water," and he feels no happiness only when slandering his fellow creatures and seeking to enrage them, thus proving, he is either "a knave or a fool." Apemantus is full of mistrust and hatred, having no belief in the practice of virtue, for the baseness of his own nature prevents him from accepting such a creed. The cynicism of Timon is an act approaching to madness, that of Apemantus is his nature, the worthlessness of which is seen through by Timon, who in their last encounter, fails not to tell him so, and justly exclaims, "were I like thee, I'd throw away myself." Apemantus having but one kind of mental vision cannot understand the nature of Timon which is evidently dualistic. He only sees the misanthropical side of Timon's character, he cannot see the philanthropical side, because he is wrapt up in his own misanthropy. Born in the lowest phase of human society, without cultivation, with soured temper and "sour-cold habit," the result of the state of poverty in which he moved and had his being, he fails to comprehend the self-denial which Timon displays on discovering the treasure. The hard words which Timon hurls at his churlish head are all richly deserved, and they contain great justice and truth in their characterisation—

> "Thou art a slave, whom fortune's tender arm,
> With favour never clasp'd; but bred a dog.
> Hadst thou, like us from our first swath, proceeded
> The sweet degrees that this brief world affords
> To such as may the passive drugs of it
> Freely command, thou wouldst have plunged thyself
> In general riot; melted down thy youth
> In different beds of lust; and never learn'd
> The icy precepts of respect, but followed
> The sugar'd game before thee.
> Thy nature did commence in sufferance, time
> Hath made thee hard in't. Why shouldst thou hate men?

They never flatter'd thee; what hast thou given,
Poor rogue hereditary? Hence, be gone!—
If thou hadst not been born the worst of men
Thou hadst been a knave and flatterer."

The character of Flavius, the prudent steward, is most admirably pourtrayed; it is one of a class which is often dwelt upon by Shakspere and who has frequently developed that high quality in man, fidelity. Flavius is worthy to rank with Enobarbus, with Adam and with the faithful Kent, for "he can endure to follow with allegiance a fallen lord." Though his lord Timon is forsaken by his "monstrous friends," the parasites who fed upon his wealth, causing him to feel the chilling frosts of poverty, Flavius still will follow his fortunes and exclaims "let me be your servant." He is the "one honest man" of the tragedy, honest in intent, purpose and deed, and this honesty causes him to be round with Timon, and to tell him that he is acting unwisely and that his means will not allow such continuance of wastefulness. He has endured reproof when he hath brought in his accounts, still will he persevere and place before his "dear loved lord," the unpleasant fact, that all his means will lack "a half to pay his present debts." Frankly and manfully he tells his master that he is trusting to a broken staff when he relies upon his so-called friends, who, when he has sought to move them to relieve the difficulties of Timon, "they do but shake their heads," and he is not one whit the "richer in return." With "distasteful looks," he hath been received and "with certain half-caps and cold-moving nods," that have froze him "into silence." When all is lost by Timon, Flavius still clings to the fortunes of his master, cheers his fellow-servants, "broken implements of a ruined house," gives them their money, rejoices they "are fellows still, serving alike in sorrow," bids them adieu,

"not one word more,"
Thus part we rich in sorrow, parting poor."

He will after his lord, for he knows he has nought

" with him to
Supply his life, or that which can command it.
I'll follow, and enquire him out:
I'll ever serve his mind with my best will,
Whilst I have gold, I'll be his steward still."

This resolve he fails not to carry out, for he seeks his master, begs him to accept "his grief," and while his "poor wealth lasts to entertain me as your steward still." His service is composed of love and truthfulness, and animated by duty to his "honoured lord," he displays his zeal by still wishing to serve without "any benefit," "either in hope or present;"—all that he wishes, all that he desires, is not that he may be made wealthy by such service, but that his lord, should he have the "power and wealth." He would that Timon should be again what he formerly was, and he would be best requited by his lord making himself rich.

# AS YOU LIKE IT.

THE first appearance of this comedy in print was in the folio of 1623. It was entered in the Stationers' Registers, August 4th, 1600, but some obstacle arose to prevent its publication. The comedy of *Much Ado about Nothing*, and the play of *Henry the Fifth*, were similarly placed at the same time. The incidents of the comedy were in all probability derived by Shakspere from Lodge's novel of Rosalynde: Euphues Golden Legacie, first published in 1590, reprinted in 1592, and again in 1598.

Shakspere has closely followed the incidents of the novel. The usurping king, the elder brother in exile, to whom "men of great worth resorted," the discovery of Rosalind by her father, the happy marriage of the princesses with their lovers, the shepherdess coy and her loving shepherd. These in Lodge's tale are but mere sketches, in the comedy, they are complete pictures, for the hand of Shakspere has so finished them, that they are redolent with life and beauty. The characters of Jaques, Touchstone and Audrey were added by Shakspere, and the life and wit of Touchstone adds materially to the interest, and lightens up by its brilliancy the sober parts of the comedy. The catastrophe of the novel and the comedy are very differently managed. In the former, the usurping king raises a large army and goeth forth to fight, is met, and slain by the sojourners in the forest, and the rightful monarch is seated in his place. In the comedy, Shakspere only describes the gathering, and effects a change in the moral nature of the usurper, by the influence of persuasion; thus causing the comedy to end more happily than the novel, which is marked by strife and war, with its blood stained horrors. From the mouth of Jaques de Bois, the forest duke learns the result, that

> "Duke Frederick, hearing how that every day
> Men of great worth resorted to this forest,
> Address'd a mighty power; which were on foot,
> In his own conduct, purposely to take
> His brother here, and put him to the sword:
> And to the skirts of this wild wood he came;
> Where, meeting with an old religious man,
> After some question with him, was converted
> Both from his enterprise, and from the world;
> His crown bequeathing to his banish'd brother,
> And all their lands restor'd to them again
> That were with him exiled."—*A.* v. s. 4.

This comedy is one of the most delightful among Shakspere's productions. It is one with which all classes are charmed, for the various phases of human character, which go to make up the world, are here to be found. The location of the comedy and its time, lend an almost inexpressible charm, for we are in the forest of Arden, in glorious summer time, when leaves are green, skies are blue, bright flowers are springing, heavenward lifting their heads, and the lark, heaven's own chorister, pours forth his splendid song. The grouping and contrasting of the characters are of the most pleasing kind, the language is rich, full, and flowing, and the snatches of melody with which the comedy is interspersed, are numbered among the finest lyrics in our tongue. It is one of those pieces which remind us of our youth, when we loved to roam beneath the wide-spreading branches of umbrageous trees, to wander through green lanes, to repose in quiet dells, to seek acquaintance with bosky bournes and green shaws, where sights pleasant to gaze on could be seen, and where

"Floods of softest music fell upon the never-tiring ear."

This comedy is one in which old age can find delight. The character of Adam, the part which Shakspere himself is said to have played, cannot fail of pleasing the aged and winning their sympathies, for the sunny side of a good long life is most beautifully pourtrayed. On the other hand, youth, yielding up to the warm impulses which course through its system, abandons itself to love and pleasure;—abandons itself, to revel in the delight of the inner world, for casting off the external coating which it has gathered in the false atmosphere of a court, and with the contact of every day life, it revels in the delight of the beautiful and true: and more than all, in displaying that secret chord of harmony, which under the name of love, binds all hearts in one common bond, eliciting one common chorus from all classes, whether king or clown, peer or peasant.

There is a charm of the sweetest nature to be found in this pastoral drama. From the usurping duke, with his constant fretfulness, the result of his crime, to the doting fondness of Audrey for that wit-owner, clever

Touchstone, all serve to fill and complete a picture, sketched and filled in only as a Shakspere and none other could do. From palace to greenwood, and from greenwood to palace, the characters shift and go, yet they are still with the same truthfulness pourtrayed. In the contrast between the life at court and the sylvan life of the banished duke lies the great charm of this play. It is this which wins our sympathies and causes us to pass into the characters as they come before us. The artificial life of the one and the natural life of the other, are placed in exquisite contrast, certainly to the advantage of the latter, and we think with the exiled duke

"This life more sweet
Than that of painted pomp? Are not these woods
More free from peril than the envious court?
And this our life, exempt from public haunt,
Finds tongues in trees, books in the running brooks,
Sermons in stones and good in every thing."—*A.* ii. s. 1.

In this pastoral drama all the characters yield to the power of love. Oliver and Orlando, who open the piece, and who are at deadly enmity with each other, through Celia and Rosalind become reconciled. Orlando, the noble and generous, is not so tainted as Oliver, who seeks his brother's life, and promises Charles the wrestler a guerdon, if, when he wrestles with Orlando, he will so throw him that he shall not trouble him any more; even he, the murderous Oliver—murderous in thought and wish, if not in deed—obeys the influence of the young god, and when he sees Celia, falls in love with her and she with him, so both are "heart in heart."

The courtly, witty Touchstone, the motley, that Jaques the cynical, met in the forest, and who worsted the would-be moralist, even he can love; and he determines to marry with Audrey, "who, tho' no slut, thanks the gods she is foul." Love works its change with them, and have her he will. "A poor virgin, sir, an ill-favour'd thing, sir, but mine own. A poor humour of mine, sir, to take that no man else will. Rich honesty dwells like a miser, sir, in a poor house; as your pearl in your foul oyster."

Phœbe and Silvius, Orlando and Rosalind, are each enlinkt in the same golden cord. The loves of the two latter being the turning point of the comedy, the scenes in which they appear, and the scenes in which they are referred to, are among the most beautiful ever penned by the master bard. They are redolent with playfulness, gentleness, and love; the wind, the trees, the flowers are all infected with this spirit, for

"Love, indeed, is light from heaven,
A spark of that immortal fire
With angels shared,—to mortals given,
To lift from earth our low desires."

Orlando is the true type of gentleness and manliness. It is his manliness which breaks out and desires of his brother a better and higher degree of education than he has given him. He says, "The spirit of my father grows strong in me, and I will no longer endure it; therefore allow me such exercises as may become a gentleman." That his father was honorable we have Duke Frederick's word; and that Orlando respects his father is seen, firstly, in the speech replying to his brother, "I am no villain: I am the youngest son of Sir Rowland de Boys; he was my father, and he is thrice a villain that says such a father begot villains." Again, in the third scene of Act I. the same feeling bursts forth, when he exclaims,

"I am more proud to be Sir Rowland's son,
His youngest son ; and would not change that calling,
To be adopted heir to Frederick."

Orlando's gentleness is shown in the scene in the forest with Adam. The old man, faint from want of food and from the weakness of age, can proceed no further. Orlando cheers him with words of comfort, almost womanly in their kindness. Ultimately he quits the scene, sustaining the burthen of the old man, by carrying him away, thus displaying his strength and manliness, combined with his gentleness.

The desire of preserving Adam's life makes Orlando forget his gentleness of manners, and he threatens loud when he rushes into the presence of the banished Duke. Yet he is soon brought back to his natural state by the gentleness of manner and import which marks the Duke's replies, for Orlando says,

" Speak you so gently ?    Pardon me, I pray you :
I thought that all things had been savage here ;
And therefore put I on the countenance
Of stern commandment.
Let gentleness my strong enforcement be :
In the which hope I blush, and hide my sword."—*A.* ii. s. 7.

The kindness and gentleness of Orlando is excellently described by his brother Oliver, who when compelled by the reigning Duke to go in search of Orlando, thus relates his own mishap to Rosalind and Celia, and the generous conduct of his brother.

" When last the young Orlando parted from you
He left a promise to return again
Within an hour, and pacing through the forest,
Chewing the cud of sweet and bitter fancy,
Lo, what befel ! he threw his eye aside,

"And mark what object did present itself:
Under an oak, whose boughs were moss'd with age,
And high-top bald with dry antiquity,
A wretched ragged man, o'ergrown with hair,
Lay sleeping on his back: about his neck
A green and gilded snake had wreathed itself,
Who with her head, nimble in threats, approach'd
The opening of his mouth; but suddenly,
Seeing Orlando, it unlink'd itself,
And with indented glides did slip away
Into a bush: under which bush's shade
A lioness, with udders all drawn dry,
Lay couching, head on ground, with cat-like watch,
When that the sleeping man should stir; for 'tis
The royal disposition of that beast
To prey on nothing that does seem as dead:
This seen, Orlando did approach the man,
And found it was his brother, his elder brother.
Twice did he turn his back, and purposed so;
But kindness, nobler ever than revenge,
And nature, stronger than his just occasion,
Made him give battle to the lioness,
Who quickly fell before him."—*A.* iv. s. 3.

It is this kindness and gentleness of manners, in combination with his manliness, that steals away the heart of Rosalind, at the same time his own is moved to loving attachment, by the kind wishes and yet kinder words of that sprightly, winning maiden.

The banished duke is courteous and overflowing with the milk of human kindness. The "uses of adversity" in his greenwood home, have taught him that calmness, that sweet repose which has become so great a part of his nature, and which causes him to feel an unwillingness to return to courtly life and courtly pleasures, when his dukedom is again proffered to him. He is not to be moved or driven from his calm and gentle manners, however harsh in their language and their actions they may be, who seek so to do. The violent demands of Orlando, he answers by gentle words.

"What would you have? Your gentleness shall force, More than your force move us to gentleness."

He would that gentleness should be the governing power, for it is with him the higher development of human nature. When reproving Jaques for his desire to

"Cleanse the foul body of the infected world,"

his calmness is undisturbed, and the gentle tone, half that of playfulness, with which the words are uttered, render the reproof more forcible. He thoroughly understands and knows the source of Jaques' desire. He is aware that it does not arise from a love of humanity, but that it arises from disgust; a disgust created in Jaques' brain by the remembrance of his early life being spent in indulging in the very vices, of which he would now "cleanse the foul body."

When once more possessing the ducal crown, he evinces no hurry to commence action in his ducal capacity. The desire of advancing the interest of his daughter and her husband, Orlando, is the chief reason of his return to his ducal palace, and he unmistakably hints, that when he has settled the succession, back he will go to the sylvan glades, exchanging his palace walls for blue skies, the song of birds and leafy canopies.

Jaques is a mere pretender. His melancholy sits not well upon him; it is a mere affectation, there is nothing earnest, nothing truthful. He would fain be your moral lawgiver, but his moral lessons are only words, they convey no feeling. He is melancholy over the poor wounded stag, he complains of the injustice of killing the denizens of the forest, he sorrows over their sufferings, but his sorrow is mere pretence, there is no real feeling in it, for he sits down and eats and fattens upon venison; upon that, which in all probability belonged to the beast whose sufferings furnished him with a text to hang a moral on. He is the great artificial of the comedy, and in every way he is foiled when he comes in contact with the natural. Orlando, Touchstone, and the singer Amiens, all in their turns so flout and beat him with his own weapons, that he readily retires from the contest. His early life has been passed in vice, and his cynicism springs from the remembrances of his vicious career. Disgusted by those remembrances, he wishes to become the world's purifier. He would go through the world to make it virtuous, not from a love of virtue, but from a morbid recollection of his own vicious proceedings. The motley "he met in the forest" moves him to action, and he tells his wishes to the banished duke, who, calmly administers a rebuke of the most truthful character. Jaques exclaims,

"give me leave
To speak my mind, and I will through and through
Cleanse the foul body of the infected world,
If they will patiently receive my medicine.
*Duke S.* Fie on thee! I can tell what thou wouldst do.
*Jaq.* What for a counter, would I do but good?
*Duke S.* Most mischievious foul sin, in chiding sin:
For thou thyself hast been a libertine,
As sensual as the brutish sting itself;
And all the embossed sores and headed evils,
That thou with license of free foot hast caught,
Wouldst thou disgorge into the general world."—
*A.* ii. s. 7.

Jaques is evidently intended as a satire upon the

would be moral philosophers, the pretenders to wisdom. He is a mere sham, whose forte lies in description, not in action, for he who is the most melancholic in words, has no reason for his melancholy, as he undergoes no trials, nor is he ever stricken by adversity.

Frederick, the usurping duke, is a harsh, ill-humoured character, mistrustful of everybody, even of his own child. He is covetous, full of gloomy fancies, suspicious of those by whom he is surrounded, and regards with hostility all honourable men. The crimes that he has committed, the banishment of his brother and the robbing of the lords who are with him banished, bring their own punishment, and he fails to find rest, contentment, or happiness. His character is well described by Celia,

> "My father's rough and envious disposition
> Sticks me at heart."—*A.* i. s. 3.

The old courtier Le Beau, also adds to the description,

> "Yet such is now the duke's condition, (temper)
> That he misconstrues all that you have done
> The duke is humourous." (capricious)

The harshness of the usurping duke is essential to the development of the plot of the comedy, for through his tyrannic mode of government, the great revolution in the character of Oliver is effected. By the stern command of Frederick, relative to Orlando, of

> "bring him dead or living,
> Within this twelvemonth, or turn thou no more
> To seek a living in our territory;"

Oliver is compelled to go in search of his brother, and during that search, his life is saved by Orlando. He also cometh in contact with Celia, whose goodness, in conjunction with the remembrance of his brother's act, beats down the "pales and forts" of his evil side, and awakens his better nature, causing him to confess his faults and to feel

"'Twas I; but 'tis not I: I do not shame
To tell you what I was, since my conversion
So sweetly tastes, being the thing I am."

Oliver and Frederick are the two unnatural brothers of the comedy, whose bad conduct appears to have its origin in envy. The superior abilities of Orlando, and the estimation in which he is held is the chief cause of Oliver's conduct. No other reason can Oliver assign, when seeking to find out the cause of his antipathy to his brother, but this, that Orlando is "full of noble device; of all sorts enchantingly belov'd; and indeed, so much in the heart of the world, and especially of my own people who best know him, that I am altogether misprised." Frederick's "rough and envious disposition" is excited to action by the high estimation in which his banished brother's daughter is held, and by hearing that "men of great worth" resort to the forest to join his brother, and "fleet the time carelessly, as they did the golden world." In both instances, their envious feelings so irritates them, that they are led into a course of hateful thoughts and deeds, from which they are ultimately reclaimed by a natural course of action. Frederick through the influence of an "old religious man," and Oliver through his love for Celia and the saving of his life by his brother Orlando, whom he so sought to destroy.

Corin, the shepherd, a type of the plain common sense of the rural world, though not an important part in this charming comedy, is yet a pleasing one. True to his calling, and the manner in which he has been brought up, he looketh not beyond; he is content with his position, and exclaims in answer to Touchstone, "Sir, I am a true labourer: I earn that I eat, get that I wear, owe no man hate, envy no man's happiness; glad of other men's good, content with my arm; and the greatest of my pride is, to see my ewes graze and my lambs suck." He is not possessed of any philosophy, nor does he aspire to possess any. The only world that he knows of, and beyond which he looketh not, is one immediately in connection with his means of living. He is possessed of strong practical sense, which he displays in his reply to Touchstone's question, "hast any philosophy in thee, shepherd? No more, but that I know, the more one sickens the worse at ease he is; and that he that wants money, means, and content, is without three good friends; that the property of rain is to wet, and fire to burn; that good pasture makes fat sheep; and that a great cause of the night is lack of the sun; that he that hath learned no wit by nature nor art may complain of good breeding, or comes of a very dull kindred."

Adam, old Adam, is one of the most pleasing characters ever drawn by the hand of the poet. He is a faithful representative of that class, so prevalent in our own country, the faithful servitor. He truly loveth Orlando, in whom he sees his late master "old Sir Rowland," and he grieves at the rude treatment Orlando receives at the hands of his elder brother, Oliver. He is all gentleness, and he would that others were so. He follows Orlando because he is so virtuous, gentle, strong, and manly, qualities that Adam himself possesses, and which causes him to admire their possession by others. His speeches are full of beautiful language breathing generosity, kindness, truth, and loyalty, and redolent with moral feeling and power. He is a splendid example of a green old age, in which youthful hopes and feelings are found existing in conjunction with the wisdom of a long practical life. His offer of his savings, his desire to become Orlando's servant, and the reasons he urges, are worthy of the character, and of the occasion. His young master to him is the first thought of his brain, for him would he lay down his life, and he begs,

"Let me be your servant:
Though I look old, yet I am strong and lusty;
For in my youth I never did apply
Hot and rebellious liquors in my blood,
Nor did not with unbashful forehead woo
The means of weakness and debility;
Therefore my age is as a lusty winter,
Frostly, but kindly: let me go with you;
I'll do the service of a younger man
In all your business and necessities."

When Orlando accepts his offer he is full of joy and exclaims,

"Master, go on, and I will follow thee,
To the last gasp, with truth and loyalty.
From seventeen years till now almost fourscore
Here lived I, but now live here no more.
At seventeen years many there fortunes seek;
But at fourscore, it is too late a week:
Yet fortune cannot recompense me better,
Than to die well, and not my master's debtor."
*A.* ii. s. 3.

Touchstone is a perfect type of his class, he is a genuine clown, with real cap and bells, yet beneath his folly lies a true vein of disinterestedness and fidelity. He cometh not to Arden from choice, but he is moved to coming by the respect in which he holds his young mistress, Celia. His leanings are towards a life at court, the ease and comfort to be found there, fit his antic disposition better than roaming among green trees and the discomforts of a forest home, yet the truthfulness of his nature lying beneath his folly, which is only his outer covering, directs him cheerfully to obey the behest of Celia and he will,

> "Jog on, jog on, the footpath way,
> And merrily hent the stile-a:
> A merry heart goes all the day,
> Your sad tires in a mile-a."*

He plays and flouts with all; each of the characters become marks for his shafts of wit to be aimed at, and each receive their share of his witty sayings. He is thoroughly master of himself, and this becomes his "coign of vantage" over the other characters, who frequently seem to be the sport of their own wilfulness and caprice, while he maintains a real independence and displays his intellectual freedom, in the power and mastery of his words. He is merry, wordy and witty, with great powers of perception,—powers that are quickened in their action by the frequent opportunities afforded him for wordy combats, and his powers are most highly developed when brought in contact with the mock moralist and would be censor of mankind, the melancholy Jaques. The self-created armour of the self-elected moralist, is pierced through and through by the sharp quips of Touchstone's wit, and the hollowness and insincerity of the pretender is most excellently shown, in the flouting he receives at the hands of this "merry motley" whom he met in the forest.

* *The Winter's Tale*, A. IV. S. 2.

The folly of Touchstone at times hardly conceals his truthfulness from those who are observant of his words. It is only those, who wrapped up like Jaques in their armour of self-complacency, that fail to perceive the motley's meaning. When the true cometh in contact with the true, as in the great scene, when Touchstone discourses upon the seven causes of quarrel, the banished duke, who is all gentleness and truthfulness, discovers his meaning, and instantly perceives that Touchstone "uses his folly like a stalking-horse, and under the presentation of that he shoots his wit." Touchstone is one of the most elevated clowns that Shakspere ever drew, and he never fails to charm his hearers. "He is gay and easy at court; he is good-tempered and at ease in the forest. He makes himself at home anywhere and everywhere, for he carries his own sunshine about with him. Touchstone is not a mere jester—a mere extractor of fun from what occurs around him; and he is not in the least a buffoon—there is nothing low or common in his composition. He has excellent sense, and the good feeling to draw truth and beauty, as well as pure humour, out of passing life."*

Amiens, the forester, and the warbler of the forest, belongs to the golden age. He follows the banished duke out of pure love. He knows the value of gentleness and truthfulness, and he takes up with the duke's fortunes, because he knows his grace is possessed of those good qualities. He would not change his present life, for he loves the mode of living; and more than that, he loveth those by whom he is surrounded. He knows the weight of man's ingratitude, and he would keep

* Clarke's *Shakspere's Characters*, pp. 55, 56.

amid green shaws, inviting others to come to him, for there will they

> "see
> No enemy,
> But winter and rough weather."

He is another instance of the true overcoming the false, for in the scene with Jaques, the latter gets flouted, Amiens hoaxing him and playing on his humour, tells him his singing "will make him melancholy," which the pretender takes literally to himself, so overweening is his vanity. Amiens is a worthy follower of his grace, who despite his banishment,

> "Can translate the stubborness of fortune
> Into so quiet and so sweet a style!"

William, the true country lout, who hath an affection for Audrey, but who is driven from his purpose by the flouting of Touchstone, and Silvius, the loving shepherd, enraptured with Phœbe, without whom he cannot live, are but very subordinate parts, yet are they so introduced, that they add materially to the interest of the comedy. Audrey, a rough country girl, a clot of the earth, devoid of thought, with no idea of life beyond that of a new gown, a merry-making and a marriage feast, adds power to the comedy by the contrast she affords in the rusticity of her manners. Phœbe the fair, yet proud shepherdess, who falls in love with Rosalind when disguised as Ganymede, by the cross purposes which such love engenders, lends an additional charm. The scornful airs which she gives herself, contrast most excellently with the manners of the young princesses when in disguise, and the mode in which she treats Silvius, her disdain and then her acceptance of his hand, completes her character, marking her most truly as a coquette of famed Arcady. Two of the most poetical passages to be found in the comedy, belong to Phœbe, the one in which she taunts Silvius, and the other full of delicacy and beauty, when she describes Ganymede:

"Think not I love him, though I ask for him;
'Tis but a peevish boy; yet he talks well;
But what care I for words? yet words do well,
When he that speaks them pleases those that hear.
It is a pretty youth: not very pretty:
But, sure, he's proud, and yet his pride becomes him:
He'll make a proper man: the best thing in him
Is his complexion; and faster than his tongue
Did make offence, his eye did heal it up.
He is not very tall; yet for his years he's tall:
His leg is but so so; and yet 't is well:
There was a pretty redness in his lip;
A little riper and more lusty red
Than that mix'd in his cheek; 't was just the difference
Betwixt the constant red and mingled damask.
There be some women, Silvius, had they mark'd him
In parcels as I did, would have gone near
To fall in love with him; but for my part,
I love him not, nor hate him not; and yet
I have more cause to hate him than to love him:
For what had he to do to chide at me."—*A*. III. s. 5.

Celia, the modest, the retiring, is in most admirable keeping. The love of her cousin, in conjunction with that cousin's loquacity and vivacity of spirits, keep her somewhat in the background, yet she is not less gifted, being full of wisdom, gentleness and sweetness. The love existing between her and her cousin is of the purest character. She believes in Rosalind, and when her father rebukes her cousin and decrees her banishment, she lacks not spirit to defend her cousin. She exclaims, describing their fondness for each other,

> "if she be a traitor,
> Why, so am I; we still have slept together,
> Rose at an instant, learn'd, play'd, eat together;
> And wheresoe'er we went, like Juno's swans,
> Still we went coupled and inseparable."

When her father will not revoke the decree of banishment, but repeats the sentence, "she is banish'd," Celia answers by saying,

> "Pronounce that sentence then on me, my liege:
> I cannot live out of her company."

Her love for Rosalind causes her to dare and to do. She cannot conceive of their being separated;—

> "Shall we part, sweet girl?
> No: let my father seek another heir."

She is fertile in her invention and prompt in her action. She decides where to go, whom to go to, and suggests means whereby the journey may be accomplished. She is in no way dispirited by the harsh conduct of her father, on the contrary, her flow of spirits becomes stronger by the occasion. She will "devise the fittest time," and "the safest way," to baffle those who may be desirous of pursuing. She will but collect her jewels and her wealth, and then she says, speaking to her cousin, as they quit the scene,

> "Now go we in content
> To liberty, and not to banishment."

Celia is equally as witty as her cousin, though she makes not so much display. The interest which her love for her cousin creates, continues throughout the whole of the comedy, and our sympathies are retained for one who could love so true, and act so kindly.

Rosalind, the winning, the loving, the witty, playful maiden, is one of those charming characters that at all times and under all circumstances fails not to please. She is the principal character of the comedy, the centre on which the chief interest turns. She is the real heroine, possessing much sprightliness, and yet withal a thoughtfulness that lends force and strength to her character. When she first appears, she is not in her true position. She is but a mere dependant, a half willing captive at her uncle's court, and her natural flow of spirits is checked by the remembrance of her father who is in banishment.

This feeling is driven from her mind by her love of Orlando, which springeth up out of pure sympathy. It is this which moves her in her first interview with him. Her sympathy is excited, and whenever such a feeling arises, love is sure to follow. The manliness and gentleness of Orlando quickens that which his unfortunate position began, and this is completed, when she learns his name and knows from whom he sprung. She says,

"My father lov'd Sir Rowland as his soul,
And all the world was of my father's mind:
Had I before known this young man his son,
I should have given him tears unto entreaties,
Ere he should thus have ventured."

This knowledge adds fuel to the fire, and she falls truly in love with him; thus affording another instance of the power of that feeling, which

"From court to the cottage,
In bower and in hall,
From the king unto the beggar
Love conquers all."*

* *Truth's Integrity, or Love will find out the way.* Early Ballads edited by R. Bell, p. 176.

The speeches of Rosalind are full of playfulness and wit, which bubbles up like a fountain, scattering its refreshing waters on all things around. She is voluble but never tiring, for her volubility is full of life and joy, and her impulses are all marked by kindness and gentleness. She never loses her maiden modesty, even when clothed in man's attire; and man's attire she surely wears—not that of a boy—if her own description can be relied upon.

"Were it not better,
Because I am more than common tall,
That I did suit me all points like a man?
A gallant curtle-axe upon my thigh,
A boar-spear in my hand; and (in my heart
Lie there what hidden woman's fear there will)
We'll have a swashing and a martial outside;
As many other mannish cowards have,
That do outface it with their semblances."

While so disguised, she never uses words nor performs any acts which are contrary to her feminine disposition. She never unsexes herself, and she as readily and as gracefully puts off her manly garments to wear her own womanly attire, as when she adopted her masculine ones to assist her in her flight.

The wit of Rosalind differs greatly from that of Beatrice's. It is not so caustic; there is much less of satire in her word-playing. It is more humourous, more mirthful, and less pointed. There is more feeling and earnestness in Rosalind than in Beatrice. The female character that most resembles Rosalind is Imogen. Both are possessed of great tenderness and sympathy,—both possess high intellectual powers,—both are heroines of their respective plays, and "in both are found the same clear and prompt intelligence—

the same consummate grace and self-possession in enacting those respective masculine parts which the exigences of their fortune compel them to assume. The deeper pathos and the graver wisdom which lend a more solemn though scarcely more tender colouring to the character of Imogen, seem hardly more than may be sufficiently accounted for by that maturer development which one and the same original character would receive from the maturer years, the graver position, and more tragic trials of the wife, in which the heroine of *Cymbeline* is set before us,—as compared with that early bloom, and those fond anxieties of youthful courtship, which we behold in Rosalind."\*

The whole of the love scenes, the manner in which the characters fall in love with each other, is done in the most masterly manner by Shakspere. He evidently intendeth their actions to support the opinion of love at first sight. The reasons for this are twofold; firstly, because of its frequent occurrence in the world, thereby showing its truthfulness; and secondly, out of compliment to one of his greatest contemporaries, Marlow, of the mighty line, to whom he alludes when he says,

"Dead shepherd! now I find thy saw of might,
'Whoever lov'd, that lov'd not at first sight?'"

In the closing scene, Jaques, true to his character, will not fall in with the measures proposed by the duke. He will away, for

"Out of these convertites,
There is much matter to be heard and learn'd."

His cynical disposition will not allow him to participate in the happiness of others; it is contrary to

---

\* Fletcher's *Studies of Shakspere*, p. 237.

the part he has assumed. True to his artificiality, and to the external manners which he hath put on, with a slight remembrance of how Touchstone worsted him in the forest, he sneers at the motley and his wife, saying,

> "And you to wrangling; for thy loving voyage
> Is but for two months victualled. So, to your pleasures,
> I am for other than your dancing measures."

On the Duke's command of "Stay, Jaques, stay," he answers,

> "To see no pastime I : what you would have
> I'll stay to know at your abandon'd cave."

The catastrophe is brought about most satisfactorily, and the comedy ends most happily. The good duke's patrimony is restored, his daughter firmly fixed with the son of his bosom friend, "the good Sir Rowland,"— his niece, enlinkt in the same bonds with Oliver, whom she hath won from his evil ways; and in the same tangled web are also enmeshed Silvius and Phœbe, Touchstone and his Audrey, their hands and hearts in fond communion joined, by

> "Hymen! god of every town."

Throughout the whole of the comedy, the poetry existing in human nature is shown forth by the master's hand. The natural is placed above the artificial; and it requires but a slight effort of the imagination, while under the influence of this charming work, once more to revel in golden dreams amid the scenes of a golden age.

# MACBETH.

THE date of the production of this tragedy is usually given in the last ten years of the author's life, about the year 1606, and it was printed for the first time in the folio of 1623. The reasons assigned by Malone for its earlier production are very vague and unsatisfactory, nor do they militate against the year now generally accepted. The materials of this tragedy were derived by Shakspere from the chronicles of Holinshed, and though he and the chronicler are occasionally at variance, yet the main incidents of the tragedy are to be found in the pages of the chronicle. The meeting of the witches, the murder of Duncan, also that of Banquo, the attempt to slay Macduff, and the death of the usurper at the hands of Macduff, are all related by Holinshed. In Shakspere taking up these incidents, he has so interwoven them in his tragedy, has so re-clothed them in the true language of poetry, and endowed them with the power of his own genius, that the truthfulness and beauty which the lines convey will never die, nor will the incidents be forgotten. In 1673, Sir W. Davenant altered, added and otherwise amended and improved this tragedy,—so at least it was said at the time,—but a greater mistake was never made. In 1731, it was again altered by Mr. Nahum Tate, who had some time before tried his "prentice hand" upon the tragedy of Lear, to the detriment of the text and the action of the play. In 1748, a special version was produced by Garrick, who pretended to restore the original text by omitting the additions and removing the mutilations of Davenant. This, however, he did not do, for though he left out many of the additions which had been made, he was guilty of many interpolations of his own, which in no way added to the grandeur and beauty of the tragedy, nor to the strength and sweetness of the poetic diction. So thoroughly did Garrick appear to understand Shakspere's intent and meaning in this tragedy, that he added a most contemptible dying speech to the part of Macbeth.

In this tragedy we see the difference between the man of genius and he of mediocrity. With the latter, this tragedy would have been but a mere chamber of horrors, producing a strong state of excitement, from which both reader and spectator would have shrank with disgust. On the other hand, Shakspere has so made use of them, even in their most striking forms, in association with the beautiful and pure, that under no circumstances do they create any emotions which are not of a healthful and pleasurable kind. It is in this power, that Shakspere stands so pre-eminent; it is this art which places him above all others, for in no other, but in him alone, is seen its pure development.

The opening of this tragedy is wonderfully finely conceived. Amidst thunder, lightning, hail and rain, the weird-sisters big with fate, prepare the reader or spectator for the supernatural influences which are to follow. The bleeding soldier, his tale of fighting, the blasted heath, the wild prophecies all serve to pave the way for the perpetration of crimes of a deeper hue and deeds of a more deadly character.

The scene in which Lady Macbeth appears, completes what the opening scenes have already foreshadowed. Her allusions to the killing of Duncan, to the natural influences by which her husband is surrounded, and to the aid which the supernatural part of the story gives him, produces that peculiar state of the brain, that it becomes prepared to receive without wonderment all the results which follow. It is in this, that the great dramatic skill of Shakspere is shown. He passes not from one extreme to the other abruptly, everything is prepared, for the interest gradually accumulates, and the brain drinks in, without the power of refusing, the deeds and actions of the character of the tragedy.

Several writers upon this tragedy have contended that the witches, whose introduction into the play takes us out of the course of ordinary life, their supernatural influence determining the action of the play, should be represented by young and pretty women on the stage, but the whys and wherefores which are urged, "pale their ineffectual fire" before the description given of them by Banquo:—

"So wither'd, and so wild in their attire,
That look not like the inhabitants o' the earth,
And yet are on't? Live you? or are you aught
That man may question? You seem to understand me,
By each at once her choppy finger laying
Upon her skinny lips. You should be women,
And yet your beards forbid me to interpret
That you are so."

The expressions "withered," "choppy finger," and "skinny lips," are refutations of the notion of their being young and pretty, while the more forcibly to point out the external character of these haggards of the night, their beards are alluded to as a reason that they are hardly women at all. This surely ought to suffice as a refutation of such an opinion, but still further, in *A.* IV. s. 1., they are called by Macbeth, "black and midnight *hags*," an expression that can not be possibly applied, nor in any way construed to apply to young and pretty women.

The tragedy of Macbeth furnishes a splendid contrast to the tragedy of Hamlet. In the latter, action scarcely advances, so slow is the movement of the principal character, who is continually resolving to act, yet never acting upon his resolution. In Macbeth, the action marches rapidly and grandly on; there is no standing still, no halting by the way, for the progress of events is swift and the catastrophe is speedily arrived at. Every character tends to develope the catastrophe and lend its aid in magnifying the qualities and nature of its completeness. The little as well as the great all help towards working out the result, which is in itself most complete.

Macbeth is made up of action, for he is the representative of activity, while Hamlet is exceedingly passive. Macbeth is all physical strength while Hamlet is physically weak. There is but little room for thought in Macbeth, he has to *do*, not to reason and reflect. In him, manly audacity and human might are strained to the utmost when he has resolved; for he dares a contest with fate having no dread or fear of the result. In the opening scene Macbeth is described as a man of worth, possessing all the requirements of a true and perfect soldier. Sword and shield never fell into worthier hands and the good use he makes of his flashing falchion, when he "unseamed" the rebel lord "from the nave to the chaps," speaks well for his prowess; speaks well for him who was "valour's minion," "Bellona's bridegroom." The truthfulness of the witches' first greeting, lends weight to their suggestions for his future greatness, and his natural promptitude of action soon causes him to set about realizing what his brain desires. His nature is one of activity; action is born within him, he cannot relapse into supineness nor sluggishness, and when he is crowned king, he still must act; he must let his thought and action proceed together. The thirst for action increases in the latter part of the tragedy, and this to a great extent is engendered by his fears. While engaged or absorbed in the performance of any deed his fears are overcome, and he rises above the dreadful consequences which he foreshadows to himself while thinking and not acting.

The chief feature in the character of Macbeth is ambition, a strong lust of power. The good parts of his nature are wholly overcome by this one particular passion, to this they all yield. His honour, his respect, his love of his fellow-creature, his desire to stand well with the world, are all absorbed by his dominant passion, ambition, the insatiate monster that ultimately destroys him. The seeds of this passion exist in him prior to his interview with the witches on the heath. The desire of Duncan's death and the wish to be king are familiar thoughts of Macbeth's before the action of the tragedy begins. He has thought this matter over and has partly resolved how and what to do. This is shown in his interview with his wife, when she taunts him for his cowardice in shrinking from the assassination,

"What beast was't then
That made you break this enterprise to me?"

His interview with the weird-like three only re-awakens the feeling that had long been slumbering within him, and from that moment the feeling gradually grows upon him and takes possession of all his faculties. After the first salutation he stands "rapt," and the greater honour which they confer on Banquo, does not destroy the feeling; it still exists within him and gives evidence of its existence when the witches have vanished, by his questioning his friend "your children shall be kings?" to which Banquo replies "you shall be king," and the impatient manner in which Macbeth answers, as if to hide the thought, which he had previously betrayed, "and thane of Cawdor too; went it not so?"

The intensity of this feeling is increased when Rosse salutes him as "thane of Cawdor," and this first confirmation of the witches' prophecies makes him become the more strongly impressed with the desire of kingly dignity and kingly power, and he also becomes convinced that the greater which they have foretold shall be fulfilled. This belief and reliance on the words of the three is shown when speaking to himself, he exclaims "the greatest is behind," and in the question which he puts to Banquo,

"Do not you hope your children shall be kings,
When those that gave the thane of Cawdor to me
Promis'd no less for them?"

The imagination of Macbeth now becomes excited and he clearly sees the ultimatum to be arrived at. His first success gives him warranty for his future successes, and his active brain immediately passes in review all the circumstances, and the course of action he must adopt. The thoughts that now arise, are of the foulest and bloodiest character, to these he doth gradually yield, for he sees no other way, but in following that "suggestion" which exacts from him the words

" Whose horrid image doth unfix my hair,
And make my seated heart knock at my ribs,
Against the use of nature? Present fears
Are less than horrible imaginings:
My thought, whose murther yet is but fantastical,
Shakes so my single state of man, that function
Is smother'd in surmise; and nothing is,
But what is not."

When he awakes from this state he rests satisfied with the results, he cares not what may happen, it will not be of everlasting duration,

"for come what may,
Time and the hour run thro' the roughest day."

In the next scene when visiting Duncan in his palace at Forres, he does not lose sight of the crown of his heart's desire. When the king addresses him firstly as "worthiest cousin," and then as " my worthy Cawdor," this kindness doth not destroy the thought nor uproot the feeling, on the contrary both are strengthened by what takes place. When Duncan declares that his estate shall be established upon his "eldest Malcolm," and proclaims him "prince of Cumberland," the necessity for prompt action reveals itself to Macbeth, who sees that unless he rapidly decides and

K

as rapidly acts, he will let slip opportunity. He perceives but one way to accomplish his wishes, and that is the death of the king, no matter by what means. He will not shrink from the performance of the "foul unnatural murther," for by no other method does he conceive that the crown can be obtained. The appointment of a successor fully determines his course of action and the resolution he has arrived at. This is made most evident by the language he uses when he is thinking aloud.

> "The prince of Cumberland.—That is a step,
> On which I must fall down, or else o'erleap,
> For in my way it lies. Stars, hide your fires!
> Let not light see my black and deep desires:
> The eye wink at the hand! Yet let that be,
> Which the eye fears, when it is done, to see."

There is much moral cowardice in the nature of Macbeth. He is prone to superstitious fears and they so work upon him, that he relents from his purposes and requires to be spurred to "prick the sides of his intent," before he will attempt to achieve that which when performed will lead to that position which his ambitious desires would have him fulfil. Those fears are soon aroused and his apprehension conjures up consequences so fearful to himself, that he determines not to attempt that to which his thoughts have long been tending. When his wife tells him he hath been enquired for by the king, he asserts his determination to "proceed no further in the business," alleging for his reasons, that Duncan of "late hath honoured" him, and that he has

> "bought
> Golden opinions from all sorts of people,
> Which would be worn now in their newest gloss,
> Not cast aside too soon."

Throughout this scene the sharp taunts of his scoffing partner once more rekindles the fierce desire, which beneath her lash, burns with such vigour that he unhesitatingly and without remorse decides to slay his "kinsman" and his king. His conscience has now become stifled, yielding at last to the more powerful will of his wife, and having resolved, his daring and active nature must have play. Strung up to do the deed, he has visions arising in his "heat oppressed brain," all marshalling "the way" he intends "to go" and shadowing the "instrument" he is "to use." In silence he would move, so that the "firm set earth," should not hear his "steps," for silence is in unison with the "present horror" of the time. The sounding bells break on this silence, and invites him to execute his purpose, "to go and it is done." When "'tis done," his fears come crowding back with renewed vigour, so that he shrinks with alarm from every sound he hears, and he imagines cries that make him quake,

"Glamis hath murder'd sleep: and therefore Cawdor
Shall sleep no more."

These ring in his ears a knell so dreadful, making his fears so strong, that mentally and physically he is so overthrown, that he cannot complete those measures necessary to the safety of himself and his wife. So strongly is he affected, so deeply is he moved, that the taunts of his cool and more determined partner fail to give him courage, and she herself is forced to perform those things which are necessary to be done. When left alone "every noise appals" him, he is frightened by the colour of his hands; their bloodiness takes away his physical vision, nor "will all great Neptune's ocean wash" away the stains. When his wife returns those fears and phantasies still cling around him, and heartily he wishes that the murdered Duncan should "wake" with the "knocking;" and though he knows he cannot, he gives expression to his thought in the words "I would thou could'st." In the interim between the perpetration of the murder and the discovery thereof, his "state" "suffers an insurrection," but the example of his wife, coupled with the wish of self-preservation and the desire of realizing his ambitious thoughts, engender a calmness of external demeanour, which hides the raging fire which burns within. When the "sacrilegeous murther" is discovered, his brain resumes its state of activity, and he readily seizes upon the occasion "to see" and judge for himself, for it affords him an opportunity to slay the "sleeping grooms," and thus remove all chances of detection. To think this, is to do it, and it is done. Weighty and manifold are the excuses he can urge in favour of the act, for "the expedition" of his "violent love outran the pauser reason." Though he does "repent" that he "did kill them," yet he skilfully argues that "in a moment like this" who could "be wise, amaz'd, temperate and furious," for "here lay Duncan," "there the murtherers," "their daggers, steeped in the colours of their trade,"

" Who could refrain
That had a heart to love, and in that heart
Courage to make his love known?"

The fainting of Lady Macbeth diverts the attention of the friends of Duncan, otherwise directing their thoughts for the instant and preventing any answer being given to the excuses of the perpetrator of "this most bloody piece of work." This incident also affords

Macbeth an opportunity of recovering his self-command and exhorting Banquo, Macduff and the rest, who are all shook with fears and scruples," to "put on manly readiness," so that they may "question" "to know it further," by meeting "in the hall together."

When the lofty seat is gained and the crown rests upon his head, still the fears of Macbeth for his own safety arise. He knows full well the "royalty of nature" which reigns in Banquo,—the "dauntless temper of his mind," the "wisdom that doth guide his valour,"—by these qualities his "genius is rebuked," and therefore he fears, that if Banquo lives, he will unmake him. His death is necessary to his safety, instinctively he feels that Banquo is his "enemy," who if he is allowed to live, will "every minute" be thrusting after his seat and life. He must be swept away, and the instruments are ready that will perform the deed. The snake's "scotched" not killed, and he would make all sure. "Both the worlds" shall "suffer" he tells his wife,

"Ere we will eat our meal in fear, and sleep
In the affliction of these terrible dreams,
That shake us nightly."

The excitement attending upon the murder of Banquo, in conjunction with his other deed, reawakens his superstitious fears and leads him "to his seeing" within the compass of his agitated brain, the ghastly form of Banquo in the banquet scene "with twenty trenched gashes in his head." He shrinks with horror from this mental vision, he is quite "unmanned in folly," and he is only brought back to his natural state by the greater fortitude of his wife, who so far restores him, that he is enabled to tell his "worthy friends" he has a "strange infirmity, which is nothing, to those that know me." Again his excitement crops up, to be allayed by the same means, and then he cannot help exclaiming

"Can such things be,
And overcome us like a summer cloud,
Without our special wonder?"

When these fears have wholly subsided and he becomes himself, his activity is awakened and he determines on a course of action that shall be conducive to his safety. He will to "the weird-sisters" to know "the worst" for his "own good."

"All causes shall give way; I am in blood
Stepp'd in so far, that, should I wade no more,
Returning were as tedious as go o'er:
Strange things I have in head, that will to hand;
Which must be acted, 'ere they may be scann'd."

This reliance upon the words of the fearful three, serves to display his moral weakness. He is not content with what he can devise to make himself secure, but he would learn from those who have already told him true, what can and will be done. He wishes to be on his guard against his enemies, to learn who they are, how their efforts may be defeated and his position made secure. He has already had fears of "the thane of Fife," for when he receives the "good caution" from the armed head, he says, "thou hast harped my fear aright." Though told to fear no "power of man, for none of woman born" can do him harm, he resolves that Macduff shall "not live," so that he "may tell pale-hearted fear it lies." The third prediction confirms him, he is fully convinced that that can "never be," for "who can impress the forest?" or "bid the tree unfix his earthbound root?" These "bodements" fully satisfy his cravings to know what can and will be done relative to his own person, and his course of conduct is now plainly marked out, it must be "bloody, bold and resolute." From this time henceforth, to think is to act, "the very firstlings of his thoughts shall be the firstlings of his hand," and though he, whom he hath been told to be aware of, "the thane of Fife," has "fled to England," he will carry out his murderous intent, by having revenge upon "his wife," "his babes," and all others "that trace him in his line." His career is now marked by unbridled violence, his thoughts are bloody and bloody are his deeds:—

" each morn,
New widows howl; new orphans cry; new sorrows
Strike heaven on the face."

He has no friends, nor must he look for any, his path is now alone, for the potent spirit that moved him to his task, that incited him to do the "deed without a name," is fallen "diseased" in mind, her bosom filled with "perilous stuff" she no longer can buoy him up, her fortitude and power is wanting, and his sole reliance is now on the predictions of the witches, to those predictions he clings as the anchor of his safety; he will not shrink, he

"will not be afraid of death and bane,
Till Birnam forest come to Dunsinane."

Nothing that arises seems in any way after this interview to alarm Macbeth, so firm is his reliance on the words of the weird-three. When he learns of further defection among his court and of the approach of the English army, he has no fears for himself; he so thoroughly believes in that which he hath been told, that the contrary is the case. Come what may, let the "false thanes" fly, he will "never sagg with doubt nor shake with fear." He is all activity, ready for the approaching struggle, in which he will bear a soldier's part, for he "will fight" till from his "bones" his "flesh be hacked." He has no dread of death, and when he learns the death of his queen, he is so unmoved, that he soliloquises on life, believes it to be "but a walking shadow."

"a tale
Told by an idiot, full of sound and fury,
Signifying nothing."

The last hope but one is now removed, for "Birnam forest" be "come to Dunsinane," yet his physical courage rises with the occasion, and he hurries to the fight resolved to "die with harness on his back." His moral courage almost breaks down when he learns that the last plank to which he clings, fails him, and that Macduff is not of "woman born." His "better part," is "cowed," and all belief in the "juggling friends" is banished from his brain. When called upon to yield, the fighting qualities of his nature re-assert their sway; his physical courage rides to its topmost height and like a gallant warrior "famoused for fight," before "his body" he throws his "warlike shield," for he "will try the last," and exclaims

"Lay on Macduff,
And damn'd be he that first cries, Hold! enough."

In furious combat with his brother thane, they quit the scene, to which Macbeth returns no more, for he is slain by Macduff, who brings to the young prince "the usurper's head," and since "the time is free," he with others of the courtly circle, whose voices in conjunction with his, hail Malcolm, as "king of Scotland."

The character of Macbeth cannot really be put in comparison with Richard III, for they have only one thing in common, ambition. Richard relies upon no one, he is himself "alone;" he possesses unlimited confidence in himself, using others only as tools to accomplish his desires, while Macbeth, on the other hand, is constantly wanting support. This phase of his character is thoroughly known and understood by his wife, who through the love she feels for him, united with her own ambition, directs and supports him in his varied acts. This necessity for some support beside his own strength, is shown in his consulting with the sisters three, and in the full reliance which he places on the predictions which they give utterance to. He could not have walked alone in his path of crime, from this want of self-sustaining power, which is most strongly evidenced in the high intellectual development of the crafty, criminal Richard.

Lady Macbeth is a strong, bold, courageous and ambitious woman, full of lofty daring, reckless as to consequences, treacherous when treachery will serve her purpose, yet so far womanly, that she is full of love for her irresolute lord. She is physically strong, not lacking astuteness, and possessing a great mastery over her husband. She goeth straight to effect her purpose, no difficulty that may or does arise will turn her aside, for when the thought has pierced her brain, awakening her ambitious desires, she suffers nought else to prevail until those wishes and desires are accomplished. All other feelings and passions are absorbed in the development of this particular one. Her brain is filled with this one thought, and everything is bent and warped to accomplish this desire. It is this which gives her courage, controls her imagination, and adds strength to the power which she already possesses over her husband. The tide of ambition carries her away, and from the instant she learns the prophecy of the weird-sisters, she resolves that such prophecy shall be fulfilled:—

"Glamis thou art and Cawdor;
And *shalt* be what thou art *promised.*"

The first speech of Lady Macbeth foreshadows her power over her husband, and it also shows her complete knowledge of his nature. She apprehends that he is too full of "the milk of human kindness" to accomplish that, to which his thoughts are ever tending, and which is a necessary result of his ambition. She would that her husband should arrive; she is impatient for his coming, knowing that when he does come, she can be the incentive which will arouse him to do the deed, which he does fear to do, and which must be done, if their thoughts and desires are to be realized. She exclaims,

"Hie thee hither,
That I may pour my spirits in thine ear!
And chastise with the valour of my tongue
All that impedes thee from the golden round,
Which fate and metaphysical aid doth seem
To have thee crown'd withal."

She is full of joy on learning that the king will bide with them that night. The golden opportunity for which she and her husband have so long been waiting shall not be lost by them. The king with her is but a sorry bird to be enmeshed in the fowler's snares. The assassination of Duncan hath often been thought of, both by herself and by her husband, and when she learns of his approach, revealing how murderous are her thoughts and intent, she says,

> "The raven himself is hoarse,
> That croaks the *fatal* entrance of Duncan
> Under my battlements."

For the fulfilment of those thoughts and desires, she wishes that the "spirits that tend on mortal thoughts," should

> "Unsex me here;
> And fill me, from the crown to the toe, top-full
> Of direst cruelty! Make thick my blood,
> Stop up the access and passage to remorse;
> That no compunctious visitings of nature
> Shake my *fell purpose*, nor keep peace between
> The effect, and it! Come to my woman's breasts,
> And take my milk for gall, you murthering ministers,
> Wherever in your sightless substances
> You wait on nature's mischief! Come, thick night,
> And pall thee in the dimmest smoke of hell!
> That my keen knife see not the wound it makes;
> Nor heaven peep through the blanket of the dark,
> To cry, "Hold, hold!" Great Glamis, worthy Cawdor."

Upon the entrance of her husband, her thoughts still running on the crown, she continues,

> "Greater than both, by the all-hail hereafter,"

and then turns to express to him the joy which the receiving of his letters have engendered. They convey to her the realization of her most ambitious hopes, they "have transported her" beyond the "ignorant present," and she feels "the future in the instant." She is impatient for action, she would go on at once, she will not let opportunity wait upon opportunity, she will seize it. She answers her husband by a question, when he says, "My dearest love, Duncan comes here to night. And when goes hence?" Here again we have proof that her thoughts have been previously occupied with the murder of the king, and the speeches which follow also bear out this construction. When Macbeth answers "To-morrow, as he purposes," she most emphatically exclaims, "O, never shall sun that to-morrow see." She is fully resolved, nought shall turn her from her purpose. She has surveyed the giddy height and she will climb it, not fearing or heeding the consequences which may result. She hath resolved upon what shall be effected, and she will take the best means of carrying that resolution into effect. She will for the time being, veil over what her thoughts and desires are, and perceiving that her husband's face "is as a book, where men may read strange matters," she bids him

"beguile the time,
Look like the time; bear welcome in your eye,
Your hand, your tongue: look like the innocent flower,
But be the serpent under it. *He* that's coming
Must be provided for: and you shall put
This night's great business into my despatch;
Which shall to all our nights and days to come
Give solely sovereign sway and masterdom."

She here strikes the note that jars not, but is in keeping with Macbeth's own thoughts, for he does not upbraid her, nor seek to check the expression of her wishes, nor does he seek to divert the current of her feeling. Assenting by his words "we will speak further" on this thought, they quit the scene, she advising him to look up clear,

" To alter favour ever is to fear:
Leave all the rest to me."

Not anything appears capable of altering her determination, within and without she is resolved upon what is to be accomplished, shall be accomplished. In scene 7, when Macbeth shrinks from the performance of his self-appointed task, and tells her "we will proceed no further in this business," giving as his reasons that Duncan had "honoured" him "of late," and that he had "bought"

> "Golden opinions from all sorts of people,
> Which would be worn now in their newest gloss,
> Not cast aside so soon."

Full of scorn and sarcasm, she replies

> "Was the hope drunk
> Wherein you dress'd yourself? Hath it slept since?
> And wakes it now, to look so green and pale
> At what it did so freely? Art thou afeard
> To be the same in thine own act and valour,
> As thou art in desire? Wouldst thou have that
> Which thou esteem'st the ornament of life,
> And live a coward in thine own esteem;
> Letting I dare not, wait upon I would,
> Like the poor cat i' the adage."

This course of talking she is thoroughly cognizant will arouse her husband, for she is well aware of his weakness, and she is also fully persuaded that her taunts will awaken his desire, will make that desire paramount, and the necessary effect is partially shown in Macbeth's hurried exclamation

> "Prithee, peace:
> I dare do all that may become a man;
> Who dares do more, is none."

She continues her scoffs and tauntings, probing his weakness to the very quick. Telling him he was a man when he "durst do it," and asking him to be "so much more the man," now "time" and "place" "have made themselves" and "their fitness" for the realization of their wishes and desires. Calling him a "beast" when he did "break this enterprise to" her, and taunting him about his fears which now unmake him for the task. Rather than she would be so infirm of purpose, she moves him by saying what she would have done having once resolved to do. She speaks of the power of a mother's love, tells him, she hath "given suck" and knows "how tender 'tis to love the babe that milks," and rising in her scoffing, she exclaims,

"I would, while it was smiling in my face,
Have pluck'd my nipple from his boneless gums,
And dash'd the brains out, had I so sworn,
As you have done to this?"

His doubts are almost all removed by her earnestness and but a faint whisper arises in his reply, "If we should fail." This last doubt is entirely removed and dispelled by the fulness of her answer, in which the way to perform the murder is shown, how its consequences may be avoided and its guilt thrown upon others.

"We fail.
But screw your courage to the sticking place,
And we'll not fail. When Duncan is asleep,
(Whereto the rather shall his day's hard journey
Soundly invite him,) his two chamberlains
Will I with wine and wassel so convince,
That memory, the warder of the brain,
Shall be a fume, and the receipt of reason
A limbeck* only:—when in swinish sleep
Their drenched natures lie, as in a death,
What cannot you and I perform upon
The unguarded Duncan?—what not put upon
His spongy officers? who shall bear the guilt
Of our great quell."

This speech determines Macbeth's course of action, dispels all his fears of the consequences that may arise and he resolves on binding up each "corporal agent" to the accomplishment of "this terrible feat." His

* An alembic, or still.

admiration for his wife is awakened by her words and by her complete control over the how and when. He becomes enraptured with her clearness of perception and her display of courage, and he cannot refrain from expressing his admiration, for he exclaims

"Bring forth men children only,
For thy undaunted mettle should compose
Nothing but males."

In this scene the physical side of the character of Lady Macbeth is freely and fully developed, nor does the mental side of her character lack illustration. She clearly depicts how and when the deed can be done, by which the object of their ambition, the crown of Scotland, can be achieved. Her perceptive faculties are more acute than those of her husband's, and she thinks and reasons less upon the consequences in the future than he does, because her reflective faculties are less strong than his. She rapidly perceives and fully displays to her husband this perception, overcomes his moral cowardice by her taunts and sneers, and so moves him by her fierce denunciations of his conduct, that he becomes "settled" in his determination to dare and to do, that he quits the stage filled with dissimulation and resolved to

"mock the time with fairest show
False face must hide what the false heart doth know."

Lady Macbeth is all action until the desired goal is reached. She halts not by the way, once having started upon the road, not anything stays or sways her from her purpose. The end with her is everything,—she has no cares about the means, they are but lightly estimated. She has no doubt of success, no scruples of conscience; "no compunctious visitings of nature," every circumstance must give way to that which she desires and which has become to her a necessity. She has no distorted visions like her husband in the dagger scene, with "gouts of blood" upon the "blade and dudgeon," and she is only prevented from perpetrating the deed herself by a physical accident, the resemblance Duncan bore to her dead father. After the murder has been committed and Macbeth's courage begins to fail, his dread of the consequences re-awakening his moral cowardice, her spirit of boldness and of going straight to the purpose, once more developes itself in the taunts and sneers which she casts upon her husband, whose fears hath imagined that some one did cry "Macbeth shall sleep no more." She says,

"Who was it that cried? Why, worthy thane,
You do unbend your noble strength to think
So brain-sickly of things;—go, get some water,
And wash this filthy witness from your hand,—
Why did you bring these daggers from the place?
They must lie there:—go, carry them; and smear
The sleepy grooms with blood."

This speech does not have the desired effect, it does not infuse the requisite amount of courage in Macbeth, he has not the heart to revisit the scene of his crimes; he shrinks appalled from that which he hath performed and is "afraid to think" upon that which he has "done." He will "go no more," and "dare not" "look on it again." Her resolution now rises to its topmost height, her physical courage is raised to its highest pitch. To her purpose firm, she owns no fear, nor feels no dread. The living, "the sleeping and the dead," are to her but toys and "pictures" that are beneath her breeding. Scoffingly vehement, she exclaims,

"Infirm of purpose!
Give me the daggers: the sleeping and the dead,
Are but as pictures; 'tis the eye of childhood
That fears a painted devil. If he do bleed,
I'll gild the faces of the grooms withal,
For it must seem their guilt."

When she returns after the disposal of the instruments of death, she exults in what she has done, and draws her husband's attention to the bloodiness of her own hands, and scoffs at him for the weakness he displays;

"My hands are of your colour; but I shame
To wear a heart so white."

Though strung up to the highest pitch yet her coolness and tranquility does not forsake her. She is fully prepared for any and every emergency that may arise, and when a knocking is heard, she fails not to direct what is to be done. Her mastery over herself, her husband, and even over the circumstances which crowd upon her, is truly great. She cheerfully states the means whereby the evidence of their guilt can be removed and how easily it is accomplished:

"retire we to our chamber
A little water clears us of this deed:
How easy is it then! Your constancy
Hath left you unattended."

When more knocking is heard she is prompt in thought, bids her husband "get on" his "night gown,"

"lest occasion call us,
And show us to be watchers."

She then exhorts Macbeth to be himself, not to let his imagination override his senses, filling him with fears of his own creation, but to be firm and true to his own nature, nor be "lost so poorly" in his "thoughts."

L

Her coolness and cleverness of acting is most excellently displayed, when she enters amid the turmoil and confusion attending upon the discovery of the murder. She enquires

"What's the business,
That such a hideous trumpet calls to parley
The speakers of the house? speak, speak."

Macduff at first will not say the cause, so completely is he deceived by her manner, that he fears he shall commit a murder were he to tell her;—her womanly nature would be overcome by the shock, for "in a woman's ear," it "would murther as it fell." On Banquo's entrance he blurts out the deed, and she, true to the part she is acting, with eye and voice of horror, exclaims "what, in our house?" And when she learns from her husband's speech of the safety of their plans, by his slaying of "the sleeping grooms," she falls into a fainting state, calling "help me hence, hoa!" as if deeply affected by the horror of the crime which has been perpetrated, and to effect which she has really been the principal instigator.

The hardihood, and boldness, the cunning and subtlety of Lady Macbeth is strongly evidenced in the second scene of act 3. She has no compunctions of conscience for the crime in which she has been a participator; unlike her husband she gives not way to "sorriest fancies;" she uses no "thought which should indeed have died with them they think on." She looks upon the past without regret, and while upbraiding Macbeth for his weakness, in yielding to his fancies and in keeping himself aloof from others, she would have

"things without remedy,
Should be without regard: *what's done is done.*"

In the deep vault of oblivion would she bury all remembrance of the past, and with thoughts solely alive to their safety in the future, and to the means whereby they shall be enabled to hoodwink and deceive those by whom they are surrounded, she would have her husband play the host with gentleness, would have him courteous and affable withal, and bids him "sleek o'er" his "rugged looks," and "be bright and jovial 'mong" his "guests to-night."

In the banquet scene her presence of mind and her fortitude are excellently developed. Her lack of reflection is also made most apparent by the great activity she displays of her perceptive powers. She has never fully weighed the consequences of the foul deed which has been committed, she only looks upon the results as they affect her present position in relation to the past action, and she readily perceives how to thrust aside the unpleasant circumstances which may arise. She is prompt in seeking to divert the attention of the court from the ravings of her husband, and readily proffers excuses for his strange conduct.

"Sit worthy friends: my lord is often thus,
And hath been from his youth: pray you, keep seat;
The fit is momentary; upon a thought
He will again be well: If much you note him,
You shall offend and extend his passion;
Feed, and regard him not."

After this apology she turns to Macbeth, sneeringly enquiring "are you a man?" and when he answers

"Ay, and a bold one, that dare look on that
Which might appal the devil :"

she scoffingly replies, knowing that such a mode of talking is the only way by which his weakness can be overcome.

> "O proper stuff!
> This is the very painting of your fear:
> This is the air-drawn dagger, which, you said,
> Led you to Duncan. O, these flaws and starts
> Impostors to true fear, would well become
> A woman's story, at a winter's fire,
> Authoriz'd by her grandam. Shame itself!
> Why do you make such faces? When all's done
> You look but on a stool."

On the second outbreak of her husband's fears arising from his strong imagination and his "thinking too precisely" on what he hath done and caused to be done, she implores their patience, and hopes the "good peers" will think it only

> "As a thing of custom: 'tis no other;
> Only it spoils the pleasure of the time."

When Macbeth partially recovers from the mental vision in which he has been entranced, and reason begins to assert its sway, he wonders that she could "behold such sights," still keeping "the natural ruby of" her "cheeks," while his "are bland with fear." Her strong physique buoys her up and the realisticness of her nature will not allow of any spiritual visitations. She upbraids him with his weakness and scoffs at the fears which he has displayed through the mental visit of "the blood-boltered Banquo." When the lord Rosse enquires "what sights" have moved Macbeth, she skilfully evades the question, requesting that "he speak not," for enquiry will make him "grow worse and worse," and wishes they would go, bidding them "good night," and kindly requests they will not stand "upon the order of your going, but go at once." In reply to their good wishes, she dismisses the court with "a kind good night to all," and then promptly answers her husband's query, "what is the night?" "almost at odds with morning." Throughout the whole of this scene, which is of a most trying character for her, she is always on her guard, always prepared for what ever may ensue. She is full of grace and queenly dignity, glossing over with such an air of charming sweetness all the stormy incidents of the scene, and thus displaying a thorough mastery over her active brain, and skilfully hiding under those guises her internal emotions.

After the banquet scene we see but little of Lady Macbeth. The murder of Macduff's family takes place and this is the last foul deed of which she has any cognizance. When next we see her, she is not sane. The activity of her perceptive powers, buoyed up by her physical nature, and the constant action for her own safety and the safety of her husband, prevent her from thinking upon the enormity of the crimes in which she has been engaged. When action ceases, these events come crowding thick upon her, and her brain, whose sphere is activity, gives way. Lacking the necessary spurs to action, she sinks into a hopeless condition of a confirmed melancholy. Even while in this state, she thinks of nought but the crimes with which she has been connected, and her actions, the washing of her hands, and her language, all turn upon her misdeeds. "Out damned spot," "yet who would have thought the old man to have so much blood in him."—"What will these hands ne'er be clean?" These and similar expressions tend to show wherein her weakness lay, in her reflective faculties; and these not being strongly developed, she has not the requisite power to sustain herself when the circumstances requiring activity cease to be. Like most of those whose misdeeds have been of a foul character, the remembrance thereof becomes vivid, laying like an incubus upon the brain, so that with "self and violent hands," she takes away her own life. There are two redeeming points in the character of Lady Macbeth, her love for her husband and the womanly feeling which prevents her from committing the murder of Duncan, from the resemblance he bore to her father. Without these she would almost be placed beyond the pale of humanity, with them she comes within its Law, and Shakspere to have done otherwise, would have been untrue to his great knowledge of humanity and to his still greater knowledge in depicting it. Her death is a fit termination to the career of the "fiend-like queen," perfectly in unison with her nature and consonant with a true development of humanity.

The aged Duncan is a weak, though good man, anxious to stand well in the estimation of his court and also most anxious to reward those whom he believes act faithfully in his interest. On the traitor thane of Cawdor, whom Macbeth slays and succeeds, he had placed the greatest reliance, for his mental weakness prevents him from finding "the minds' construction in the face." He is one of those who "think men honest that but seem to be so," and accepts as truth the protestations of love and service which they offer. It is thus he is deceived by Cawdor, for "he was a gentleman on whom he built an absolute trust." He has no fear of his direst foe Macbeth; no thoughts arise within his brain that he is likely to act in a treacherous manner, for he looks upon him as "a peerless kinsman," whose great merits he cannot sufficiently compensate, for more is due to him, "than more than all can pay." He has no thought of wrong, nor any desire to commit any. There is no meanness in his nature, his thoughts are bound in honour's bond, and those that serve him well, he "will labour" to make them "full of growing." His nature was too tranquil for the turbulent times in which he lived, and he lacked the requisite mental and physical power to hold the mastery over such fierce spirits as Macbeth and his wife. His gentleness and unsuspicious nature made him an easy victim to the craft and subtlety of the ambitious thane and his partner. His goodness makes his murder the more unnatural, adding greatly to the interest of the tragedy, and failing not to win the sympathies of the audience or reader.

Banquo is a manly, interesting and truthfully drawn character. He is not without ambition, yet he would not realize his ambitious thoughts by unholy means. He is the soul of honour, by whose principles he wishes to be governed, and though the "cursed thought" will rise within him, relative to his own and the advancement of his family, caused no doubt by the mystic prophecy of the weird-like three, his conduct and his actions are both regulated by his love of justice and his feelings of honour. He would have those thoughts restrained which his "nature gives way to in repose," and from the tablets of his brain be razed out. Prior to the murder of Duncan, he tells Macbeth he did dream "of the three weird-sisters," "who have showed some truth" towards him, and when Macbeth expresses a wish to have some words upon that business, if he "would grant the time," he readily agrees, and in reply to Macbeth's wish that he would "cleave" to his "consent," when it is, for "it shall make honour for you," he says,

> "So lose I none,
> In seeking to augment it, but still keep—
> My bosom franchis'd, and all allegiance clear,
> I shall be counsell'd."

He rapidly hits the blot of Duncan's murderer, his judgment being aided by the knowledge that he had gained at the meeting on the heath. All that was promised his brother thane has now taken place, and though he has no doubt that Macbeth has "played most foully for it," the realization engenders the thought that they may be "my oracles as well, and that he will prove "the root and father of many kings." This thought leads him to think of quitting the court and thereby ensure the safety of his son Fleance, and when he is being assassinated, this thought becomes most paramount, for with dying voice, he bids "good Fleance, fly."

Macduff is a true specimen of the qualities of the fighting men of the period, rude and rugged in his manners, plain in his speech, honest withal, with sufficient perception to discover whose hand has done the "sacrilegious murder," and to feel certain misgivings for his own safety, on which he thinketh pretty freely, for he will not "to Scone," but unto "Fife." He will not come to Macbeth's court, "denies his person" when he is sent for, and flies to England:—

> "to pray the holy king upon his aid
> To wake Northumberland and warlike Siward,—

that, by the help of these, peace may be brought to his native land. Macduff is personally brave, filled with patriotism and anxious for the well-being of his country, so much so, that he would "hold fast the mortal sword" on behalf of his native soil, bonny Scotland. There is no treachery in his nature, which is open, unsuspecting of others and therefore the more readily deceived. This is made most apparent in his interview with the late king's son, Malcolm, whose representations of himself, the opposite of what he is, so completely hoodwinks Macduff, that he becomes fully convinced of their truth, and he fails not to lament the fallen state of his country, when "the truest issue of" its "throne" "by his own interdiction stands accursed." From his breast all hope vanishes and so completely have the words of Malcolm taken possession of his brain, that when the young prince unspeaks his "own detraction," and affirms it was his "first false speaking," he cannot "reconcile such welcome and unwelcome things at once." He has thought but little of the safety of his wife and children, "those strong knots of love," for his "fears" for his country have made him unwittingly "a traitor to their interest," so that when he learns the sad fate that has befallen them, the strength of his love displays itself, making him "play the woman with" his "eyes" and when the flood-tide of his grief is over he would that "front to front," "this fiend of Scotland" stood within his "sword's length," and "if he scape heaven forgive him." His wish is soon gratified, he and the "hell-hound" meet and the last prophecy of the three sisters is fulfilled by his arm, for he not being of "woman born," but "was from his mother's womb untimely ripped," slays the foul tyrant, and restores the son of the good Duncan to the throne of Scotland.

Malcolm and Donalbain, the sons of the murdered

monarch are most carefully drawn. Though not playing an important part in the tragedy, they are both marked by great perception, quickness of judgment and rapidity of action when their judgment is formed. Soon as they know that their royal father is murdered, they both display a knowledge of human character and of the circumstances by which they are surrounded. They wisely judge by what has been done, what is also likely to be done, and knowing the weakness of their position, they determine to flee, Malcolm to England, his brother to Ireland, their "separated fortune" making "both the safer," for where they are,

"There's daggers in men's smiles: the near in blood,
The nearer bloody."

They must not wait for any "dainty leave-taking," there is no time for that, they must be prompt, seeing as they do the dangers by which they are environed, for "this murtherous shaft that's shot, hath not yet lighted;" and their "safest way is to avoid the aim." Though their flight may lend a colour to the accusations which will be made against them, and bestow a seeming show of guiltiness, it were best to put much distance between them and Macbeth. Swift as midnight they must to horse, for they feel unless they do so, they will be added to the list of victims, and thus they hold

"There's warrant in that theft,
Which steals itself, when there's no mercy left."

The correctness of their judgment is soon evidenced and the wisdom of their acts soon proved. After their flight we hear no more of Donalbain, but Malcolm returns, backed by armed thousands of stalwart Englishmen, led by the gallant Siward, "an older and a better soldier," not "Christendom gives out." They besiege the slayer of Duncan in his castle at Dunsinane, fulfilling another of the prophecies of the weird-sisters, carry it by assault, the usurper is slain and Malcolm succeeds to his father's crown.

Rosse, Lennox, Angus, Monteith and the other courtiers are true exponents of their class. They may most justly be looked upon as pure representatives of the courtly circle of the period. Trained to arms, inured to danger, in love with fighting, they thoroughly represent the rude manners of those troublous times, when the hand more frequently sought the falchion's hilt, than the pen, to settle their differences, and the rule of the sword was paramount throughout the land. These characters though of a subordinate kind are all necessary to the development and completeness of the tragedy. They are thoroughly consistent in themselves and are also thoroughly consistent in fulfilling that, which the poet, ever true to himself, designed them to do. They fill up a picture, whose canvass is not over-crowded, giving a complete and correct view of human life and of the motives by which humanity is governed, for of all those whom Shakspere hath presented in this tragedy, there are none, no not one, but what may be looked upon with human interest and viewed as faithful embodiments of the law of humanity.

The weird-sisters are most skilfully used and are really important characters in the tragedy. As a dramatic effort of the poet, they may not inaptly be compared with the Fates, or Furies of the Greek dramatists. They are the deluders of men, pattering "in a double sense" with those who seek their aid, entangling them in oracles of a dual nature. Belief in witches and in witchcraft was prevalent in the age of Shakspere, and during the period which the tragedy seeks to represent, such belief was universal. Shakspere has therefore seized upon this belief and in his exposition thereof is true as he ever is. The weird-sisters do not in themselves represent the laws of fate they are but its "metaphysical aid." Like humanity they are governed and directed by the laws of necessity, a power beyond their will. When Macbeth wrestles with fate and desires to know the worst, they ask him if he would know from their own "mouths" or "from our masters," what shall be his destiny. The weird-three are but an opposite development of the same belief which produced those wonderful fairy creations to be found in his Midsummer Night's Dream.* The government of fairies and their interference with human affairs was but another phase of witches and their masters, both of whom were considered to have their influence in determining the career and character of

* "Shakspere added a new grace to fairy lore, he almost remodelled and re-invented it. The places to which fairies were supposed to be most attached,—the green knoll, the opening in the wood, the crystal fountain; the ornaments and costume they most affected, the playful pranks in which they revelled, their dancing on the sands "with printless foot," their making of "midnight mushrooms," their gathering of dewdrops, and hanging "a pearl in every cowslip's ear," then creeping into acorn cups, then killing of "cankers in the musk rosebuds," their keeping back the "clamorous owl" that nightly wondered at them, their singing their Queen Titania asleep, their stealing the honey-bags from the humble bees, and plucking the wings from painted butterflies, their bringing "jewels from the deep" for the bewildered Bottom, and feeding him with dewberries, their putting a girdle "round about the earth in forty minutes,"—all these, and many other traits of fairy life and customs, we learn from him, and are indebted for the knowledge to the captivating enthusiasm with which he entered into this ideal world, and sported with those favourite children of his fancy."—H. G. BELL. *Biographical Introduction*, p. 26.

humankind. In this instance they possess no human sympathy, are not really in human form, and are old, wild and haggard. Amid the warring of the elements they are first introduced, and under circumstances of a similar character they disappear.

Apart from the development of human character, this tragedy contains some splendid illustrations of the author's power of observation of external nature. The description of the position of Macbeth's castle by Duncan, the confirmation thereof by Banquo, in which the characteristics of the swallow is used to justify the king's approval, could only have been written by one who must closely have observed nature under her many forms, and failed not to tender the results of his observation.

"This castle hath a pleasant seat; the air
Nimbly and sweetly recommends itself
Unto our gentle senses.
　　　　This guest of summer,
The temple-haunting martlet, does approve,
By his lov'd mansionry, that the heaven's breath
Smells wooingly here: no jutty, frieze,
Buttress, nor coign of vantage, but this bird
Hath made his pendant bed, and procreant cradle
Where they most breed and haunt, I have observ'd,
The air is delicate."

The governing power throughout this tragedy, as in that of Hamlet, is fate or circumstance. Everything is subordinate to fate. The weird-sisters are but the instruments of destiny, whose laws the whole of the characters obey. The forming and directing hand of outward and inward circumstance everywhere prevails. The web of life is enwoven, and within its threads the acts, wishes and desires of the whole dramatis personæ are moulded and directed. The governing principles of human nature in this great work are truly displayed, and so clearly are they presented that a more faithful rendering of humanity was never effected.

Under whatever form this tragedy is considered, it is one among the grandest that has ever been produced. The various characters spring into existence and are created by the wonderful knowledge which the poet possessed. From the depths of his own brain he has evolved the characters and by the force of his wondrous imagination made them entirely his own. He has endowed them with a reality, abounding in life and nature. None other but he who produced Hamlet and Lear could have written this truly great work; great in its irresistibleness, and great in its rapidity of action. The grandeur of its poetic diction and picturesqueness coupled with its truly living representations of persons, incidents and places, must for ever place it in the foremost rank of the works of its inimitable producer the "myriad-minded" Shakspere.

# KING JOHN.

—◇◇—

THIS play forms a fitting prologue to Shakspere's great dramatic chronicle, and it is unquestionably based upon an elder play of that name, which had been known to the English stage more than forty years prior to Shakspere's play. The elder work was written by Bale, a furious protestant bishop, whose production holds an intermediate place between the moralities and historical plays. In 1591 another play under this title was produced, but the name of the author is not known. Two other editions of this spurious play were published one in 1611, and one in 1622. Shakspere's play, in which there is no mention of Magna Charta was produced in 1596, and was first printed in the folio of 1623.

This is one of the most interesting of the great series of historic plays, for it is full of variety, force and splendour, and the poetic side of the principal characters, so necessary to dramatic fitness, is most excellently preserved. The darker shades in the character of King John are partially lightened up by Shakspere, for he makes the king to be the representative of the country and the exponent of her policy. The cares and troubles of John are not alone his personal cares and troubles, but they are the cares and troubles of the English nation. In the king we see the nation and his deeds are made to represent the national will. The king is an incarnation of the national interest, and it is as an incarnation of that feeling, that he is always treated with respect, even by his opponents, despite the follies and crimes of which he has been guilty.

The closing scene of John's life is most masterly drawn and it fails not to win our pity for the dying king, whose "heart is cracked and burned," and whose life is "turned to one thread, one little hair," which breaks when he learns from the lips of his cousin, that the power on which he had trusted for the defence of his kingdom, was with his treasures, "in the night," "all unwarily devoured by the unexpected sea."

It is a great advantage to this play, a strong element in its success, that its chief interest should be of a national character. Its appeals are thus of a higher character than when appealing to motives of a personal nature, for they affect the spectator and the reader nationally, animating and developing their patriotic feelings and causing them to watch its course with much concern and interest, for the fortunes of their country are involved, either for evil or for good, in the fortunes of the king, who thus becomes the representative of the national policy.

Constance is most truthfully pourtrayed, for she is full of maternal love, and it is the strength of this feeling goaded by ambition, which produces so large an amount of activity in her nature. She is violently passionate when she cannot accomplish that which she desires, and she rails loudly and curses deeply when thwarted in her wishes. This is a weak point in her character, leading to disastrous results to herself and to the cause of her "oppressed boy," yet this weakness is truly womanly. Her upbraidings of Austria are of the bitterest kind, so much so, that she loses friends, dispirits her son and defeats her own purpose. She presents a most forcible contrast in her changes of mood, which are of a varied character, from the extreme height of passion and bitterness to the tenderest depths of maternal love. She is imperious, the result of her grief, for "grief is proud," and " to the state of " her " great grief "

"Let kings assemble, for my grief's so great,
That no supporter but the huge firm earth
Can hold it up here I and sorrows sit;
Here is my throne, bid kings come bow to it."

She fully believes in the right of her son Arthur to the throne of England, and she is also fully convinced that he does "deserve a crown," for did not "nature and fortune," at his birth join to make him great. Her fears for his success engender doubts of the honesty of John and Philip, for hath "not France forsworn," and is not "fortune corrupted, changed and won" by hourly adulterating with his " uncle John." Her pride and her maternal love may be said to be the basis of her character, in which the power of imagination holds no mean sway. Whatever may be the nature of her passion, whether soft and subdued, or moved to vehemence of the strongest kind, the development of her imaginative power, charged as it is with rich poetic colouring, sheds a true feminine grace over her whole character, completely winning our sympathies and enlisting our opinions in favour of her claims.

When all chances of Arthur's success are entirely overthrown and there is no probability of her wishes and desires being accomplished, for circumstances run contrary to her purpose, the full strength of Constance's maternal love is evidenced in the tenderness of her address to the cardinal legate, when her son is taken prisoner and held in custody by his uncle John. She says,

> "Father cardinal, I have heard you say,
> That we shall see and know our friends in heaven.
> If that be true, I shall see my boy again;
> For since the birth of Cain, the first male child,
> To him that did but yesterday suspire,
> There was not such a gracious creature born.
> But now will canker sorrow eat my bud,
> And chase the native beauty from his cheek,
> And he will look as hollow as a ghost,
> As dim and meagre as an ague's fit;
> And so he'll die; and, rising so again,
> When I shall meet him in the court of heaven
> I shall not know him: therefore never, never
> Must I behold my pretty Arthur more.
> *Pand.* You hold too heinous a respect of grief.
> *Cons.* He talks to me that never had a son.
> *K. Phil.* You are as fond of grief as of your child.
> *Cons.* Grief fills the room up of my absent child,
> Lies in his bed, walks up and down with me,
> Puts on his pretty looks, repeats his words,
> Remembers me of all his gracious parts,
> Stuffs out his vacant garments with his form:
> Then have I reason to be fond of grief.
> Fare you well; had you such loss as I,
> I could give better comfort than you do."

The nature of the young prince Arthur, is evidently unfitted for the rudeness and force which marks this period of our history. He is boyish and innocent, quiet in his expressions, gentle in his manners, and he feels that he is not worth "the turmoil" that will be made on his account. He is full of pathos and he weeps at the thought of the sorrow and suffering that must be undergone by others, of the blood that must be shed, should "the blast of war" be blown in his behoof. He would rather be laid in his grave than these things should occur, and he would fain "be content" were he "out of prison" to "keep sheep," for he would then "be merry as the day is long." He is full of affection and simplicity and in the scene with Hubert, when pleading for his eyes, his speeches are full of true pathos and are marked by great dramatic power.

The character of Hubert in his relation to the king is most consistently drawn, for he is a complete courtier, desirous of obeying his sovereign's behests, and he thereby becomes a ready instrument in carrying out the king's will. He is loyal to the king, because in doing so, he is loyal to the state. He is loyal in obedience to his feudal oath and from habitual service, till it hath become with him a necessity. Owing to this latter reason, he, does not like Salisbury and some others of the barons' revolt against the king, and it also prevents him from committing a breach against his country, and preserves his nationality. He is fully cognizant of the craft and subtlety of John, being thoroughly versed in the sinuous policy of his master, and he readily understands the insinuations and murderous intent of the king towards young Arthur, Constance's "fair son." He is won to the purpose by his duty, by the admission of John "we do owe thee much," by the king's strong wishes for his welfare, coupled with the advantages promised wherewith the "king's means to pay" his love. The "good respect" and the love that is expressed for him, causes him to give that pledge, that whatever the king may bid him "undertake," though "death were adjunct to the act," "by heaven," he "would do it." The violence of the times, for it was a barbarous age, have given to Hubert that external roughness and harshness, which he himself thinks prevails within, in this he is however mistaken, for the better part of his nature is not altogether dead, there is a leaven of humanity left, and though he resolves to commit the murder, when he attempts its committal, he is deterred therefrom by the pleadings of the young prince. His latent power of goodness is awakened, he is not proof to the earnest appeals of the fair boy, his resolution is broken down, and though he knows he must undergo "much danger" for not perpetrating the deed he "will not do it for all the treasure that thine uncle owns." This is probably one of the greatest dramatic scenes ever penned by Shakspere, for the two extremes of pity and terror are most wonderfully pourtrayed. It must be ranked among the finest productions of the "Swan of Avon," stamping him as a master that completely understood the nature of humanity and the development thereof.

The character of cardinal Pandulph is not only essentially true in its relation to humanity, but it is also true to history. The Annals of the monastery of Burton, recently published, show how thoroughly correct Shakspere is in his delineation of this papal prelate. Haughty and arrogant, the result of his vanity and the office which he held, Shakspere fails not to pourtray these features of his character, and he justly puts in his mouth, language by which the desires of the dictatorial priest are fully developed; language which cannot fail to awaken in a discerning and patriotic audience, an intense disgust and hatred of papal pride and papal intolerance.

Faulconbridge is a rough, good-humoured and thoroughly honest man, by nature noble. He is proud of his martial courage, and still more proud of his descent from the lion-hearted Richard, whose characteristics he in a great degree possesses. He is a complete representative of our national character, for he is compounded of cheerfulness, a lively wit, common sense and an intense love of his native land. He is eager and bold, filled with a love of glory and the achievement of gallant deeds by the force of arms. His natural powers soon fit him for his new position, and he readily assumes the seriousness and the dignities of his occupation. Nothing can win him from the cause he espouses; he is a complete thorough-going partisan, and his great courage and daring render him invaluable as a servant to the weak, irresolute John.

Salisbury is a purely natural man, strong in love, a true friend, an excellent neighbour, but no politician. Lacking politics, Salisbury does not attract much attention until the close of the history. He is a man of feeling, not of reasoning powers, and by his feelings he is mostly actuated and directed. When leagued with France against his native land, and having good grounds for such alliance, his feelings will crop up, and he cannot withhold his lamentations which are strongly embued with patriotic feeling. He says,

"Such is the infection of the time,
That, for the health and physic of our right,
We cannot deal but with the very hand
Of stern injustice and confused wrong.
And is't not pity, O my grieved friends,
That we, the sons and children of this isle,
Were born to see so sad an hour as this."—*A*. v. s. 2.

Salisbury is somewhat surprised at the prospects of

his sovereign, his inattention to politics prevented him from forming anything approaching a correct idea of the king's strength, for he says,

"I did not think the king so stored with friends."

When he is made aware of the intended treachery of France, in the words of the dying Melun, his private wrongs become entirely subservient to the love of his native land. He fails not to take warning, reverting back to his former allegiance, and the honour and safety of England is affirmed.

Both Philip of France and he of Austria, are true representatives of their class. They are selfish and calculating, caring not whether their actions are right or wrong, so long as they will be benefitted by the course of action which they resolve on. In the nature of their kingliness they take oaths, make promises and then as readily break them. They think only of themselves, and their immediate class. They do not seek to advance the interest of the whole, but only their own self-interest, which they consider to be the state. Within the circle of their crowns is concentrated every thing that has a tendency for the promotion of their own advancement, at the same time they are quite oblivious to the advantage of the people. They are firm believers in the divinity that doth hedge a king, though their frequent oath-breakings and acts of rapacity completely demonstrate the fallacy of their belief.

The grouping of the characters is most exquisitely managed, the picture is in every way complete. No other hand but Shakspere's could have drawn it, and no other brain but his could have pourtrayed with such dramatic power the varied characters of this history, which teaches us a most important lesson, a lesson that should be remembered by all those who are desirous of promoting the welfare of a nation, that no hostile sword, no appeal to a foreign power can ever heal the domestic wounds of a state. The cure must come from within, it lies not in outward intervention. What Faulconbridge exultingly says of his native land, admits of general application:

"This England never did, nor never shall,
Lie at the proud foot of a conqueror,
But when it first did help to wound itself.
Now these, her princes, are come home again,
Come the three corners of the world in arms,
And we shall shock them: nought shall make us rue,
If England to itself do rest but true."

# RICHARD II.

THE precise date of the appearance of this tragedy cannot be determined. Whether it was written three or four years prior to its publication, or whether it was published immediately after its production upon the stage, are questions which now cannot be definitely settled. The first edition was printed by Valentine Simmes, and published by Andrew Wise, under the title of the "Tragedie of King Richard the Second," in the year 1597, and this edition is looked upon as the most accurate of all the quartos by some of the editors of Shakspere. Richard II. is one among the number of plays mentioned in the list of Francis Meres, published in 1598, in which year a second edition, also printed by Simmes, was published by Andrew Wise.

In 1608 a third edition of the tragedy was published. This edition was considerably enlarged, the Parliament scene and the deposing of King Richard receiving great additions. In fact, "all that part of the fourth act in which Richard is introduced to make surrender of his crown, comprising 154 lines, was never printed in the age of Elizabeth." This edition was printed by W. W. for Matthew Law, and bears the following title: "The

Tragedie of King Richard the Second, with new additions of the Parliament Sceane, and the deposing of King Richard. As it hath been lately acted by the King's Servants at the Globe, by William Shakspere." In 1615 a fourth edition in 4to. was published, and the tragedy is also contained in the folio of 1623, in which edition it was for the first time divided into acts and scenes. In 1634 it was again published in 4to. In 1691 it was altered, under the title of "The Sicilian Usurper." In 1720 it was again altered by Lewis Theobald, and again in 1722 by James Goodhall.

Another play bearing the same title was in the possession of the company acting at the Globe Theatre, and it has been thought that this was also a production of Shakspere's. This play, however, differs so materially in its construction, that it is not in any way probable that one man would have written both. It commences at an earlier time than the play of Shakspere's, the incidents are altogether different, and there is a greater amount of savageness and barbarity than can be found in Shakspere's Richard II.

The chronicles of Hall and Fabian served as the text-book for the chronicle of Holingshed, from whose pages Shakspere derived this play, for the incidents follow very close on the rendering of Holingshed, though in spirit, language and characterization, the play is wholly Shakspere's. He has endowed the musty records of the old chronicler with a vitality that will never die; and he has also developed in this poetic play a knowledge and a love of humanity which is ever a prominent characteristic of the poet. There is one particular feature with which this history abounds, and which fails not to win our sympathies. It is pregnant with true pathos, and under every circumstance, whether of situation or moral development of character, it is most loftily sustained. That Richard II. is an early work of the great master is evidenced by the everrecurring rhymes, a style and mannerism which Shakspere wholly abandoned in his later works.

Richard II. is not really the first of Shakspere's historical plays, for King John precedes Richard in an historical point of view upwards of a century; but it is the first of those eight splendid chapters of Shakspere's dramatic chronicle, which carries us from the cause, through all the incidents, to the close of our great Civil Wars,—the war of the Red and White Roses, which, from the reign of Henry VI. to the death of Richard III, and the union of the great houses of York and Lancaster under the sovereignty of Henry VII., devastated our land, cut up our nobility, and to a great extent gave to our countrymen that fierce hardihood and martial bearing, at that time the terror of foreigners, and at the present day is still one of the leading characteristics of our sturdy sons. In the perusal of the chronicle of the dramatist we are enabled better to understand the period which he seeks to represent than we are in any of the so-called histories. It is not a dry detail of the wars in which our country has been engaged, the famines we have undergone, the pestilences with which we have been afflicted; but it shows in what manner the sovereign reigned, and how the power of the parliaments, which had their origin in the reign of an Edward, were gradually gathering their strength in the weaknesses and follies which Richard displayed. In it is also shown the marked progress of mankind, and if in a future period, a dramatic poet were to attempt an historical play of our own times, he would have to pourtray the Parliament, not the Queen and her court, because under existing circumstances the Parliament alone represents the people, and is the criterion of our period.

In the paths of history alone can be found the rule whereby men are to be guided and nations governed. If we view the historic field in its proper light, we shall find it to be the lofty height from which can be viewed the follies, vices, fashions, forms, customs, and manners of society. History stands in the same relation to life, as the loftiest peak is to the searcher after the picturesque, who, were he to keep to the ravine, the gorge, or the plain, would loose one-half in his search. Let him, however, place himself upon a lofty peak, and vale and valley, hillock and hill, mount and mountain, are there before him, his eye drinking in the wondrous sight and discharging its copious draughts upon the brain. Just so does history. By its magic wand the past starts into existence; we learn of other men and other times; we are taught there have been men before us, imbued with the same feelings, moved by the same passions, and governed by motives of a similar character as ourselves, though existing and developed under entirely different circumstances. Thus we are led to this point, when contemplating ourselves, that, as we look upon the past, so will future generations look upon our acts on the world's wide stage in a similar manner.

In the chronicle of Shakspere everything is endowed with a human aspect, and it is this humanity that gives the poet such marked pre-eminence over the mere historian of fact. It is the spectrum by which he unfolds to our gaze the wisdom, follies, and vices of our progenitors; plucking aside with nerveless hand the veil of antiquity, and showing that, like us, they were but children of Nature—beings obeying and fulfilling to the best of their ability, considering the peculiar circumstances in which they were placed, the law of humanity. Impressed with these views, pervaded with these ideas, one cannot fail of perceiving how infinitely superior is the poet's chronicle to the relation of the mere historian. To the philosophy of history doth the poet rise, and gives strength and wisdom for our guidance in the future. With this view the eight plays become but chapters of one great work, to which we may not inaptly apply *King John* as the prologue, and *Henry VIII.*, that play of pomp and magnificence, as the epilogue. A worthy close to so worthy a commencement, in which the continuation is equally as good.

The tragedy of *Richard II.* is not by any means so well known as that of *Richard III.* It has not been so much presented on the stage, nor is it so melo-dramatic in its construction as to win the popular taste like that of the crooked-back tyrant.* Until its revival by Charles Kean, some eleven years ago, it was almost unknown to the playgoers of the present generation. In this tragedy there are no imaginary characters, like that of the Bastard in *King John;* they are all purely historical, their names and the incidents of the play

---

* *Richard III.* as written by Shakspere, is almost unknown to the British stage, Mr. S. Phelps being the only manager who has restored Shakspere's own play during the present century. Colley Cibber's hash is the one constantly played, and is very popular with star-actors, who care less for the poet's lines than they do for making points. The difference between Cibber's version and Shakspere's is very great; Cibber's being a mass of incongruities, whole scenes being borrowed from other plays, and many of Shakspere's characters omitted.

being found in the pages of the historian. The interest of the tragedy hinges upon the character of the King, for in his character is found the history. In thus presenting character, the essentials of dramatic poetry are preserved, and the poet at the same time relates the history of the period. The tragedy opens with the quarrel between Bolingbroke and the Duke of Norfolk, which occurred in 1397, in the twentieth year of the reign of Richard. With consummate skill, is drawn the character of that class, who thought and acted upon the principle that the sword was the proper weapon to rule mankind. In this scene we see at once the distracted state to which the affairs of the nation had been brought by a fierce, turbulent nobility, and the discord which existed between the members of the royal family is fully exemplified. The King, seated upon his throne, waiting for the appearance of the "accuser and the accused," thus describes them,

"High stomach'd are they both, and full of ire,
In rage deaf as the sea, hasty as fire."

Upon the entrance of the diverse parties, the class to which they belong, and upon whom, for a long period of our history rested the government of our land, is beautifully pourtrayed. We have their humbleness to the symbol of royalty, painted by their tongues, while their fierce bickering, the result of their martial pride and power, is admirably shown forth. It is not in the language of clowns and jesters that they accuse and retort, but in language characteristic of their high position in the then state of society. Vauntings of their own worth and the abnegation of all other classes is the prevailing feature. They bandy terms like practised tilters in the world of tongue, fighting skillfully with words, and at the same time are equally ready to fight with sword, lance and shield for the truth of what they so loudly and fiercely affirm. Bolingbroke "fiery in haste and hot with speed," calls Norfolk,

> "a traitor and a miscreant;
> Too good to be so, and too bad to live;
> Since the more fair and crystal is the sky,
> The uglier seems the clouds that in it fly.
> Once more, the more to aggravate the note,
> With a foul traitor's name stuff I thy throat;
> And wish, so please my sovereign, ere I move
> What my tongue speaks, my right drawn sword may prove."

To which Norfolk in rage made hot, retorts,

> "Let not my cold words here accuse my zeal:
> 'Tis not the trial of a woman's war,
> The bitter clamour of two eager tongues,
> Can arbitrate this cause betwixt us twain;
> The blood is hot that must be cool'd for this.
> Yet can I not of such tame patience boast,
> As to be hush'd and nought at all to say:
> First, the fair reverence of your highness curbs me
> From giving rein and spurs to my free speech;
> Which else would post, until it had return'd
> These terms of treason doubled down his throat.
> Setting aside his high blood's royalty,
> And let him be no kinsman to my liege,
> I do defy him, and I spit at him;
> Call him a slanderous coward, and a villain:
> Which to maintain, I would allow him odds,
> I meet him, were I tied to run a foot
> Even to the frozen ridges of the Alps,
> Or any other ground inhabitable,
> Wherever Englishman durst set his foot.
> Meantime, let this defend my loyalty—
> By all my hopes, most falsely doth he lie."

The war of words continues, until so harsh and discordant become the two peers, that the king, perceiving no other way to remove the hate which rankles in their breasts, decides, that

> "At Coventry, upon Saint Lambert's day:
> There shall your swords and lances arbitrate
> The swelling difference of your settled hate:
> Since we cannot atone you, you shall see
> Justice design the victor's chivalry.
> Lord marshal, command our officers at arms
> Be ready to direct these home alarms."—*A.* i. s. 1.

The hatred borne between Bolingbroke and Norfolk, is truly typical of this fierce period, and is, in itself, a forerunner of those calamitous wars of the red and white roses, which commenced in the reign of Henry VI. and were only brought to a close by the victory of Richmond at the battle of Bosworth Field, in whom the red and white roses were ultimately united. Hatred of each other was not confined to the males of this period. Among the gentler sex it existed with an intensity nearly equal to that which was found among the men, though the results of its action were less deadly. Shakspere, true historian as he is, has not lost sight of this fact. That it was forcibly impressed upon his brain, we have evidence in this play, when he makes the Duchess of Gloster revile her husband's brother, "time-honoured Gaunt," in her wish,

> "O sit my husband's wrongs on Hereford's spear,
> That it may enter butcher Mowbray's breast!
> Or, if misfortune miss the first career,
> Be Mowbray's sins so heavy in his bosom,
> That they may break his foaming courser's back,
> And throw the rider headlong in the lists
> A caitiff recreant to my cousin Hereford."—*A.* i. s. 2.

Richard, by historians has always been represented as weak, credulous, cunning, criminal, irresolute and rapacious. A counterpart of the irresolute John in his mode of action, at one time heaping insult on the heads of his nobles, and at another time, completely subject to their wishes and desires. By turns fawning and yielding, then harsh and tyrannous, winning neither their love nor their admiration, governing only to be feared or despised. Faithfully are all these failing represented by Shakspere's play, and yet despite these failings, he teaches us to pity, and wins from us our sympathies for the fortunes of the fallen monarch. These very infirmities cause him to creep into our affections; they are allied with the beautiful parts of Richard's character, and they show how slight the partition between the highest and lowest parts of our nature. These failings are common to humanity, they belong to all members of the human family and their universality excites our sympathies, and moves us to pity and forgive the weakness of Richard.

The passionate weakness of Richard is frequently evinced. It is distinguished by displays of puerile conceits and childish expressions. In *A*. III. s. 3, the king says,

"We'll make foul weather with despised tears;
Our sighs, and they shall lodge the summer corn,
And make a dearth in this revolting land."

Then he proceeds to talk of "shedding tears" to fret a "pair of graves," until finding his remarks are but wantonly received, he exclaims,

"Well, well, I see,
I talk but idly, and you mock at me."

This weakness is still more forcibly developed in the same act, when he learns of the landing of the crafty Bolingbroke. Instead of marching straight to meet his foe with a warrior's stride, and seeking to effect his overthrow by the action of the sword, he evokes the

earth not to feed his enemy,
> "Nor with thy sweets comfort his ravenous sense:
> But let thy spiders, that suck up thy venom,
> And heavy-gaited toads, lie in their way,
> Doing annoyance to the treacherous feet
> Which with usurping steps do trample thee.
> Yield stinging nettles to mine enemies,
> And when they from thy bosom pluck a flower
> Guard it, I pray thee, with a lurking adder,
> Whose double tongue may with a mortal's touch
> Throw death upon thy sovereign's enemies."—s. 2.

Other examples of the king's weakness of character can easily be found. One most forcible is afforded in the scene, when the poor groom, the only one faithful out of the king's mass of retainers, speaks of his "yearning heart," on seeing Bolingbroke bestride Richard's favourite roan. The king touched by the grief of the groom, and his own sorrows, rails upon the horse and then upon his position, saying
> "I was not made a horse;
> And yet I bear a burthen like an ass,
> Spurr'd, gall'd and tired by jauncing Bolingbroke."
> A. v. s. 5.

The answer of Richard to Scroop on hearing of his favourites, Bushy, Wiltshire, and Green, having made peace with Bolingbroke, is another proof of his weak and passionate nature. The peace which they have made is that of the grave, for they have been executed by the orders of Bolingbroke, and the king sees not through the reply of Scroop, when he says,
> "Peace have they made with him indeed, my lord!"

He still thinks them alive, and he bursts out into invectives against his faithful friends—who for their faithfulness to his fortunes, have passed into the valley of death. He calls them

"Villains, vipers, damn'd without redemption!
Dogs, easily won to fawn on any man!
Snakes, in my heart-blood warm'd, that sting my heart!
Three Judases, each one thrice worse than Judas!
Would they make peace? terrible hell make war
Upon their spotted souls for this offence."—*A.* III. s. 2.

When Richard learns of the defection of his uncle York, another phase of the weak parts of his character is most admirably developed. The violent invectives in which he indulged against his three favourites, give way to the apathy of despair. His intellect becomes completely prostrate, all desire of action is lost, and he wails the general popularity of his rival and his own unpopularity.

"What comfort have we now?
By heaven, I'll hate him everlastingly
That bids me be of comfort any more.
Go to Flint castle: there I'll pine away;
A king, woe's slave, shall kingly woe obey.
That power I have, discharge, and let them go
To ear the land that hath some hope to grow,
For I have none:—Let no man speak again
To alter this, for counsel is but vain.
*Aum.* My liege, one word,
*King R.* He does me double wrong
That wounds me with the flatteries of his tongue.
Discharge my followers, let them hence.—Away,
From Richard's night to Bolingbroke's fair day."

The contrast between Richard and the cool, astute, calculating, and selfish Bolingbroke, is forcibly marked. At every point we see the advantages which the matured intellect of Bolingbroke possesses over the weakness of the king; a weakness which is yet further confirmed by the exclamation of Richard when looking in the glass:

"hath sorrow struck
So many blows upon this face of mine,
And made no deeper wounds? O flattering glass,

> Like to my followers in prosperity,
> Thou dost beguile me! Was this face, the face
> That every day under his household roof
> Did keep ten thousand men? was this the face
> That, like the sun, did make beholders wink?
> Was this the face that fac'd so many follies,
> And was at last out-fac'd by Bolingbroke?"—*A.* IV. s. 1.

The next speech of the deposed Richard is also fraught with this feeling. The shadow of his sorrow overwhelms him, and forces upon him bitter memories and bitter thoughts, awakening reflections which redound not to his advantage, and which compel him to admit the correctness of his rival and his conqueror's remark,

> "The shadow of your sorrow hath destroy'd
> The shadow of your face."

Richard is struck with his rival's words; they are in unison with his own thoughts. He would hear them once more, for he says,

> "Say that again.
> The shadow of my sorrow? ha! let's see:—
> 'Tis very true, my grief lies all within;
> And these external manners of laments
> Are merely shadows to the unseen grief
> That swells with silence in the tortur'd soul;
> There lies the substance: and I thank thee, king,
> For thy great bounty, that not only giv'st
> Me cause to wail, but teachest me the way
> How to lament the cause."

The thought of what he was, of what he is, and his knowledge of the causes which have brought about his present position, are too much for him to withstand. He dreads that his foe should know his weakness, this connected with his anxiety to be free from the presence of Bolingbroke, moves him to "beg one boon," and then he will away to trouble his haughty cousin "no more."

The moral cowardice of Richard is most beautifully displayed by Shakspere. Like his father, the Black Prince, he lacks not the physical courage to fight, in that respect, he is no coward. On the other hand, in the moral world, his fears are always uppermost, by those he is governed, lacking the coherence of thought requisite for self-government. This lack of moral power is not lost sight of by the dramatist, in it he is true to history. In his coinciding with the historian, he however goes beyond him, for he more ably developes this want in the kingly character. In the scene of the banishment of the two peers, Richard moved by his fears and anxious for his own safety, would embitter—not subdue the quarrel. He would have them continue " the tempest of their home-bred hate." He would not they should

" Embrace each other's love in banishment,"

and in order that he may be the more secure in his royal seat, he would bind them by their vows, and ere they leave the kingly presence, they must pledge their knightly words. He says,

" Lay on our royal sword your banish'd hands;
Swear by the duty that you owe to God,—
Our part therein we banish with yourselves,
To keep the oath that we administer :—
You never shall, so help you truth and God!—
Embrace each other's love in banishment;
Nor never look upon each other's face;
Nor never write, regreet, nor reconcile
This louring tempest of your home-bred hate;
Nor never by advised purpose meet
To plot, contrive, or complot any ill
'Gainst us, our state, our subjects, or our land."

A. I. s. 3.

That Richard was violent in temper, meets with the concurrence of all writers, nor has Shakspere departed from the historic relation in this respect. This failing in the kingly character is pourtrayed by York, when standing by the death-bed of "time-honour'd Gaunt," in the line

"For young hot colts, being rag'd, do rage the more."
*A*. III. s. 1.

This feeling is still more forcibly displayed by Richard himself, who is carried away by the violence of his temper, a violence aroused and brought into action by the reproaches of the dying Gaunt. So strong is the passion of the royal Richard, that he forgets the respect due to age, and to the near relationship which existed between him and Gaunt. The king is completely carried away by the turbulence of his passions, and he calls his relative and adviser,

"a lunatic, lean-witted fool,
Presuming on an ague's privilege,
Darest with thy frozen admonition
Make pale our cheek, chasing the royal blood
With fury from his native residence.
Now, by my seat's right royal majesty,
Were thou not brother to great Edward's son,
This tongue that runs so roundly in thy head,
Should run thy head from thy unreverent shoulders."
*A*. II. s. 1.

Richard in his state was extremely costly and extravagant. His means were lavished upon favourites and upon frivolities, which greatly served to alienate from him the people's love. To meet the demands of his courtiers, the king was compelled to levy fresh imposts upon the people, and even these imposts were found to be insufficient for his purpose, though the greater part of his reign was passed in peace. On the breaking out of the Irish war, which occurred about the time of Gaunt's death, the king forcibly seized upon the estates and coffers of his uncle. This act, the result of his violent temper, was in direct opposition to the wishes of his uncle York, whose sense of duty to the crown made him overlook the wrong done to his brother's house. This act was the " crowning mercy," for not the slightest doubt can exist, that it was mainly instrumental in bringing about the downfall of Richard. This taken in conjunction with his treatment of the commons, whom he

" pill'd with grievous taxes,"

and the "new exactions," which daily were devised, awakened the heads of that party, which ultimately became famous throughout our history as the Lancastrian, inciting them to action, and combining all classes in the movement against the tyranny of the king. The fear of this is shown in the speech of York, who strongly advises the king to forego his seizure of the estates of Gaunt. York pathetically appeals to his royal nephew, and thus beautifully observes:—

"You pluck a thousand dangers on your head,
You lose a thousand well-disposed hearts,
And prick my tender patience to those thoughts
Which honour and allegiance cannot think."

To this Richard replies,

"Think what you will; we seize into our hands
His plate, his goods, his money, and his lands."

York, annoyed at his nephew's harshness and obstinacy, yet still more annoyed at the consequences which he foresees will follow such a course of conduct, consequences of the direst nature to the weak monarch, retires from the kingly presence, but not without continuing the same idea, and seeking to advise the king to adopt another and a wiser course. He says,

"I'll not be by the while: my liege, farewell:
What will ensue hereof, there's none can tell;
But by bad courses may be understood
That their events can never fall out good."—*A.*, II. s. 1.

That Richard was criminal in his conduct most historians agree. If not the actual perpetrator of murder, he was the undoubted cause of the murder of his uncle Gloster. Yet what other course of action was open to the king, it is difficult to decide. Gloster was a bold, bad, overbearing and turbulent man, who had consented to the deposing of the king, whose safety in a great measure depended upon the capture of Gloster, who was seized, taken to Calais and there strangled. This instance of Richard's criminality, and which even Froissart, the king's chief defender is compelled to admit, is still further confirmed and endorsed by the old chroniclers Hall and Holingshed. Shakspere has not departed from the historic view, for in two allusions to Gloster's death, he fixes the guilt upon Richard. The first occurs when Gloster's widow meets John of Gaunt, and strives to excite him to revenge his brother and her husband's death. Gaunt answers her, by speaking of the king as

"heaven's substitute,
His deputy anointed in his sight,
Hath caused his death."—*A.* I. s. 2.

The second reference to Gloster's death occurs after a violent speech of the king, when threatening Gaunt that he will take his life, to which the aged noble answers

"My brother Gloster, plain well meaning soul,
Whom fair befal in heaven 'mongst happy souls!
May be a precedent and witness good,
That thou respect'st not spilling Edward's blood."
*A.* ii. s. 1.

There cannot be any doubt that the character of Richard as drawn by Shakspere is literally a true one. The weaknesses, the frivolities, the storm of passion, the rapacities, and favoritism which distinguish his reign, are all to be found in the tragedy of the poet as well as in the pages of the historian. It is not only in the mere meagre field of facts and incidents that we discover the truthfulness of the pourtrayal of Shakspere's Richard. In the higher attributes of history, the poet is the truest historian, for he presents the most correct analysis of the king's character, displaying to a great extent the motives by which Richard was actuated and governed, and in the largeness of his comprehension completely developing the working of the human heart. It is this, which, despite the deformities of Richard's character, causes us to feel pity for his misfortunes. His very infirmities are of that nature that they take hold of our affections. "His heart is by no means hardened against himself, but bleeds afresh at every new stroke of chance; and his sensibility, absorbed in his own person, and unused to misfortune, is not only tenderly alive to its own sufferings, but without the fortitude to bear them. He is, however, human in his distresses; for to feel pain and sorrow, weakness, disappointment, remorse and anguish, is the lot of humanity, and we sympathize with him accordingly. The sufferings of the man make us forget that he ever was a king."*

* Hazlitt's *Characters of Shakspere's Plays*, pp. 79, 80.

Richard is not deficient in perception; it was not from a lack of mental qualifications that he fell, but rather from the non-activity of his mental powers. It was the want of energy, of continuity of action, and the lack of perseverance that lost him his throne. Had he have displayed the same amount of promptitude in the revolt of Bolingbroke, as he did in the revolt of Wat Tyler, history would in all probability have told a different tale. He would have been "skilful enough to have lived" and "the foul and ugly mists," with which he was enshrouded by the wiles of his cousin would have been dispelled. Shakspere shows this failing, the chief weakness in the king's character, by the comparison he institutes in the third act of the play. It occurs in a conversation between the gardeners of the king, the under one asking his chief,

" Why should we, in the compass of a pale,
Keep law, and form, and due proportion,
Showing, as in a model, our firm state,
When our sea-walled garden, the whole land,
Is full of weeds; her fairest flowers choked up,
Her fruit trees all unprun'd, her hedges ruin'd,
Her knots disorder'd, and her wholesome herbs
Swarming with caterpillars?
1st. Gard.                    Hold thy peace:—
He that hath suffered this disordered spring
Hath now himself met with the fall of leaf;
The weeds, that his broad-spreading leaves did shelter,
That seem'd in eating him to hold him up,
Are pluck'd up, root and all, by Bolingbroke;
I mean the earl of Wiltshire, Busby, Green.
Serv. What, are they dead?
Gard.                        They are;
And Bolingbroke hath seiz'd the wasteful king.—
Oh! what pity is it,
That he had not so trimm'd and dress'd the land,
As we this garden! We at time of year

> Do wound the bark, the skin of our fruit-trees,
> Lest, being over-proud with sap and blood,
> With too much riches it confound itself;
> Had he done so to great and growing men,
> They might have liv'd to bear and he to taste
> Their fruits of duty. Superfluous branches
> We lop away, that bearing boughs may live:
> Had he done so, himself had borne the crown
> Which waste of idle hours hath quite thrown down."
> s. 4.

Richard was possessed of good intellectual powers, his perceptive faculties being above the average. He lacked not the faculty of discrimination, and at times he evinced great promptitude in action, seizing the right moment, and displaying talent of no mean order. Shakspere loses not sight of this side of Richard's character, for, with a truthfulness which is all his own, and which he never fails to display, he hath put in the mouth of the king, language which implies a deeper knowledge of himself, of those by whom he was surrounded, and a keener perception of the motives for their course of action, than has been usually assigned to the weak, vacillating monarch. In the speech of the King to Aumerle, we perceive how thoroughly he understands the character of Bolingbroke, whose conduct awakens his perceptive powers. He says:

> "Ourself and Bushy, Bagot here, and Green,
> Observ'd his courtship to the common people:—
> How he did seem to dive into their hearts,
> With humble and familiar courtesy:
> What reverence he did throw away on slaves,
> Wooing poor craftsmen with the craft of smiles,
> And patient overbearing of his fortune,
> As 'twere to banish their affects with him.
> Off goes his bonnet to an oyster wench;
> A brace of draymen bid God speed him well,
> And had the tribute of his supple knee,

With "thanks, my countrymen, my loving friends;"
As were our England *in reversion* his,
And he our subjects' next degree in hope."
*A.* i. s. 4.

Of the perceptive powers of the King there is another forcible example to be found in his reply to York, who implores Richard not to heed the words of Gaunt, telling the King that

"He loves you, on my life, and holds you dear,
As Harry, duke of Hereford, were he here."

To which Richard answers,

"Right, you say true : as Hereford's love, so his;
As theirs, so mine; and all be as it is."—*A.* ii. s. 1.

The knowledge which Richard possesses of the character of Bolingbroke leads him to perceive the ambitious yearnings, despite the outward humbleness which Bolingbroke at times assumes. This knowledge, coupled with the knowledge of his own weakness to repel the proud lord, produces sorrow and grief at heart and causes the deposed monarch to speak like a frantic man. In reality no longer a king, he despises the bended knee and suppliant form of the wily Bolingbroke, and tells him,

"Fair cousin, you debase your princely knee,
To make the base earth proud with kissing it:
Me rather had my heart might feel your love,
Than my unpleas'd eye see your courtesy.
Up, cousin, up; *your heart is up*, I know,
Thus high at least [*touching his head*] although your
  knee be low." *A.* iii. s. 3.

Richard in his adversity displays great powers of perception; powers which have been quickened into activity by the varied and strange circumstances in which he has been placed. The better part of his nature is developed by his misfortunes. He is chastened by his sorrows and rendered more human, thus winning our sympathies and gaining our pity and our admiration. His removal from the kingly dignity destroys the overweening vanity which marked his earlier career, and it teaches him to look within, and there find the causes which have produced his fall. He is stung to the quick when Northumberland seeks to thrust on him the paper for his signature, telling the deposed monarch the Commons will not be satisfied till it be done, and Richard answers,

"They shall be satisfied : I'll read enough,
When I do see the very book indeed
Where all my sins are writ, and that's myself."
*A.* iv. s. 1.

The death of the king is admirably managed, and is in perfect keeping with his character. The fierce valour which blazes up at the words of the keeper, the snatching of the sword and the slaying of the attendants, are deeds all in unison with this man of impulse, this creature of storm and calm. The closing words of Richard are truly in accordance with his character, they are in keeping with one who could speak of angels fighting on his behalf, and then relying upon his own efforts. Of one, who at one moment was sunk in a state of the lowest despondency, and then could joyfully depart from this life with the assurance and faith contained in his exclamation,

"Mount, mount my soul! thy seat is up on high,
Whilst my gross flesh sinks downward, here to die."
*A.* v. s. 5.

Shakspere has briefly, yet most excellently pointed out the manners of Richard's court :—the base flatterers by whom he was surrounded, the extravagance displayed in the number of his retainers, which in the king's household alone, formed no mean army. From the royal mouth we have the number, for the king describes himself as one who,

> "every day under his household roof
> Did keep ten thousand men."

The inordinate desire of display in dress, the foppishness which characterised the external appearance of the handsome king, and the other follies which crept into his court, and which had chiefly been imported from the land of song and sunny skies, fair Italy, these things are most forcibly shown; a few lines of the master's work conveying most truthfully the state and manners of the court of Richard. The example is found in the speech of York when addressing Gaunt,

> "then, there are found
> Lascivious metres, to whose venom sound
> The open ear of youth doth always listen;
> Report of fashions in proud Italy,
> Whose manners still our tardy apish nation
> Limps after in base imitation.
> Where doth the world thrust for a vanity,
> So it be new, there's no respect how vile—
> That is not quickly buzz'd into his ears."—*A.* II. s. 1.

The rude habits and the unchecked indulgence in vicious pleasures, some of the characteristics of the period are not forgotten by Shakspere. He shows that all classes, from the highest to the lowest, were affected by the coarse manners of the time. In Bolingbroke's enquiry for his son, the future sovereign of the realm, gallant Harry of Monmouth, the victor of Azincour, we have the vices of the age faithfully depicted. For three months he has not seen the young prince, and Bolingbroke tells his attendants when directing them to go in search of prince Harry, to

> "Inquire at London, 'mongst the taverns there,
> For there, they say, he daily doth frequent,
> With unrestrained loose companions—
> Even such, they say, as stand in narrow lanes
> And beat our watch, and rob our passengers:
> While he, young, wanton, and effeminate boy,
> Takes on the point of honour, to support
> So dissolute a crew."

The consort of the deposed Richard is most exquisitely drawn by Shakspere. She is a gentle, loving being, a character which no one fails to admire; and her disposition is of such a nature, that it steals upon our senses, wins our sympathies, making us feel pity for her misfortunes, and evoking our admiration for the constancy of affection she evinces for her husband. When Richard is deposed from his high estate and committed to the Tower, her love for him above all other things stands forth. Nothing can overcome this feeling, with her it is all paramount; it is the "be-all and the end-all" of her existence.

Her marriage with Richard was a most unfortunate step for her; unfortunate in its results, and in the fact, that the alliance was unpopular with the English people. The twenty-five years' truce which had been agreed upon to celebrate the event, was regarded with aversion by the great majority of the English nation, and it served in no mean degree to alienate their affections from Richard, and transfer them to his antagonist, the cool and crafty Bolingbroke. The state of feeling which existed between the French and the English nation at the time of Richard, and that which exists now, affords a striking contrast. Our ancestors, at this early period of English history, looked upon France and the French people as their natural enemies, whom they were bound at all times to fight. To harry and scour the French territory, destroying life and property, was one of the sworn duties of the English people. This feeling has only subsided in the last few years, and that through a better understanding of the relations which one country should hold towards another. Within the last fifteen years, side by side, shedding their best blood like sworn brothers in the deadly strife, have fought the brave men of France in conjunction with the gallant sons of our fatherland. At the present time we are striving by all possible means to cement still closer the bond of union which already exists, and the conduct of the English government and of the English nation during the late Franco-Prussian War, has won the esteem and approbation of the French government and people.

Shakspere, by some writers, has been blamed for making so womanly a character of the consort of Richard. At the time of Anne's marriage, 1396, her age was eight years, and Richard was deposed in 1399, at which time his wife would be eleven. Shakspere, however, has great authority for the character he has drawn, even in its relation to historic truth, and still greater authority in the poetic world for the beautiful exposition of humanity presented in the character of Richard's queen. Her love of her husband is first shown in the anxiety she evinces and displays when " her lord, the king," is gone to Ireland. Her attendant Bushy tells her she

"is too much sad:
You promis'd when you parted with the king,

> To lay aside life-harming heaviness,
> And entertain a cheerful disposition.
>
> *Queen.* To please the king I did: to please myself
> I cannot do it; yet I know no cause
> Why I should welcome such a guest as grief,
> Save bidding farewell to so sweet a guest
> As my sweet Richard; yet again, methinks,
> Some unborn sorrow, ripe in fortune's womb,
> Is coming towards me; and my inward soul
> With nothing trembles; at something it grieves
> More than with parting from my lord the king."
> *A.* II. s. 2.

These forebodings—the result of her ever thinking upon her husband, are speedily realized,—they are fulfilled when Green informs her of banished Bolingbroke having "set footing in this land." This intelligence fully convinces her of what will follow, for she exclaims,

> " So, Green, thou art the midwife to my woe,
> And Bolingbroke my sorrow's dismal heir:
> Now hath my soul brought forth her prodigy;
> And I, a gasping, new deliver'd mother,
> Have woe to woe, sorrow to sorrow join'd."

The dignity and grace of the queen is admirably shown forth in the garden scene of the tower, when she rebuketh the gardeners for speaking of the deposition of the king. Yet her queenliness soon yields to her womanly feelings and to a wife's fears. This is evidenced by what the gardener observes after she hath quitted the scene. He says,

> "Here did she drop a tear; here in this place,
> I'll set a bank of rue, sour herb of grace:
> Rue, even for ruth, here shortly shall be seen
> In the remembrance of a weeping queen."—*A.* III. s. 4.

Her parting with her husband is extremely beautiful, and shows the loving-kindness and goodness of her character. Nought can eradicate and destroy the love she feels for the king. The chilling hand of adversity has fallen upon her husband's head, and loth is she to leave him with whom she has mated for life. The "fair rose" indeed has withered, yet she would wash it "fresh again with true-love tears." Weeping, she says,

"And must we be divided? must we part?"

She implores Northumberland not to sever her from her husband, but to

"Banish us both, and send the king with me,"

to which the rebel lord replies,

"That were some love, but little policy."

Again, she asks to be allowed to accompany her lord,

"Then whither he goes, thither let me go?"

All her requests are refused and she is compelled to part from the king, with but a loving kiss, which she repays with interest, exclaiming,

"Give me mine own again; 'twere no good part,
To take on me to keep and kill thy heart.
So now I have mine own again, begone,
That I may strive to kill it with a groan."—*A.* v. s. 2.

The character of John of Gaunt, the duke of Lancaster, is one of the finest in the play. His intense love of his country, his desire to see her renowned above all others, prevents him from ever leaving the party of the king. He believes in the sacredness of royalty as exemplified in the person of Richard, and also in the well-being of his country, depending on the due observance of the laws. This feeling, while it strongly attaches him to the cause of the king, also directs and moves him to rebuke and administer wholesome advice to the weak and credulous Richard. What a splendid contrast between the wisdom of Gaunt, and the frivolity and levity of Richard, is furnished in *A*. 2. s. 1. Gaunt is dying, and York, his brother, wishes him not to upbraid the king, telling him,

" For all in vain comes counsel to his ear."

To this Gaunt replies

" O but they say, the tongues of dying men
Enforce attention like deep harmony :
Where words are scarce, they are seldom spent in vain ;
For they breathe truth, that breathe their words in pain.
He that no more must say, is listen'd more
  Than they whom youth and ease have taught to glose ;
More are men's ends mark'd, than their lives before :
  The setting sun, and music at the close.
As the last taste of sweets, is sweetest last,
Writ in remembrance, more than things long past :
Though Richard my life's counsel would not hear,
My death's sad tale may yet undeaf his ear."

The king enters, and in a mocking tone, enquires " how is't with aged Gaunt ?" who responds in a speech playing upon his name. After two or three bantering speeches between Richard and Gaunt, speeches in which the frivolity and capriciousness of the king prevail; the dying duke bursts forth in the following splendid lines, as an answer to the king's remark of

"I am in health, I breathe, and see thee ill.
*Gaunt.* Now, He that made me knows I see thee ill,
Ill in myself to see, and in thee seeing ill;
Thy death-bed is no lesser than thy land,
Wherein thou liest in reputation sick :
And thou, too careless patient as thou art,
Committ'st thy anointed body to the cure
Of those physicians who first wounded thee."

What a magnificent rebuke to the folly of Richard, whose weakness is completely exposed in his committal of the cure of the state, of the body politic, into the hands "of those physicians who first wounded" it. How beautifully Gaunt depicts the greatness of the king's illness over his own. Gaunt is but an individual suffering, his own death being of no consequence, while the ills which the king's misgovernment has brought about, are of such magnitude, that with the king's

> " death-bed, is no lesser than thy land
> Wherein thou liest in reputation sick."

Gaunt further proceeds to tell the king of the evil results which flow from his system of favoritism, and says,

> "A thousand flatterers sit within thy crown,
> Whose compass is no bigger than thy head;
> And yet, incaged in so small a verge,
> The waste is no whit lesser than thy land."

Here again, the dying noble desires the well-being of his native land above all other things. To him, his country is his parents and his friends. Above all things the land of his birth,—above all things, the preserving of its honour, its position and its worth. He acknowledges no other land like this "precious stone set in the silver sea." To him, sunny Spain, with its groves of citron and her dark-eyed maids,—fair France, with her lilies and her blooming demoiselles, and Italy, the land of song and sunny skies, all these are nought when compared with England, the home of bravery, honour and virtue. Of Spain, Italy, and France, Gaunt possessed no mean knowledge. He had visited them, sojourned there, and fought on their soil with honour to himself and to his country. The experience he had gathered during his sojourn, only served to increase his love and admiration of his native land. The high estimation in which he held the land of his birth, is evidenced in the conclusion of the same speech, when he says,

"Why, cousin, wert thou regent of the world,
It were a shame to let this land by lease;
But for thy world, enjoying but this land,
Is it not more than shame to shame it so."

The faithfulness of Gaunt to the cause of Richard, is also shewn, when the duchess of Gloster, his brother's widow, upbraids him for his apathy in not revenging her husband, and his kinsman's death. Nothing can move him from his determination to abide by the cause of his nephew. Her railing does not in the slightest degree change his loyalty, nor incite him to act in opposition to the king. He tells her,

"God's is the quarrel; for God's substitute,
His deputy anointed in his sight,
Hath caus'd his death; the which if wrongfully,
Let heaven revenge; for I may never lift
An angry arm against his minister."—*A.* i. s. 2.

The character of Gaunt stands out in fine relief, when contrasted with Gloster, Northumberland, or any of the turbulent barons of the period. In him all desire of self-aggrandisement, is lost; it has given way to a real love of the land which gave him birth, a love which displays high national feeling, indelibly stamping his character as that of a true patriot. The words which Shakspere has given to "time-honoured Gaunt," are of such sterling value, possessing the real ring of the true metal, that they ought to be imprinted on the brains of every inhabitant of the united kingdom.

"This royal throne of kings, this scepter'd isle,
This earth of majesty, this seat of Mars,
This other Eden, demi-paradise;
This fortress built by nature for herself,
Against infection and the hand of war;
This happy breed of men, this little world;
This precious stone set in the silver sea,

Which serves it in the office of a wall,
Or as a moat defensive to a house,
Against the envy of less happier lands;
This blessed plot, this earth, this realm, this England.
This nurse, this teeming womb of royal kings,
Fear'd by their breed, and famous by their birth,
Renowned for their deeds as far from home,—
For Christian service and true chivalry,—
As is the sepulchre, in stubborn Jewry,
Of the world's ransom, blessed Mary's son;—
This land of such dear souls, this dear dear land,
Dear for her reputation through the world,
Is now leas'd out—I die pronouncing it—
Like to a tenement or pelting farm:
England, bound in with the triumphant sea,
Whose rocky shore beats back the envious siege
Of watery Neptune, is now bound in with shame,
With inky blots, and rotten parchment bonds:
That England, that was wont to conquer others
Hath made a shameful conquest of itself.
Ah, would the scandal vanish with my life,
How happy then were my ensuing death.—*A.* ii. s. 1.

The moral reflections uttered by Gaunt in this scene relative to the probable result of Richard's conduct, are truly beautiful. Not only were they applicable to his time, but they are applicable to all times, conveying in a few lines, a lesson, which the whole of mankind would be none the worse for studying. How true is the exclamation of the poet Keats, that

"A thing of beauty is a joy for ever,"

and how excellently is this assertion verified by the language of Gaunt. Its merit is of the highest order, for the idea is so sustained and continuous, and the language is so in unison with the thought, that the creation is really beautiful. From the lines, like a figure from the canvass of the painter, starts forth moral beauty, and remains "a joy for ever." The aged patriot says,

> "His rash fierce blaze of riot cannot last;
> For violent fires soon burn out themselves;
> Small showers last long, but sudden storms are short;
> He tires betimes, that spurs too fast betimes;
> With eager feeding food doth choke the feeder;
> Light vanity, insatiate cormorant,
> Consuming means, soon preys upon itself."

Northumberland in this play is but a mere sketch, which the dramatist eventually and most truthfully completed in Henry IV. He is an ambitious, restless, and selfish man; a thorough hater of peace. Only amidst strife, plots and turbulence does he enjoy existence. Upon the battle-field, with the blast of war blowing in his ears, he revels with delight, and his son, the gallant Harry Hotspur, is a worthy fighting descendant of such a fighting sire. Of the rest of the baronial and knightly characters, with two exceptions, they are men of words, ready to give the lie and back it with their swords. The quarrel scene in the 4th act, is but a bandying of foul names and foul words:—of boastings, and of hurling of gauntlets, none of which are redeemed, for Bolingbroke observes,

> "Lords appellant,
> Your differences shall all rest under gage,
> Till we assign you to your days of trial."

The bishop of Carlisle is a distinct character, and one which contrasts most favourably with some of the other dignitaries of the play. Under every phase of fortune he remains faithful to Richard. He persistently abideth by the king's course of action, and even after others have given up the struggle he ceases not from action. Of all the followers of Richard, he alone has the courage to defend the fallen monarch. His consistency of conduct winneth the respect of his adversaries, and when he is taken prisoner and brought before Bolingbroke, charged with having conspired against his life, he is dismissed by the usurping monarch, who says,

> "Carlisle, this is your doom;—
> Choose out some secret place, some reverend room,
> More than thou hast, and with it joy thy life;
> So, as thou liv'st in peace, die free from strife:
> For though mine enemy thou hast ever been,
> High sparks of honour in thee have I seen."—*A. v. s. 6.*

Of the Duke of York, uncle of the king, it may with justice be said, that he had neither the energy nor the ability to play a conspicuous or important part in the struggle between the barons and the king. He was too much attached to the sports of the field, and to retirement upon his estate, to be capable of lending force or strength to either side. His whole conduct is marked by indecision; he could not resolve, and this lack of resolution prevented him from adopting any definite course of action. His irresolution did not proceed "from thinking too precisely upon the event," but from a want of thought, due to a deficiency of mental calibre and insufficient training. When left in charge of the realm, he having been deputed regent during the absence of his nephew Richard, in Ireland, the weak side of his character is soon made manifest. When he learns of the landing of Bolingbroke he knoweth not what to do, nor whither to go, and most truly doth he depict his own character in the language which he uses when describing his position. He says,

> "Here am I left to underprop his land,
> Who weak with age cannot support myself."
> "what a tide of woes

> Comes rushing on this woeful land at once!
> I know not what to do."
> "Gentlemen, will you go muster men? If I know
> How, or which way to order these affairs,
> Thus disorderly thrust into my hands,
> Never believe me."
> "All is uneven,
> And everything is left at six and seven."—*A.* II. s. 2.

Richard II. is undoubtedly one of the finest of Shakspere's historic plays. It is a grand opening chapter of his great dramatic chronicle, for it presents all things in their true historic light, and embues them with that true human interest which is the keystone of success. The historical relation of this play is continued through the reign of Henry IV. by Shakspere, in two parts. Though the actual period of time which this play extends over is but three years, yet what a field, what a vast extent of view it doth present. What various passions, emotions, and sentiments it calls into existence, moving and acting upon ourselves as if we were engaged in the strife, instead of being mere spectators, gazing through the glass of Father Time. Taken individually and collectively, the characters form a group upon which speculation will busy herself in analyzing the motives, determining the results, and in calculating how, and in what way, we have been and are affected. Life's mirror is here presented, and by its reflection, like the lantern of Diogenes, we perceive that the figures are composed of clay and brass, silver and gold. That the good and the bad are bound up in each other; and we are to some extent shown the means, which the advances of civilization prove, whereby the condition of humanity has been and can be bettered. The rude clamour of the barons, enough "to fright the isle from its propriety," and the upheaving of the masses under Tyler, were forerunners of that great and earnest cry for social reform which the improved intelligence of our people is seeking to realize. The liberty of thought and speech which we now enjoy, the removal of serfdom and villeinage, are results which have flowed from the conduct of our ancestors. In the reign of Richard II. the seed which had been sown by Simon de Montfort, *viz.* the creation of Parliaments, was nourished and cultured by the Commons, who also, by their unity of action, succeeded in establishing the principle of the right of Parliament to vote and check the disbursements of the monies of the State. The infringement of this principle by Charles I. brought his head to the block, and established the power of the great and good Protector, Oliver Cromwell.

In the reign of Richard, as evidenced in the play, we see the natural result of the misgovernment of the king. We see that a great and wonderful change of feeling towards the reigning house came over all classes, both lord and knight, burgher and peasant. In the revolt of the villeins under Wat Tyler, which occurred some fourteen years prior to the opening of this play, 1397, so bitter was the animosity of the people against the house of Lancaster, that they compelled all men, with whom they were brought in contact, to take an oath never to seat one of that house upon the throne of England. Yet by the tyranny, the vices and follies of Richard, this feeling was destroyed, and Bolingbroke, the son of John of Gaunt, of the house of Lancaster, was hailed as a deliverer by the great body of the English people.

Northumberland in this play, is the outline of that

greatness and power, which some of the barons attained during the feudal times. Northumberland is the forerunner of him, of the bear and ragged staff, who in an after period of our history, was one of the principal actors among the ever-changing scenes on the ever-shifting stage of life. Warwick was to the 15th century, what Napoleon the Great was to the 19th,—a putter up and knocker down of kings. Northumberland was to Bolingbroke—what Warwick was to Henry VI. and Edward IV. The growing up of these barons and the expansion of their power, was a natural result of the system under which they lived. The families of a Neville, of a Clifford, of a Percy, and others, arose from the turbulence of the times, and for awhile, assumed a dictatorial power over the sovereign, a power sometime in the ascendant, and at others not, but which power was eventually destroyed, when the great Warwick fell upon the bloody field of Barnet. The pomp and magnificence of dress—another distinguishing mark of the period, ran into great extravagance during the reign of the unfortunate Richard. The splendour and richness of costume, the paraphernalia of war which characterized the lists at Shrewsbury, serves to show how great was Richard's delight, how strong was his desire for display,—a desire which was productive of injury to himself, assisting in evoking the ferment which ended with his dethronement. Every scene of the play affords ample scope for reflection; for whether we consider the incidents, the intrigues, the state of morals, the growth of parliamentary power, the extension of the principles of freedom, the unlocking of the priestly influence by the translations of the bible, the turbulence and lawlessness of the knights and mail-clad barons, it forms a picture whose lines are forcibly impressed upon the brain ; a volume, whose pages are pregnant with true wisdom, and it also serves to

"form a scene,
Where musing solitude might love to lift
Her soul above this sphere of earthliness,"

and in the bright future, read the happy destiny of human kind.

# RICHARD III.

The tragedy of Richard III. was first produced in the year 1593, and it was first printed and published in 4to. in 1597, under the title of "The Tragedy of King Richard the Third. Containing His treacherous Plots against his brother Clarence; the pittiefull murther of his innocent nephewes; his tyrannicall vsurpation; with the whole course of his detested life, and most deserued death. As it hath beene lately Acted by the Right honourable the Lord Chamberlaine, his servants. At London, Printed by Valentine Sims, for Andrew Wise, dwelling in Paules Churchyard, at the sign of the Angell." Five other editions were published in 4to., prior to the production of the complete dramatic works of Shakepere in folio, in 1623; one in 1598, in 1602, in 1605, in 1612, and in 1622. Two editions in 4to. were also published after the first folio, one in 1629 and one in 1634. In the folio edition, the title was altered to "The Tragedy of Richard the Third; with the landing of Earle Richmond, and the Battell of Bosworth Field."

There was an elder play of Richard III., published by Thos. Creede, in 1594, its title running as follows: "The Tragedie of Richard the third: Wherein is shown the death of Edward the fourth, with the smothering of the two young Princes in the Tower: With a lamentable end of Shore's wife—an example for all wicked women. And lastly, the coniunction and ioyning of the two noble houses, Lancaster and Yorke. As it was played by the Queenes Maiesties Players. London Printed by Thomas Creede and are to be sold by William Barley, at his shop in Newgate Market, neare Christ Church doore." This play bears no affinity to Shakspere's Richard III., for it is wholly different in its construction, and after the scene in which Edward the Fourth dies, the "story is thenceforward most inartificially and clumsily conducted, with a total disregard of dates, facts, and places, by characters imperfectly drawn and ill sustained. Shore's wife plays a conspicuous part; and the tragedy does not finish with the battle of Bosworth Field, but is carried on subsequently, although the plot is clearly at an end." Richard in the elder play, is a coarse, unvarnished ruffian, possessing none of the subtlety nor the intellectual power which marks the character of Richard, as drawn by Shakspere. The language of the elder play is partly prose and partly very ponderous blank verse, and in no way can it be compared with the splendour of language which is found in Shakspere's production.

In this great tragedy the mind is preferred to the body, above all things the mental power, to that, every thing must yield. The mental superiority which Richard possesses, and feels he does possess, gives a strong dash of irony to all his utterances. The conventions of society, though Richard pretends to respect them to answer his own purposes, he thoroughly despises, and no matter the instrument or the means, so that they serve his desires and promote his interest, he cares not what the world may think or say, he is himself, alone!

Richard being thoroughly conscious of his own mental superiority, enabled him accurately to discriminate and weigh the powers of those by whom he is surrounded. To be wise is to be strong, and his strength laid in his superior knowledge. His quick sharp wit, his great powers of dissimulation, and his resolve to spare neither friend nor foe that stood in his path, gave him " a tower of strength," greater than "the king's name," and which at every opportunity and under every circumstance he never failed to avail himself thereof. Those with whom he is brought in contact, he seizes on as stepping-stones towards the height which his ambition is desirious of climbing to, and no matter what has to be performed to reach the giddy height, reach it he will. His physical deformity preys upon his inward sense, though he laments it not, for it serves as an incentive to hurry him on in the path he has chosen. He has "no delight to pass away the time," by looking on his " own deformity," and since he "cannot prove a lover," he will " prove a villain." He hates "the idle pleasures" of the day, and by

"inductions dangerous,
By drunken prophecies, libels and dreams,"

he determines to commence his course of action by setting his

" brother Clarence and the King
In deadly hate the one against the other."

The stupid Clarence, the vapouring Hastings, and the ambitious Buckingham, are but tools of his iron will, which he uses and destroys to effect his purposes. His " naked villany he will hide

" With old ends stolen out of holy writ,
And seem a saint, when most he plays the devil."

The scene with Lady Anne, displays his powers of speech, the expansiveness of his intellectual powers and his wonderful self-reliance. It is this combination which enables him to effect so much, and elevates him so greatly above the pigmies by whom he is surrounded. His spring of action is ambition, and hypocrisy is the chief instrument in the development of his schemes. His hypocrisy is not of the sneaking kind, it is of the intellectual, giving him the power to conceal his aims, and to hoodwink those that stand in his way. There is nought of cowardice in his nature, he is constitutionally brave,—brave without being rash, but resolving to be a villain, he conceals his villany, cloaking thoroughly the end he desires to arrive at.

Though Richard possesses a recklessness of thought, there is a weak place in his character, and in the scene before he loses his life and crown, his superstitious fears are awaked by his ghostly visitations, and the terrors which they create, overmaster for a time the self-reliance which he has hitherto displayed. The entrance of Catesby and the intelligence he brings of the advance of Richmond's army, soon arouses his shattered energies, and he joyfully prepares for the final struggle—a struggle in which he displayed a vigour of action marked by the greatest bravery, as if "greatness would be greater than itself;" and thus defiant he passes away, winning sympathy, in spite of the great depravity he throughout his career displayed.

The tragedy as written by Shakspere, is vastly different from the hash of Colley Cibber's, now generally enacted on the stage, the latter opening with the last scene of Henry VI., while Shakspere's opens with the soliloquy of the principal character, in which the keynote of the whole tragedy is struck. The thoughts and intents of Richard, relative to his brother Clarence, are realized in the first and second acts; so is also his desire fulfilled of marrying the Lady Anne, whose husband and father he had previously killed. The wooing scene in the 1st act, is a splendid example of the knowledge of humanity which Shakspere possessed, and also of the great mental power with which Richard is endowed. In the third, we have his simulation of anger at pretended wrongs done to himself; then we have the entrance of Queen Margaret who loads him with curses, and yet he is triumphant over all. Everything makes for him,

> "I do the wrong, and first begin the brawl;
> The secret mischief that I set abroach,
> I lay unto the grievous charge of others."

Richard is prompt in action; the act follows the thought; no sooner does he decide than the deed is performed. Clarence must die, the warrant is ready and the murderers are at once sent to accomplish their work, after being told not "to hear him plead,

> For Clarence is well-spoken, and perhaps
> May move your hearts to pity, if you mark him."

The fate of the imprisoned Clarence is beautifully foreshadowed in that wonderful prophetic dream which he relates in the following scene. The fear of Richard is partly realized, for one of the assassins is moved to pity by the words of Clarence, but the other, intent only on the reward promised by Gloster, and possessing less of the milk of human kindness, first stabs and then drowns him "in the malmsey-butt within." The language throughout the whole of this act is of the loftiest character, far different to that served up by Cibber in his version of this tragedy. The lines are full and flowing; there is no abatement in their vigour, for the language and thought are in unison with each other, and the true height of poetry and passion is constantly sustained.

The historic relation according to the chronicles is not strictly observed by Shakspere in this tragedy, for he perpetrates an innovation by the introduction of Margaret, the consort of Henry VI., she at that time being exiled from England. The completeness of the tragedy would have been marred by the absence of Margaret,—for one of the grandest characters of the period would have been absent from the picture, whose beauty is added to by the words which she utters, when replying to Gloster's questioning, and which in themselves contain sufficient excuse for the author's innovation. Gloster says,

"Wert thou not banished on pain of death?"

to which she replies,

"I was; but I do find more pain in banishment,
Than death can yield me here by my abode."

She is the only one that reads the aim and intent of the wily Gloster, and this he well knows, for he rather fears her words lest they should awaken in others the thought which she herself doth think, and which her words pourtray, when cautioning the queen and her court, she says,

"Poor painted queen, vain flourish of my fortune!
Why strew'st thou on that bottled spider,
Whose deadly web ensnareth thee about?
Fool, fool! thou whet'st a knife to kill thyself.
The time will come that thou shalt wish for me
To help thee curse that poisonous hunch-back'd toad."

And again,
> "Take heed of yonder dog!
> Look, when he fawns, he bites; and when he bites,
> His venom tooth will rankle to the death:
> Have not to do with him, beware of him;
> Sin, death, and hell have set their marks on him,
> And all their ministers attend on him."—*A.* i. s. 3.

With the exception of the character of Margaret, the historical relation is strictly preserved, and the facts of history are given with great exactitude, and can be as safely relied upon for their data, as any so-called history of the period. But apart from this, the poet has endowed each of his characters with a vitality that is not to be found in the pages of the historian, and this he has been enabled to do by his searching out the inner truths and nature of humanity, as well as looking only to the outward, or external. In this manner, the pages of the poet are more true than those of the historian, for he rises to one higher and universal truth which he has gathered from a series of historical facts, and thus we have truth and poetry, each becoming the handmaiden of the other, going hand in hand to the advantage of the reader of history and the lover of poetry.

Shakspere apparently intended this tragedy to mark with strong distinctive features, the close of a strong distinctive period. The fearful career of crime which Richard indulged in, is a most apt termination to the wars of the Red and White Roses, and which completed the ruin of the armed aristocracy and became the commencement of a new civil order. All classes were affected with the taint of the times, and so strong were the passions of the people and the governors, that they became restless, turbulent and unruly, producing a terrible state of anarchy and destruction, and which state was destroyed by the death of Richard, and the ascension to the throne of the Earl of Richmond, under the title of Henry VII., who united both the houses, and whose reign was remarkable for the progress of the English people.

In the second act, events march rapidly on to the advantage of the designing Gloster. No sooner is the intelligence of Clarence's death conveyed to the court, than Edward himself shuffles off his mortal coil, leaving only in the way of his crafty brother, his two sons—the Prince of Wales and the Duke of York. Richard, assisted by Buckingham, who now becomes his principal confidant, seizes upon every opportunity, and by their joint warrant, the Lords Rivers and Grey and Sir Thomas Vaughan, are sent prisoners to Pomfret Castle. This act alarms the Queen for the safety of her children, and she "will to sanctuary," for she can perceive the downfall of her house, for

> "The tiger now hath seized the gentle hind;
> Insulting tyranny begins to jet
> Upon the innocent and aweless throne:
> Welcome destruction, death, and massacre!
> I see, as in a map, the end of all."—*A.* II. s. 4.

The third act is the beginning of the end. It is easy to perceive that the cherished desires of the crooked-back duke will soon be gratified. Everything is being prepared for his elevation, at the same time the end is not far off. Events are hurrying on, and one by one he removes from his path those who are in any way in opposition to his will. Hastings, his bosom friend, is sacrificed, and no wonder, for he is a weak, vain, inefficient man; inflated, without the necessary ballast to preserve his life in such troublous times. Closely connected with Gloster, the latter thoroughly knows and understands his character, and consequently despises him. He carefully enmeshes the butterfly lord, and by a master stroke of policy obtaineth his condemnation and death. There is nought criminal in the character of Hastings, for he fully resolves to stand by the late king's

"heirs in true descent,"
And will not give his "voice on Richard's side,
God knows I will not do it, to the death."

The overweening confidence of Hastings prevents him from escaping the fate he otherwise might have avoided. He possesses not the power to understand the character of Gloster, for he firmly believes

"there's never a man in Christendom
That can less hide his love or hate than he!
For by his face, straight shall you know his heart;"

and he perceives not the intensity of dissimulation which marks Gloster's character. Hastings is more in love with life when nearer death, than in any other period of his existence. He says, in reply to Stanley,

"My lord,
I hold my life as dear as you do yours;
And never in my life, I do protest,
Was it more precious to me than 'tis now:
Think you, but that I know our state secure,
I would be so triumphant as I am."—*A.* III., s. 2.

This self-joyousness and exaltation leads him to disregard the warnings he receives, and to place implicit confidence in his friend Catesby, who brings about his utter ruin. He does not heed the words of Stanley, who

"did dream the boar did raze his helm,"

but on the other hand, he did disdain "it and did scorn to fly" until it is too late, and he quits the scene lamenting his own folly which led him to believe in the "momentary grace of mortal men;" and, he is led to the block to meet the same doom as had already fallen on the heads of Rivers, Grey and Vaughan, who all

"at Pomfret, bloodily were butcher'd."

The remainder of the third act is occupied with the coquettings of Buckingham and Gloster with the lord mayor and citizens of London. The latter are so practised on and deceived by the assumed humility and the external show of piety which Gloster displays, that they proffer and beg his acceptance of the crown. This, he at first refuses, but on their warmly entreating him a second time, Gloster reluctantly assents to have fortune buckled to his back, "to bear her burthen."

The character of Gloster when made king, undergoes a great change. He hath lept into the seat he hath so long been sighing and playing for, and now fixed in his "coign of vantage," he no longer dissimulates; he wears no hypocritical garb, but he goes direct to his purpose. He is not to be turned aside by any compunctions of conscience from preserving the position he has attained. He will have none with him that wish to examine too closely into his desires and acts, all such he will banish from his presence, he will only hold

"converse with iron-witted fools,
And unrespective boys: none are for me
That look into me with considerate eyes."

Such as these he will have, for he can bend such to his purpose; with them there will not be any scruples relative to the acts they may be called upon to perform. Unscrupulous himself, his instruments must be of the same character, or else things will not be as he desires. He is fully resolved on keeping the throne, nor does he shrink from any crime, however deep or deadly, to render himself secure in the royal seat. His proposal of the murder of the young princes to his friend Buckingham, is put partly as a test to that courtier, who hesitates, betrays a fear of consequences which may result from the achievement of such a deed, though he of all others has been the chief instrument by whose assistance the crafty usurper is seated on the throne. Buckingham recoils from the plain speaking of his master, when he says,

"I wish the bastards dead;
And I would have it suddenly perform'd."

He asks for time, the consequences are such that he cannot accept them at once, he would have

"some breath, some little pause, my lord,
Before I positively speak herein;
I will resolve your grace immediately."

Richard has resolved upon the death of his nephews; it is necessary to his safety they should cease to be, and when "high-reaching Buckingham grows circumspect" and refuses to fulfil his wishes, he soon finds means to accomplish his desires. He questions his page,

"Boy!
Know'st thou not any whom corrupting gold
Would tempt unto a close exploit of death?"

And, when he learns of one—"a discontented gentleman," whom gold would "no doubt tempt him to anything,"—sends for such a one at once. He will not delay, nor will he shrink from having the deed performed. He now resolves upon the most desperate resorts, for in conjunction with the murder of the princes, he plans the death of his queen and the marrying of his brother's daughter. He firmly believes the doing of these deeds is necessary to his safety, and that is sufficient cause for him to have them done. It behoves him so to act, for he says,

> "it stands me much upon,
> To stop all hopes whose growth may damage me.
> I must be married to my brother's daughter,
> Or else my kingdom stands on brittle glass.
> Murder her brothers, and then marry her!
> Uncertain way of gain! But I am in
> So far in blood that sin will pluck on sin."—*A.* IV. s. 2.

Richard and Macbeth are both examples of promptitude of action, and also of resolve to do anything and everything that may be thought by them necessary for their own safety. They both plunge into crime with the same object, both are moved by ambition, both seek their self-preservation by the committal of more crime, both are imbued with the same ideas, and both give expression to the feelings by which they are moved,

> "For mine good,
> All causes shall give way; I am in blood,
> Stept in so far, that, should I wade no more,
> Returning were as tedious as go o'er:
> Strange things I have in head, that will to hand;
> Which must be acted ere they may be scann'd."
> *Macbeth, A.* III. s. 4.

The desire of Richard to marry his brother's daughter, is not fulfilled, for he is outwitted by her mother, Queen Elizabeth, who listens to his warm pleadings and apparently consents to grant his wish, though firmly resolved to prevent it. The cunning, crafty usurper, is here beaten by his own weapons, and he readily falls into the snare which the queen lays for him, when she says,

"Shall I go win my daughter to thy will?
I go. Write to me very shortly,
And you shall understand from me her mind."

The whole tragedy is full of action, but more particularly so in the last act; event follows event in rapid succession, and the whole of our faculties are awakened and absorbed in the bustle and active agitation with which this act is crowded. Destiny rides upon the storm, and Richard, strong in courage and in mental power, striving to bend all things to his will, yields only to the fate,—the inexorable.

The versification in this tragedy is one grand sonorous march; one constant flow without a break or impediment. The thought, passion and imagery, are in unison with each other, and the diction is most appropriate to the occasion. The hand of the master is traceable throughout the whole of the tragedy, and the wealth of his genius has been lavished upon its production. It is characterised by great ease; there is no apparent effort in its pourtrayal; everything yields to the directing influence of Shakspere's genius, which from first to last is truly astonishing.

# HENRY VIII.

THIS is the last of Shakspere's historic plays, and it forms a worthy epilogue to his dramatic chronicle. The date of its production hath long been a disputed question, but it is now currently assigned to the year 1605, and it was first printed in the folio of 1623. In all probability it was produced at the Globe Theatre in the summer season of the above mentioned year. The production of this play has been placed by some writers in the latter part of the reign of Elizabeth, but both external and internal evidence lean towards the conclusion, that it was written and produced in the early part of the reign of James I. The internal evidence, viz. the allusions to the "aged princess" and the prophecy by Cranmer have been said to be interpolations by Ben Jonson, in 1613, yet no evidence has been advanced in support of the assertion. These so called interpolatory passages are not in any way in the manner of the learned Ben; they are quite distinct from his style, and this fact, in itself, ought to destroy his claim to be the author. The allusions to the king contained in the speech of Cranmer are not personal allusions to the character of James, but to the character of his government, which sought to "make new nations" as evidenced by their attempts at the colonization of Virginia. This was a movement in which James took an especial interest, and more particularly in relation to this important settlement, and the poet without undue flattery might ascribe to the king, through his executive, the power "to make new nations." The speech is in the last scene of the play and its whole tenour, for the glories of the reign of Queen Bess are promised to be continued to her successor, goeth to support the position that the play was not produced earlier than the year 1605, and that it belongeth to the reign of the pedant James. After speaking of the greatness of the virgin queen, the lines proceed

> " Nor shall this peace sleep with her: But as when
> The bird of wonder dies, the maiden phœnix,
> Her ashes new create another heir,
> As great in admiration as herself;
> So shall she leave her blessedness to one,
> (When heaven shall call her from this cloud of darkness,)
> Who, from the sacred ashes of her honour,
> Shall star-like rise, as great in fame as she was,
> And so stand fix'd: Peace, plenty, love, truth, terror,
> That were the servants to this chosen infant,
> Shall then be his, and like a vine grow to him;
> Wherever the bright sun of heaven shall shine,
> His honour, and the greatness of his name,
> Shall be, and make new nations: He shall flourish,
> And like a mountain cedar, reach his branches
> To all the plains about him:—Our children's children
> Shall see this, and bless heaven."

This play is not "merry" nor "wanton," but "sad, high, and working;" full of "noble scenes," magnificence, pomp and "earthly glory." In its pages once more we see the old nobility of the realm attempting to play the most important part in the nation's welfare. The Duke of Buckingham is chief among his companions, who pride themselves upon their blood, and not only is he versed in matters of the sword, but he is learned, wise in council, with an expansive mind, the result of much culture and observation. Unfortunately Buckingham is impetuous, he cannot hide the hostility he feels against Wolsey, who galls him by the mode and manner he acts towards the court, "without the privity of the king." Buckingham is "high reaching," and in conjunction with his fellows wishes to restore the old authority of the nobles. He most thoroughly detests the upstart Wolsey, whom he calls a "butcher's cur," and regrets he has "not the power to muzzle him." Both Buckingham and Norfolk know full well the nature of the crafty cardinal, his "malice and his potency," and also that "he is revengeful," prone to mischief and "able to perform it." They are fully cognizant of the deeds of this "keech," "this holy fox or wolf," for his acts hold in check these blood-proud peers. The "ambitious finger" of the "count cardinal," is the thorn that is constantly pricking the sides of haughty Buckingham and his brother peers, who are vexed that "a beggar look, outworth's a noble's blood." The wisdom and better judgement of Buckingham is overborne by the spleen and vexation which he feels against Wolsey, and knowing that he has "gone to the king," resolves "to follow and outstare him." This he does not do, for "the fire of passion" with which he is moved is allayed by the reasons of Norfolk, and he then unfolds his plan whereby he means to ensnare this "top-proud fellow," but unfortunately for himself, by "practice and device," he is caught in his own net. The death scene of Buckingham is one of the most beautiful and affecting ever written by Shakspere.

The character of Wolsey is essentially true to history. He is the architect of his own fortunes, winning his way by the force of his intellectual faculties, and by his powers of dissimulation, to the annoyance, disgust and hate of the nobles of the court, who do not fail to perceive the fostering care he receives at the hands of the king. He is full of ambition, and by "the force of his own merit makes his way," and wins "a place next to the king." He is full of pride, covetousness and love of pomp, altogether incompatible with his sacred calling, and the practice of these unholy matters ultimately lead to his overthrow. He is devoid of truth, in love only with himself, for the king's honour he "does buy and sell" as he pleases "for his own advantage." He is a practiser of dissimulation, under which mask he conceals the malice of his nature. He is munificent to his servants, all of whom he strives to advance, for in them he has the willing tools to carry out his will. He bribes the confidants of his foes, and buys them over to serve his own purposes. He is full of rapacity and oppresses the commons with enormous taxes, which he greedily consumes and devotes to promote his own desires. By the practice of deceit he obtains credit for actions not his own, but belonging to others, for when the commons refuse to pay the levy and remonstrate with the king, who on hearing of their case directs a free pardon to all that have denied "the force of this commission," Wolsey true to his craft, tells his secretary,

"let it be nois'd
That through our intercession this revokement
And pardon comes."

He is opposed to the nobility, from the fact, that he is despised by them, and he strives all that he can to subjugate them to his will. He seeks to destroy them as a class, not that the country will be served by such destruction, but that he will have less opponents and enemies in his path. The leader of the nobles he overthrows, by the evidence of his surveyor, whom he hath corrupted and bought over to his purpose; nor does this act content him, for he attempts to lord it over his sovereign, to whom he stands so deeply indebted. The highest ecclesiastical appointments in the land he seizes on, becomes the papal legate and ultimately aims at the Papal chair. Though of mean descent himself, he thoroughly despises all others of that class, especially if they possess the virtues of humanity, for though a priest, he holds that man "a fool" who "would needs be virtuous." He allows none to think for themselves, and he will only be surrounded by those that follow his desires, yield to his wishes and obey his commands; and these must not be of the common class, for he will "not be griped by meaner persons." The object and purpose for which he amasses great riches, "the piles of wealth he hath accumulated," were to "fee" his "friends in Rome," so that he might "gain the Popedom," and thus be higher than his natural sovereign. This ambitious desire, engenders mental blindness, and which leads firstly to his failure relative to being Pope, and it also leads to his final overthrow, for his "contrary proceedings" in the matter of "the divorce" become "unfolded." He would that Henry should marry "the French king's sister," "no Anne Bullen for him." He knows that she is "well deserving" but she is a "spleeny Lutheran," "not wholesome to the Papal cause," and he would "his holiness" should "stay the judgment of the divorce." This persistency of opposition to the gratification of the king's amorous desires, awakens Henry's hostility to the cardinal, whose spell is out, for "the king hath found"

> "Matter against him that for ever mars
> The honey of his language."

With all his knowledge of the king's character there was this one particular phase, viz., Henry's sexual passion, that he had entirely overlooked. He had never accurately weighed nor discriminated the strength of this passion, and this oversight, coupled with his negligence, in putting his "main secret in the packet" he "sent the king," causes Henry to break with him, deposing him from his high estate, commanding him to surrender the great seal to his direst foes, and confines him "to Asher house." True to his nature, which is made up of dissimulation, craft and hypocrisy, he quits the scene doling forth precepts of virtue which he himself did never act upon during his life, and punished those who had been fools enough so to do.

The character of the king, as drawn by Shakspere, is not particularly flattering to the amorous monarch, whose dalliance with the fair sex partook more of the animal portion of his nature than any development of the feeling of love. There is no attempt to disguise the "tyranny together working with his jealousness," the cruelty and the sensuality of Henry's conduct, though such deeds and actions are not prominently thrust forward. The self-will and passion of which the king was to a great extent a slave, are faithfully pourtrayed, so is also his intense implacability, for it is said and justly so that Henry never forgave an enemy; for he was entirely "void and empty from any dram of mercy."*

Of Anne Bullen we see but little. There is not much of her character pourtrayed, but sufficient is shown to intimate that she is fully capable of bearing the honours which are being thrust upon her, and though she "would not be a queen for all the world," she is well able to play a queenly part. She bears "a gentle mind," and beauty and honour in her are mingled. Her chastity and good humour are thoroughly exhibited and her completeness of mind and feature is of that high class, that

"She will outstrip all praise
And make it halt behind her."†

The character of Katharine is charmingly and truthfully drawn. She is full of womanly goodness and virtue, true in her love for her husband and full of gentleness. "She bore a mind that envy could not but call fair," and those with whom she associated and by whom she was surrounded are of the most virtuous kind, so that her bitterest enemy can say nought against her virtue. Her husband she loves "with that excellence that angel's love good men with," "loved him next Heaven," and almost forgot her "prayers to content him." She readily obeys his wishes and desires with but one exception, and that is the attempt to divorce her from him with whom she had been mated for twenty years. This arouses her womanly nature and she fails not to castigate the arrogant cardinal, refusing "to be judged by him," and rising in her queenly dignity, declines "ever more upon this business" to "make

* Merchant of Venice, Act iv. Sc. 1.   † The Tempest, Act iv. Sc. 1.

appearance in any of their courts." The death scene of the outraged Katharine is particularly beautiful, for in her last moments, full of true gentleness, she forgives her bitter enemy, Wolsey, fails not to wish joy and happiness to her late husband, hoping "that he may for ever flourish," and bids Capucius that he will "tell him, in death I bless'd him, for so I will."

# SHAKSPEREAN JOTTINGS.

CYMBELINE.—The date of the production of this grand romantic drama, for it can hardly be called a tragedy, cannot be said to be definitely ascertained. It was seen by Dr. S. Forman, the astrologer, either in 1610 or 1611, for he has recorded the witnessing thereof, though he does not name the day nor the theatre at which it was played. The historical materials were found in Holinshed, who mentions the names of the king and his sons, but no trace of their adventures in the drama can be found in the pages of the historian. The fortunes of Posthumus and Imogen, the wager, the treachery of Iachimo, were probably derived from the Decameron of Boccaccio, though the position of the characters who lay the wager is different in degree. The old dry bones of others, in this instance, Shakspere has endowed with vitality, and enriched with the charms and graces of his own consummate powers. Cloten is an original portraiture, made up of contradictions, full of self-conceit, which is mainly engendered by his position and the gross flattery of the courtiers by whom he is surrounded. He is tainted with brutality and folly, yet not lacking all the qualities of humanity, for at times he displays a manliness of nature, which fails not to stamp him as one of human kind.

Both the young princes, the brothers of Imogen, are distinguished by their simple-hearted goodness, and this is most fully developed by the training which they receive from Belarius, by whom they are brought up in a knowledge and love of the natural and true. The yearnings for a wider field of distinction which they feel, are but promises of true wisdom and greatness, which is ultimately fulfilled. Their mixed character is excellently and faithfully described by their aged counsellor, when he says they are " the sweetest companions in the world," and

"They are gentle,
As zephyrs, blowing below the violet,
Not wagging his sweet head; and yet as rough,
Their royal blood enchaf'd, as the rud'st wind,
That by the top doth take the mountain pine
And make him stoop to the vale."

They are apparently both alike in character, yet they are not truly so, for the elder Guiderius is the most impetuous and passionate of the two, and upbraids the more gentle Arviragus, who uses richer and more flowing language, for playing " in wench-like words with that which is so serious."

The character of the queen, " a crafty devil who coins plots hourly," is the blackest among the whole of the women ever drawn by Shakspere. She is remarkable for her coolness, her cunning, her hypocrisy and her treachery, being truly "a woman that bears all down with her brain." She lusteth for power, in which everything is included, and her desire for Cloten to marry Imogen, proceeds from her love of dominion. In the development of her wickedness, she cares not who may suffer, so that she obtains her desire. She needs no broker when practising her deceit; her "cunning sin" can "cover itself withal," for she can attempt slowly to poison her husband, yet watching him with the tenderest care. She too is not lacking in her expression of friendship for Imogen and Posthumus, well knowing that by her pleading for the persecuted pair, she will be increasing the king's anger against them, and thus under the guise of friendship which "is constant in all other things," she will be "tickling where she wounds." She can wet her "cheeks with artificial tears," and frame her "face to all occasions." Her brain is "more busy than the labouring spider," and her "serpent heart," is "hid with a flowering face."

Imogen is one of the most charming, artless and lovely female characters that Shakepere ever produced. There is none other more exquisite among the whole range of his creations. She is all grace, it is not that she is beautiful in form and feature, her true beauty consists in her purity, her tenderness, her artlessness and the depth of her love, all these are finely conceived and most beautifully displayed. Her outward qualities charm each beholder, but her inward qualities are of a loftier character, and it is these which give her the power by which she acts. The purity of her nature instinctively divines what is the true course of action, and she is never at fault in the mode she adopts. The language which she uses is of the truest nature, true to her divine purity, and the love which she has for Posthumus. Love with Imogen is all in all. She is all love, it is her every-day thought, in fact, her religion. Her character is made up of love; and her husband, "a man worth any woman," is the "bright particular star" upon whom her love is concentrated. With her goeth the affections of the audience, who are moved in like manner with herself. With her sorrows they sympathise and in her joys they equally participate. She is the centre round which the lesser characters all revolve, for they all serve to heighten by the force of contrast, the purity of her thoughts, and to develope the charming grace, innocence and truthfulness of her nature.

THE WINTER'S TALE.—This comedy was first printed in the folio of 1623, and the first record of its production is an entry in the manuscript diary of Dr. S. Forman, which exists in the Ashmoleum museum. It was played at the Globe Theatre on the 15th of May, 1611. It was the custom for the king's players, to which company of actors Shakspere belonged, during the spring and summer season to play at such theatres as the Globe, which was open to the sky, and in the winter they played at the private house in Blackfriars. Greene's History of Dorastes and Fawnia served Shakspere to found this play upon, and his version is a vast improvement upon the work of Greene. Though he has adopted many of the incidents of Greene's story, in no way has Shakspere adopted his language. The termination is also different, displaying more judgment and evincing more power than is found in the novel. The characters of Autolycus, Antignous, the Clown Shepherd and Paulina have been added, and are entirely the creations of Shakspere, for no characters of their class are found in Greene's story.

Some writers have wished to place this comedy among the historical works of Shakspere, but it may more truly be termed a tragic-comic pastoral, for the oracle of Delphi decides the tragic catastrophe and prepares the reader for the happy conclusion of the piece. The jealousy of Leontes is of a totally different kind to that of Othello's. Leontes' passion proceeds from within, while Othello's passion is brought about by the whisperings of the crafty Iago. Othello is not prone to jealousy, the subtlety of his ancient and the outward circumstances by which he is surrounded, evoke the passion with him, while Leontes has no outward incidents to serve this purpose; things external do not give rise to nor develope this passion with him, for he is naturally affected by it, owing to the suspiciousness of his nature. Leontes is the dupe of his own imagination, Othello is the dupe of Iago, who fans into a flame all the elements of mistrust with which he has sought to surround the gentle, loving Desdemona. Hermione is thoroughly conscious of her own innocence, strong in her moral power, full of dignity, grace, honour and duty. She is calmness personified when she learns the worst, and this calmness is the result of her innocence and of her belief in the ultimate triumph of her cause. She defends her honour most eloquently in words, yet still more so by her acts. Perdita possesses fully the nature of her mother. She has the same calm dignity, the same repose, the same resignation and power of self-denial. Both mentally and in her physical aspect, she is a true copy of the wronged Hermione.

King Lear.—This tragedy was produced at the Globe Theatre in the spring of 1605. There was an elder play which was entered on the stationers' books in

1594, and there is no doubt that Shakspere derived some hints therefrom, particularly in relation to the character of the faithful, enduring Kent. From Holinshed's chronicles the chief materials have been derived, though the catastrophe of Shakspere's tragedy differs from all others. Three editions in 4to. were published in 1608 of Lear, which is one of the greatest of all tragedies, for it is composed only of tragic elements. Though complex in its arrangements, it is faultless. Parental love and filial ingratitude are the leading feelings of the tragedy, and out of their development is evolved all the results of the tragedy. The fool is a splendid set-off to the sorrows of the fallen monarch, and he also serves to render those sorrows more impressive than they otherwise would be. The introduction of the fool is a wonderful example of the dramatic skill of Shakspere, and shows how clearly and completely he was versed in true dramatic construction.

The character of Cordelia is one of the most beautiful of the great master's creations, and one of the most difficult for any actress to represent. The actress who may undertake this part must be perfectly natural, she must not descend to any of the trickeries of her art, she must be gentle, kind, innocent and affectionate, "of all compounded," with a sweetness in her articulation, for the voice of Cordelia is "ever soft, gentle and low; an excellent thing in woman." Cordelia is full of truth and constancy to the truth, and she cannot heave her heart into her mouth, for the truth "nor more nor less" will she speak, whatever be the cost. Her "fortunes" may be marred, yet gently though firmly she says in answer to her father's query, "I love you and most honour you," and then adds

"Why have my sisters husbands, if they say
They love you all? Haply, when I shall wed,
That lord whose hand must take my plight shall carry
Half my love with him, half my care and duty:
Sure, I shall never marry like my sisters,
To love my father all.
*Lear.* But goes thy heart with this?
*Cor.* Ay, my good lord.
*Lear.* So young, and so untender?
*Cor.* So young, my lord, and true."

The wrong which her father enacts towards her when he disclaims all "paternal care," holds her "as a stranger" to his heart, and leaves her "shorn of her fair proportion," does not ruffle her gentleness, for when saying farewell to her sisters she bids them "use well our father." When she learns of the ill treatment which her father had received from her "two sisters," it does not move her anger, she does not indulge in rage, there is no "hideous rashness" in her nature; what they have done only moves her "patience and sorrow," and in a true womanly way she yields to her feelings, and then resolves that nothing shall be wanting on her part to save her father, for above everything rises her filial feeling. She has no thought for herself, "no blown ambition incites her to arms," on the contrary she is moved to action by "love, dear love," "our aged father's right," and by her natural hate of all wrong doing. She would that the "kind gods" should cure the "great breach" and wind up "the untuned and jarring senses" of her dear father. She knows by whom this ill result has been wrought, but in the tenderness and gentleness of her nature she does not revile her "two sisters," who have caused the "violent harms" in the "reverence" due to her father, and she fervently hopes that the "medicine" of "restoration" will hang upon her lips, so that by kissing she may repair the wrong. Though defeated in battle, her object is accomplished, for she feels and knows that she has saved her father from "the rack of this rough world."

---

TWELFTH NIGHT.—In 1601 this comedy was produced, and on the second of February 1602, it was acted on the celebration of the Readers' Feast at the Middle Temple. It was first printed in the folio of 1623. Two Italian plays, composed upon a novel of Bandello's, are said to be the source from whence Shakspere drew the serious incidents of his comedy, and there is some slight resemblance between the story told in each play and that told by Shakspere. It was however not from these plays that Shakspere derived such incidents which he has used, when they suited his purpose, but from an old translation of the novel itself. There is no affinity of language or ideas to be found in the Italian plays, nor in the novel, when compared with Shakspere's comedy, who has drawn entirely upon his own interminable resources for the poetry and diction, of this, one of his grandest character plays. The comic characters, Sir Toby Belch, Sir Andrew Aguecheek, Malvolio, and others are pure creations of the poet. Self esteem is the chief feature of Malvolio, whose character is truly described by Maria, when she says, he is "an affectioned ass, that cons state without book, and utters it by great swaths: the best persuaded of himself, so crammed, he thinks, with excellencies." This description is also confirmed by his mistress, the lady Olivia. Feste is the opposite of the conceited steward, for he possesses all the good qualities which Malvolio affects, and only affects, while he pretends not to possess them.

A MIDSUMMER NIGHT'S DREAM.—This comedy was produced in the year 1595, and was first printed and published in the year 1600, by Thomas Fisher, a second edition printed by James Roberts, was published in the same year. The custom, "more honoured in the breach than in the observance," of charging Shakspere with deriving his plots from the works of other authors, hath not been failed to be made, in regard to this truly poetical play, though in this instance, it is not sustainable, for no work is yet known from whence Shakspere could have derived his plot. It has been said that Chaucer's Knight's tale and Plutarch's Life of Theseus, furnished hints that Shakspere profited by, but in neither of the named sources, is there the slightest trace of a similar story to that which is told in the comedy. There cannot be a doubt that the source of this comedy, is to be attributed to Shakspere's great knowledge of folk lore, his complete acquaintance with the superstitions of the day, and from his own luxuriant imagination sprang the conception and the development of this lovely dream, which is a splendid poetic effort of a great poet's brain. The characters are all finely and truly conceived, and the language of each is consonant with the character. Throughout the whole of the comedy, there is a vein of the highest poetry that charms both the reader and the spectator, for it is equally fitted for the closet or the stage, and it is as delicate in its conception as it is beautiful in its execution. Bully Bottom, the weaver, is full of self-esteem. He never doubts his own capacity, and he would undertake all and everybody's business, so confident is he in his own powers. His colleague Quince, and the rest of the "rude mechanicals," in conjunction with himself, form a rough contrast to the delicate play of the fairies. The material world is here opposed to the ideal; the unimaginative to that which is most fanciful, and this contrast serves to give a prominence to both.

Much Ado About Nothing.—In 1600, this comedy was first published in 4to., and it was not again printed till it appeared in the folio of 1623. The serious portion of the plot of this comedy, it is said, may be traced in the 5th canto of Ariosto's Orlando Furioso and in Spenser's Faery Queen, book 2, canto 4, but the chief portion of its plot, was in all probability derived from a novel by Bandello, to which Shakspere has added, however, the principal parts. The gentle Hero, a jewel so rare that "the world" cannot "buy such;" Claudio who hath so "borne himself beyond the promise of his age," and the exquisite word-talkers, witty and pointed, Beatrice and Benedick, are Shakspere's own coinage. The comic portions of the comedy are entirely the work of Shakspere, the inimitable Dogberry, and his choice companions of the watch, the worthies Verges, Sexton and Seacole are his own, and deeply we stand indebted to the bard for those exquisite creations. Even the incidents of the original tale he has varied at his pleasure, and made them more subservient to the dramatic interest. The characters of Beatrice and Benedick are foreshadowed in his Biron and Rosaline, the latter being his early attempt, the former, the finished production of his master mind. In the first two acts, silentless and retirement are the distinguishing features in the character of Hero, and she thinks with Claudio that

"Silence is the perfectest herald of joy."

The talkativeness of Beatrice and Benedick are the necessary contrast to the reticence of Hero and Claudio, without which the dramatic composition would not be effective nor true.

---

THE TAMING OF THE SHREW.—In 1594, a comedy was published having for its title, "A Pleasant conceited Historie called the Taming of a Shrew," but, it bears little or no relation to Shakspere's comedy, which was first produced in 1596, and first printed in the folio of 1623. The name of the author of the elder play is not known, and the comedy is a very poor production, lacking humour and character. Shakspere made but little use of the incidents contained in the work of his predecessor, nor did he derive any of his characterization from the elder play. The life and spirit which marks Shakspere's "Taming of the Shrew," is entirely his own, for there is nought approaching it in the crude effort of the earlier damatist, neither is the poetry of the same nature, the diction of Shakspere being immeasurably superior.

The character of Petruchio, is admirably conceived and most completely developed. The great knowledge which Shakspere possessed of human nature, has made him thoroughly consistent in his drawing of Petruchio, who possesses humour, is coarse, unscrupulous, full of determination, resolved to have his own way, and possesses a strong admiration of, and a still stronger desire to possess "wealth," which is the "burden" of his "wooing dance." If "wealthily" he wives, then "happily" he marries, and when told of one that is "rich, and very rich," he will have her, though she were "as curst and shrewd as Socrates' Xantippe." He also has a personal liking for Katharine, his "superdainty Kate," "the prettiest Kate in Christendom," which feeling takes root at the first interview and gradually crops up. Tame Kate he will, to do this he has resolved, and in all probability effects his purpose more securely by this means than he would have done by his hectoring blustering manner. The tamed one evidently perceives, beneath the rude external, traces of love, and by those traces, though subtle, faint, and indistinct, she herself is personally attracted, and thus is made to own, when speaking of her sex, that she is

"asham'd that women are so simple,
To offer war, where they should kneel for peace;
Or seek for rule, supremacy and sway,
When they are bound to serve, love and obey."

---

ANTONY AND CLEOPATRA.—This tragedy was produced at the commencement of the year 1608 and was first printed in the folio of 1623. The materials were in all probability derived from Sir Thomas North's translation of Plutarch. The tragedy is written in the matured style of Shakspere and the dignity and manliness of Antony is preserved throughout. Though the atmosphere of the tragedy is of a sensual character, there is no attempt to make it alluring. In no form or way has the author made vice attractive, nor is any sympathy excited for the proceedings and the fate which befalls Antony and his bewitcher, the voluptuous Cleopatra.

This tragedy should be read with that of Romeo and Juliet. They both treat of and relate to love, the latter, being one of the purest and most perfect representations of the feeling in its natural state ever written; while in Antony and Cleopatra, the mere animal passion of love apart from affection, pervades the whole tragedy, which rivals Lear, Hamlet, Macbeth, and Othello, in the power and strength of its language, in the truth of its construction and in the correctness of its portraiture of character.

THE TEMPEST.—The Tempest is a remarkable instance of the true romantic drama. It is addressed to the imaginative portion of man's nature, and is unique in its kind. The excitement of the opening scene prepares the mind for everything which follows, and the sympathy which we feel for the characters does not proceed so much from the circumstances in which they are placed, for its source can be traced within, it being our sympathetic imagination that is awakened.

The character of Prospero, is marked by a strong love of humankind and redolent in the practice of humanity. Possessed of the power to punish those whose usurpation had driven him from his throne, his country and his friends, he seeks not to do so, but satisfied with their penitence, he takes them back into his friendship. To their evil action he opposes good deeds, for malevolence he returns benevolence.

The fair Miranda is one of the most exquisite creations in the whole range of the Shaksperean drama. She is a fit compeer for Cordelia, Perdita and Desdemona,—one of those quiet natures whose mental worth is closed as in a bud; whose depth of character is concealed like the fire of the diamonds, until occasions serves and reveals the strength and beauty of her inner life. She is full of pity, and her training, which has been without intercourse with the outer world, has taught her the two virtues, modesty and pity, both of which she never fails to practice.

The deeds of Prospero and the acts of the dainty Ariel, whose characteristics are tenderness, speed and grace, remove the drama from the world of reality, and they, in conjunction with its poetic thoughts and its true poetic language, create for awhile a world of fancy, in which our imagination revels in the very madness of pleasure and delight.

No work is known from whence Shakspere could have drawn the incidents of this most charming play. From within himself—from the vast stores of his own imaginative powers, did Shakspere get both language and incident of this most marvellous poem. Everything is in harmony; the rough manners of the boatswain are quite truthful and dramatic, they are not too extravagant, and they serve as an excellent contrast to the polished manners and expressions of the king and his courtiers.

This romantic play is usually ascribed to be the last of Shakspere's productions, and if so, it is a remarkable instance of the vigour of his powers, and also remarkable for the firm grasp which the day-dreams of his youth, held of his powers in the days of their maturity.

HAMLET.—The character of Hamlet is of the highest type, no further refinement is scarcely possible, either in the circumstances in which he is placed, or in the niceties and subtleties by which he is moved. In this early work, 1588, Shakspere had learned to subordinate all the characters in a drama to one, spreading one feeling over the whole. This was a great advance in dramatic art, and the play of Hamlet is remarkable for its unity, being most excellent in its dramatic construction and one of the noblest poems the world has yet known.

In the character of Hamlet we have the development of thought instead of action. The deep-thinking of the young prince prevented action, for the consequences of action are all foreshadowed in his thinking. The action of the tragedy drifts towards Hamlet, instead of its being a result of a course of action resolved on by the young prince.

Man and his destiny is the burden of the tragedy of Hamlet. The endless perplexities of life, its hopes and fear, its melancholy, and the thoughts which "come like shadows," stand face to face with the silent, immoveable and impenetrable world of destiny.

Hamlet is the story of a life, in it is represented the various phases of human existence. There would not be harmony in all its parts if the grave-digging scene was omitted. The picture would not be perfect; one phase of humanity would be unrepresented and the completeness of the work would be marred. Life is an enigma, an uncertainty, and this tragedy is a development of it. It teaches us a lesson and causes us to accept life with its uncertainties, and shows that the whole is harmonious and complete; that nought transpires but what contains a lesson which we should profit by.

---

The deeper nature of Hamlet overpowers the shallowness of Polonius. The young prince at once interprets the character of the old courtier, and being throughout a hater and detester of falsehood, he despises and contemns the fawning courtier, who has been all through "his life, a foolish prating knave."

---

> "To be, or not to be,—that is the question:—
> Whether 'tis nobler in the mind to suffer
> The slings and arrows of outrageous fortune,
> Or to take arms against a sea of troubles,
> And by opposing end them?"

Shakspere has been charged by some writers with being guilty of great incoherence of thought in this passage, they saying, the train of reflection does not take its natural or logical course. To this opinion I cannot subscribe. The condition of thought sought to be pourtrayed is that of doubt, and while that state exists, incoherency is a result to be calculated on. It is only when those doubts are satisfied,—when in fact the pros and cons of the question have been fully argued, and a clear fixity of opinion is obtained, that we can expect coherence of thought. Shakspere has thus most justly—because truthfully, in those lines displayed his almost infinite knowledge of the action of the human brain.

---

The character of Sir John Falstaff is one of the most remarkable in the whole range of the comic drama.

It stands by itself, independent of all other characters, both in Shakspere, or any other writer. Its true characterization is found in what Falstaff says of himself, the "brain of this foolish-compounded clay, man, is not able to invent anything that tends to laughter, more than I invent or is invented on me. I am not only witty in myself, but the cause of that wit is in other men."* To analyse the character of Falstaff in all its fulness, would not only be difficult, but it would also be unacceptable, for in the performance of such an analysis, much of its comic power, which lies in its unintentional wit and in its dry humour, would be destroyed. There is great fancy, deep truthfulness, merriment unrestrained, the choicest wit, an abundance of liveliness, and an almost inexhaustible variety to be found in the character of the fat knight.

---

MERCUTIO is one of the most brilliant characters that Shakspere ever created. He possesses a strong humourous perception, and is talkative in the highest degree, for he "speaks more in a minute, than he will stand to in a month." His confidence in his own powers is unbounded, and he was "very well beloved of all men." He is a prime jester, dashing, wordy, yet not lacking meaning, and he is most sarcastic on the follies of his compeers. He is compounded of wit, fancy and valour, and they are so dexterously displayed in this marvellous creation, that they stamp it as one of the finest specimens of the bard's power of characterization. Mercutio quickens the action of the tragedy, and gives it a vitality which greatly heightens the interest.

* Henry IV. Part II, *A.* 1, s. 2.

In a state of madness the patient knows not physical suffering, his mental powers are so coiled within, that he is impervious to feeling the vicissitudes of nature. The storm may howl, the thunder may roar, yet the elements disturb not, nor can they overpower the cankerworm which gnaws within and which shuts out all other fears, hopes and pains. In depicting insanity, the wonderful truthfulness of Shakspere is pre-eminent. He appears to have grasped the whole range of mental phenomena without effort, and to have truly understood and pourtrayed the workings of insanity. The madness of Lear and Ophelia is singularly true to nature, and its truthfulness is shown in his faultlessness of treatment. When the aged monarch appears, he never alludes to his physical suffering, he is completely overpowered by mental sorrows, and he has no recollections of peril, nor has he any feeling of pain. This disregard of physical suffering is also shown in the Queen's description of the death of Ophelia. The fair girl floats down the stream undisturbed by her impending fate,

"Her clothes spread wide,
And mermaid like, awhile they bore her up:
Which time, she chaunted snatches of old tunes,
As one incapable of her own distress."

---

The gloom of winter, the joy of spring, the warmth of summer, and the ripeness of autumn, pass away, for such is the course of nature's action, yet they each leave behind their silent lessons, full of meaning for the benefit of humanity. The trees and flowers bloom, and have their being, and though like the seasons, their lessons are silent, yet are they pregnant with meaning to the true observer of nature. He fails not to read the lessons which they teach, and he garners it up with true wisdom, till broadcast he scatters his knowledge to the advantage of humanity. Shakspere is a brilliant example of this power to read and understand the silent lessons of nature. He neglected nothing that he came in contact with; all things he observed; saving and hoarding up all he saw and heard, illustrating his own words, "Let us cast away nothing, for we may live to have need of such a verse."*

Shakspere had no respect for hypocrisy, the "serpent heart hid with a flowering face." With nerveless hand he exposes "the goodly apple rotten at the core." The evil results which flow from the practice of hypocrisy, the bane of political and social life, he unsparingly points out. The "holy leer," the "wolf in sheep's array," he most unflinchingly condemns, and he unmasks the hypocrite tongue which speaks without the heart. He never holds back nor fails to apply the lash to this most "cunning sin," which is but "a sort of homage that vice pays to virtue." Bigotry had no terrors for him: free in spirit and endowed with unlimited charity, he vindicated the rights of man and woman both fearlessly and lovingly. Shakspere studied both men, nature and books, and fortunately for humanity, he read them all with advantage.

SHAKSPERE'S MORALITY.—The morality of Shakspere is built upon nature and reason, independent of all religious considerations, for as Bacon banished religion from science, so Shakspere has done the like in the

* Troilus and Cressida, *Act* IV. s. 4.

development of his art. He never attempts at preaching morals by direct precept, for he seems to write without moral aim, thus showing the highest development of his art, which consists, not in direct teaching, but by living, acting impulses, by illustration and example. The relation of Shakspere's poetry to morality and moral influence upon men, is most perfect, and nothing higher has been asked of poetry than that which Shakspere rendered. One noble impulse does more towards the ennobling of men, than a hundred good precepts, and a bad passion is best subdued by the excitement of a better. Shakspere differs from most other poets, especially those of modern times. His powers of self-command were unquestionably of the highest order, and the strong development of this power prevented him from committing the fault so prevalent among many poets, of inventing passions and bestowing upon them such attractions, so that we are apt to be led morally astray. The constant aim of the Shaksperean drama is the purification of the passions, and this is the true aim and action of tragedy. Fear and sympathy are both excited, and this excitement serves to purify these and similar emotions of the brain. Shakspere's poetry is moral; he took up life as a whole, and he, into himself absorbed more of the moral element of life than any other poet has ever done.

---

Shakspere's Religion.—No definite religious creed can be assigned to Shakspere. Both Protestant and Catholic claim him as their own, yet he belongeth to neither. His religion could not be bounded by any church, for it was like his genius, universal. The clearness of Shakspere's perceptive and the great strength of his reflective powers, prevented him from doing homage to any form of superstition, whether coarse or refined. He acknowledged no particular form of faith, but lived in the belief of the goodness of humanity, of which he was, and is, the most powerful exponent. He set aside all religious consideration and took a complete secular view of life,* pointing out the consequences of immoral acts, and above all things doth he extol the love of humanity, as the true law for the guidance of human kind, the love of whom pervades the whole of his works, and it is the development of this love, that marks him as the poet of humanity, which is the sentiment of sympathy universally applied. When we seek to elevate the human race, when we experience pleasure in seeing and striving to make others happy, and when our feelings compel us to share their pains and sorrows, we are carrying out the law of humanity. All this is constantly taught by the poet, and this teaching fails not to beget that due reverence and love for the author which can never die. To the lines of Shakspere can we turn for guidance and solace, resting assured there is more real knowledge of humanity and a truer love of humankind to be found in his pages, than in any of the sermons ever delivered

* Men and women are made to drain the cup of misery to the dregs; but as from the depths into which they have fallen, by their own weakness or the wickedness of others, the poet never raises them in violation of the inexorable laws of nature, so neither does he "put a new song" into their mouths, or any expression of confidence in God's righteous dealing. With as precise and hard a hand as Bacon did he sunder the celestial from the terrestial globe, the things of earth from those of heaven; resolutely and sternly refusing to look beyond the limits of this world, to borrow comfort, in suffering and injustice, from the life to come."—*The Quarterly Review*, No. 261, p. 46.

by clerical men, or in any other volume that has ever been written, the bible not excepted.

SHAKSPERE'S CONTEMPORARIES.—Coleridge speaks of Shakspere's contemporaries, as "giants," but this opinion, I conceive, to be an erroneous one. Not any of the dramatic poets of Shakspere's time, nor any of the those that preceded or followed him, can in any way be compared with the incomparable master. Marlowe, evidently the greatest among the contemporaries of Shakspere, is not of lofty stature. The great besetting fault among the dramatists of the period, was a love of the horrible, and in the display of this coarse taste, Marlowe, Massinger, and most others revelled. No single work can be adduced which approaches the great master either in power, invention, skill of handling, sweetness and knowledge of humanity. It is only in isolated scenes, or in scattered passages, that any of Shakspere's contemporaries has reached the Shaksperean height, and that rarely. No instance can be furnished of any of their flights of power or grandeur being sustained beyond mere passages. Their works have been, and still are considerably over-rated. This is demonstrated in the fact, that none of their phrases have ever become familiar in our mouths "as household words," like those of Shakspere. Not a passage, not a line, not a single happy expression took root among those with whom they lived, nor have they took root with any generation since their time. This failing to secure a lasting place in the common utterances of the English people, affirms the position, that they did not possess those gigantic proportions which have been so frequently claimed for and ascribed to them. The position which their works now occupy, being chiefly known by the detached specimens strung together by Charles Lamb, is another important proof of the weakness of their powers, and at the same time, a strong argument against their giant developments.

---

SHAKSPERE AS AN ACTOR.—Upon the merits of Shakspere as an actor, there has existed, and still does exist, a wide difference of opinion. Many have held that he was but an inferior actor, playing but parts of a lesser degree, and in no instance rising higher than the part of "Adam," in "As You Like It," or the "Ghost" in the tragedy of Hamlet. Both these parts are really of a higher character than most persons generally assign, they require a more than ordinary amount of ability to properly sustain them, and it is but seldom upon the modern stage that they are well played. The "Ghost" in Hamlet, is a part which only Shakspere could have played, for none but himself could have conceived and understood the mode and manner in which a spirit could and would talk. Rowe, who edited an edition of Shakspere's works, 1709, says he never rose higher than the part of the Ghost in Hamlet, while Chettle says, he was "excellent in the quality he professeth." By Wright we are told that "he was a much better poet than player," and by pleasant gossiping Aubrey, we are told he did "act exceeding well." Stage traditions, however give him a much higher position as an actor, for he is said to have been the original Mercutio in "Romeo and Juliet," a character, which judging from his works, is an outline of his own, embracing the fire, energy, sweetness, and all the other attributes of his genius. It is also said of him, that Queen Elizabeth being present at the playhouse, so engrossed was Shakspere in the kingly part he was personating, that he failed to notice the presence of her majesty, who dropped her glove to excite his attention, upon which he immediately picked it up, adding the following extempore lines to his speech:—

"And though now bent on this high embassy,
Yet stoop we to take up our cousin's glove."

Whatever may have been his merits as an actor, the success he attained, affords pretty good proof that his position was a high one. Most of his contemporaries spoke of his success, and in most of his pieces it is known, that he played parts. Had he have been but an indifferent actor, he would not have been attached to the king's company of players, performing before the court of James I. If Downes, who was the prompter of the day, can be relied upon, Taylor and Lowen, two of the original actors in Shakspere's pieces, were instructed in their various parts by the poet himself, and those instructions were afterwards handed down to Betterton, by Sir W. Davenant, who attributed Betterton's success in the parts of Henry the Eighth and Hamlet, in a great measure to those instructions. These circumstances, coupled with Hamlet's advice to the players, warrants the conclusion, that Shakspere, was as great in practice as he was perfect in theory.

SHAKSPERE'S BIRTHDAY.—It is most remarkable, yet no more remarkable than true, that no public recognition has yet taken place in acknowledgment of the greatness of the genius of Shakspere, and the influence his works have had in the formation of the national character. Our progress as a nation, is in a great measure, owing to the works of the bard of Stratford, who taught that the common good is the highest aim, and the only one for the activity of man to be directed to. The world is the great school in which mankind must be tested, and those only can be perfect, who have been "tried and tutored." Possessing a world-wide reputation, "the best among the rarest of good ones," his name is not held in that respect and honour in his own country, that it deserves to be. His works are "familiar in our mouths as household words;" they impregnate the ordinary conversation of the day, and his thoughts direct, mould and form the thoughts and manners of our time. In Germany, his natal day is celebrated with great rejoicings. The literati of that nation devote their intellectual energies to the development of his works, and numerous are the essays which are published, as a rule, on the 23rd of April. Much feasting is also held in celebration of his name, while in England, with the exception of the annual dinner at Stratford-upon-Avon, no rejoicing is held in general recognition of the "myriad-minded poet." It is to be regretted that this should be so; it is also to be regretted that our people should be wanting in this respect, for "how poor an instrument may do a noble deed," and what deed could be nobler than paying honour to him, who hath conferred greatness and honour upon our country. It is much to be regretted that our people pay their external devotions, more to those who have conquered with the sword, than those who have conquered with the pen,—to those who have directed armies and achieved victories upon the battle-field, than to those whose works have built up and formed the character of the people of this great nation, foremost among whom standeth the name of William Shakspere, whose fame, "folds in this orb of the earth." It is to be hoped that in the progress of society—and it can really be affirmed that society has progressed, intellectually and morally, and is still progressing, that the time is not far distant, when the people of the United Kingdom will not fail to observe the birthday of Shakspere as a national festival, for on the people must this task devolve. Those in high places, and those who are possessed of ample means, set no example, nor take any steps to accomplish such a purpose. From "poor men's cottages," not "princes' palaces," must the public expression of thankfulness come, for the manifold advantages which have accrued to our nation, from the productions of the incomparable swan of Avon.

SHAKSPERE'S NON-OBSERVANCE OF THE UNITIES.—Owing to Shakspere's non-observance of the unities of time and place—though he strictly observes unity of feeling, the true law of unity—he has been called by many critics a barbarian, wanting art; a wild, untutored genius, without learning, poor in scholarship and void of a knowledge of classic lore. This class of critics, agreeing with nothing but what coincided with the peculiarities of their education, contended for the full observances of the unities, from the simple reason that the Greek dramatists always observed them. They entirely lost sight of the circumstances attending the introduction of the unities, and the nature of the Greek drama, when contrasted with that of Shakspere. The introduction of the unities was an innovation equally as great as Shakspere's disregard of them. The Greek dramatists introduced that which was in unison with their feelings and in keeping with the spirit of their stage. In their dramas, they appealed chiefly to the reason of their hearers through their outward senses, inasmuch as they supposed an ideal state, instead of referring to an existing reality. On the other hand, the Shaksperean drama appeals to the imagination; to that power which looking within, contemplates our inward nature and its relation to humanity.

Though the productions of the Greek dramatists contain many passages of surpassing beauty, yet there is a want of dramatic power. This want arises from their seeking to represent men as they should be, while the drama being a poem accommodated to action, its object and aim is to represent the phases of human life; to display the motives of human action, and to show the effects of various circumstances upon the human race; to unravel the pages of old time's mighty book, and to unmask the human character with all its follies and vices, its hopes and sorrows, its varied aspirations, its meanness and its greatness, and thus teaching a lesson of great moral worth.

For Shakspere to have preserved the unities of time and place in his dramas, he must have introduced long speeches, describing events, such speeches being equivalent to the chorus of the ancients. Had he have done this, instead of the presence of character and the realization of the event, we should have had a wondrous amount of word-painting, which in itself would have overwhelmed the progress of the drama. For Shakspere to have strictly followed the unities of time and place, he could not have shown Macbeth upon the heath with the weird-sisters, in his castle, his interview with his wife, the murder of Duncan, his coronation, and his death, years after. He could only have shown but one phase of Macbeth's character, and one action during the day. This would have borne no more relation to the true Macbeth, than does the classic drama of antiquity bear to the real life of the world, in which storms and calms, clouds and sunshine, misery and happiness are seen commingling together.

---

THE PERIOD OF SHAKSPERE.—It was a remarkable period, that, in which the poet Shakspere was born; remarkable not only with regard to our own country, but also to the other nations of Europe. The exigencies of the time required great men, and they came in all their varied phases, adding strength to the mentality of their own age and force to the character of the nation to which they belonged. The external and internal circumstances of our nation at this time, were of an extraordinary character, and the quality of the men, both mentally and physically, who enacted their parts, was fully commensurate with the requirements of the age. During the fifty-two years that Shakspere moved and had his being upon this earth, the number of great men in all walks of literature, in the arts and in the scientific world was truly astonishing. Such a combination of talent, such an array of genius was never before witnessed, nor can any other fifty-two years' of the world's history hardly furnish forth a parallel. No period of our own history, either preceding or following this time, can present such a glorious array of great and wise men, whose works redound to the honour of our native land; for leaving out the lesser lights which flourished during those days, have we not Bacon for our philosopher; Burleigh for our statesman; Shakspere and Spenser for our poets; Drake, Frobisher, Davis, Howard and Grenville, for our admirals; Gresham for our merchant; Andrews, Hall, and Hooper, for our theologians; and Knolles, Speed and Stow, for our historians.

On the continent, among painters who have achieved a world wide reputation, there existed coeval with Shakspere, Titian, the master of colour; Annibal Carracci, he who painted the Three Maries; Rembrandt the painter of contrast, of deep shadows and strong lights; Cuyp, whose delightful landscapes with drowsy cattle are the pride of fenny Holland; Claude, the ethereal, the limner of sunlight and beauty; Salvator Rosa, he of the wild and terrible, whose dark caves and darker men are so full of picturesque beauty; Zurbani Henera, the master of the great Velasquez, and others whose works remain memorials of their love of truth and beauty. To particularise the great painters who came into the world and went out of it, and others who flourished during the Shaksperean period, would be a task of some length; sufficient to mention the names of Teniers, the elder, Tintoretto, Paul Veronese, Nicolas Poussin, Spagnoletto, Vandyke, Snyders, Reni Guido, and Abraham Bloemart.

In the world of astronomy we have a trinity of giants in the names of Tycho Brahe, Kepler and Galileo Galilei. Descartes, the eminent philosopher, whose works created a revolution in the world of thought, flourished during this period. Tasso, the poet,—he, whose immortal song of Jerusalem Delivered, has filled the world with delight, and Montaigne, the great essayist, were contemporary; so was Rizzio, Camoens, the Portugese poet, author of the Lysiad, Lope de Vega, the prolific dramatist of Spain, and Calderon, the eminent Spanish poet, of whom Schlegel says, "a poet, if ever man deserved that name," was co-existent with the "sweet swan of Avon."

In directing our attention to this period, whether we confine our view to our own country or extend it to the continent of Europe, we cannot fail to perceive its greatness. The immense activity which was displayed in the mental world, the rude shocks which existing notions received, the upheaving of the religious element, and the planting and culture of the right of private judgment in those days, presents points of such a forcible character, that they will be remembered "to the last syllable of recorded time." The state of English society during this period, was of a very peculiar nature, and Shakspere, as evidenced by his works, was thoroughly acquainted with and understood the age, which was essentially dramatic. "In set speeches, in conversation, in grave state papers, the mythical and the legendary were mixed up with the historical and the present, as if all were alike real, and all intimately blended with one another. The vivid imaginations of men supplied the connecting links and brought the picture home to the mind, instead of setting it off at greater distance, as is the tendency of modern criticism to do. The common ground of all was the supposed humanity of all; varying, indeed, according to time, climate, circumstances, but in all essentials one and the same with themselves and those around them."\* Filled with a love of humanity, wherever found, Shakspere failed not to respect the popular will, and his great knowledge and foresight taught him that this was a gradually extending power. Though not wholly despising the royal prerogative, he felt, and he wrote what he felt, that it must gradually decline before the growth of popular opinion.

The power of feudalism all but expired with our great civil wars, which resulted in the throne of England being occupied by the House of Tudor, under whose supremacy, the English character became wholly freed from the evil consequences of feudal influence and the papal authority. The spirit of enterprise, one of the strong characteristics of the English nation, developed itself with marvellous rapidity. The industrial power of the English people began to be nurtured and soon made itself felt and acknowledged. The outward power of the nation gradually expanded and many of the internal obstacles to trade and commerce were removed.

Our allegiance to Rome which had been partially thrown off in the reign of the sensual Henry VIII., was not completed till the reign of his daughter Elizabeth: nor was the English power consolidated till the Spanish nation under the direction of its fanatical and murderous sovereign, Philip, in its religious zeal and bigotted fury, thought to conquer this isle and restore it to the dominancy of the papal Pontiff. This inconsiderate act awoke the energies of the English people; brought into operation the latent power of

---

\* The Quarterly Review, No. 261, p. 41.

the nation, and afforded the sublime spectacle of a whole people rising to do battle for their hearths, their homes, their country, and their creed. Such an instance was not lost sight of by our bard, for proudly he sings of this

"Eden, of this demi-paradise,
This precious stone set in the silver sea;"

and, exulting in the results produced by English valour and English skill upon the so-called invincible armada of Spain, exclaims:

"Come the three corners of the world in arms,
And we shall shock them. Nought shall make us rue,
If England to itself do rest but true." *

* King John, *Act* v. s. 7.